CHRISTIAN FAITH AND OTHER FAITHS

STEPHEN NEILL

CHRISTIAN FAITH AND OTHER FAITHS

THE CHRISTIAN DIALOGUE WITH OTHER RELIGIONS

Second Edition

OXFORD UNIVERSITY PRESS

Oxford University Press, Walton Street, Oxford OX2 6DP

OXFORD LONDON GLASGOW NEW YORK
TORONTO MELBOURNE WELLINGTON CAPE TOWN
IBADAN NAIROBI DAR ES SALAAM LUSAKA ADDIS ABABA
KUALA LUMPUR SINGAPORE JAKARTA HONG KONG TOKYO
DELHI BOMBAY CALCUTTA MADRAS KARACHI

ISBN 0 19 283011 2

First published by Oxford University Press, London, 1961
Second edition first published as an Oxford University Press paperback, 1970
Reprinted 1977

Reprinted lithographically in Great Britain by
Ebenezer Baylis and Son Ltd
The Trinity Press, Worcester, and London

PREFACE TO THE SECOND EDITION

THIS book contains, in expanded form, the Moorhouse Lectures delivered in Melbourne Cathedral in 1960. The material of six of them was used again in lectures on the Sam. P. Jones Foundation in the Candler School of Theology, Emory University, Atlanta, Georgia. In extending to me the invitation to deliver the lectures, the Most Reverend Frank Woods, Archbishop of Melbourne, expressed his wish that the main theme of the lectures should be the relationship between Christian faith and non-Christian systems of belief, a subject of obvious relevance in an Australia which almost overnight had become aware of its involvement in Asian affairs, and was admitting to its universities hundreds of students from Asian countries.

I gladly accepted the Archbishop's proposal, but found myself in consequence in a certain dilemma. To produce yet another outline of the non-Christian faiths in their classical forms would have been easy, but hardly profitable, when so many excellent books of this type already exist. It seemed right to attempt the far harder task of asking what these religions mean to their adherents today, and to attempt to understand them from within as they are understood by those who continue to find in them a way of life. I have written frankly as a Christian. But I am whole-heartedly committed to the method of dialogue eloquently set forth by, among others, Canon Kenneth Cragg. Real dialogue is possible only if all the interlocutors are committed, resolute and uncompromising; only so are we able to uncover to one another the riches of the religious inheritance into which we have ourselves entered.

After I had delivered the lecture on Buddhism, I was touched when I received from the Secretary of the Buddhist Association of Victoria a courteous note, thanking me for the correct and sympathetic interpretation which I had given of that faith. The fact that the book has had to be reprinted three times in six years, and is now being prepared for reissue in paperback form, encourages me to hope that others, Christian and non-Christian, may have had the same experience.

For the purposes of this edition the whole book, including the bibliography, has been carefully revised and brought up to date.

One chapter has been completely rewritten. Chapter VII, which in earlier editions appeared as 'The Gospel of Marx and the Gospel of Christ' has been extended to cover other forms of secularism, some of which in the modern world seem to have extended their influence even more widely than Marxist Communism.

S.N.

September 1969

ACKNOWLEDGEMENTS

The quotations from W. C. Smith's *Islam in Modern History* in Chapter III are included by permission of the New American Library, New York, that from C. C. J. Webb's *Studies in the History of Natural Theology* in Chapter IV by permission of the Clarendon Press, Oxford, and the two from J. V. Taylor's *Growth of the Church in Buganda* in Chapter VI by permission of the S.C.M. Press Ltd.

CONTENTS

		PAGE
	PREFACE	V
I	THE PROBLEM SET	I
II	THE KING OF THE JEWS	20
III	ISLAM IN CRISIS	40
IV	RENASCENT HINDUISM	70
V	THE DOCTRINE OF THE LOTUS	99
VI	THE PRIMITIVE WORLD	125
VII	FAITH AND NO FAITH	153
VIII	THE EXISTENTIAL PILGRIMAGE	180
IX	CHRISTENDOM	207
	BIBLIOGRAPHY	235
	INDEX	241

CHAPTER I

THE PROBLEM SET

A HUNDRED and ten years ago, in 1860, the first really representative missionary conference of modern times was held at Liverpool. Full records were kept, and reading the lectures and the discussions to-day one is almost in the position of a listener at those proceedings of long ago. Much of what passed strikes a curiously modern note. The vocabulary has changed—we no longer speak of native Churches— but many of the concerns are exactly the same as those discussed at the most recent meetings of the World Council of Churches. There is, however, one notable difference. Hardly a word was said about the non-Christian religions with which the missionary has to do in his daily practical work; we could hardly imagine such a lacuna in the proceedings of a missionary conference to-day.

A good many reasons could be given for this apparent indifference. Those present at the Conference were concerned principally with their own problems as preachers of the Gospel in strange lands,[1] and with the developments in the Churches that were growing up under their guidance. Many of them were dealing with primitive peoples whose religious ideas may not have seemed to them very important. But perhaps the main reason was that, even in 1860, the great religions of the East were still very imperfectly known. Max Müller's great series of *The Sacred Books of the East* still lay in the future—the first volume was published only in 1875. Carlyle, in his enthusiastic but uncritical study of Muhammad in *Heroes and Hero-Worship* (1841), had broken through the traditional Christian attitude of reserve, if not of hostility, in relation to 'the false prophet', but in a style which was not likely to commend his work to pious missionaries. In 1860 Sir William Muir had not yet completed his great work of producing the first critical biography of Muhammad to appear in English.[2]

The situation we face to-day is as different as could well be imagined. All the religions of the world have been minutely studied,

[1] Only one representative of a younger Church, an Indian clergyman, was present at the Conference of 1860.

[2] A great deal of pioneer work, particularly in the study of the classical languages of the East, had, of course, been accomplished before 1860.

some of the best work having been produced where Western science has co-operated with the intuitions and inner apprehensions of the Eastern mind. All the greatest works have been translated into all the main languages of Europe. Selections have appeared in paperback form and are easily available. More than we perhaps realize, something of Eastern, and particularly of Indian, thought has become part of the unconscious furniture of our minds.

Hard upon comparative philology, the study and classification of languages, followed what is often called 'comparative religion' but should more correctly be called 'the comparative study of religions'. One of the first tasks was to classify religions according to the main recognizable types. Here Nathan Söderblom (1866-1931), famous in other fields as one of the great leaders in the ecumenical movement, made a notable contribution in the clear distinction that he drew between the prophetic and the mystical types of religious approach. Inevitably and rightly from their own point of view, those engaged in such comparative studies included Christianity as one of the phenomena to be studied, classified and compared, no less than the other forms of the religious experience of mankind. Thus, for instance, in his *Orpheus* (1909), a book very well known fifty years ago, Salomon Reinach ended his work with a combined study of Judaism and Christianity, which he regarded as only slightly variant forms of one of the principal types of religion.

Christian reactions to this approach were on the whole favourable. Ideas of evolution were in the air, and had been transplanted without due thought from the sphere of biology in which they belong to many other aspects of human life, where they are perhaps less appropriate. It chimed well with new ideas of tolerance to think of Christianity as playing its part in man's age-long search for God; Christians would naturally hold that it was the highest manifestation of the divine that had yet been accorded to the human race, but need not necessarily exclude the thought that it might be a resting-place on the endless pilgrimage of man rather than his permanent home. A great many points of similarity between the Gospels and other faiths —the wisdom of the Rabbis no less than the wisdom of the East—had emerged. The Gospel claim to uniqueness seemed to be less firmly founded than had earlier been supposed by Christians, and philosophical arguments in favour of its absoluteness appeared inconclusive.[3]

[3] See, for instance, an extremely interesting discussion of the views of Ernst Troeltsch (*Die Absolutheit des Christentums und die Religionsgeschichte*, 1901) in H. Kraemer, *Religion and the Christian Faith* (1956), pp. 63-67. Troeltsch makes use of the remarkably self-contradictory phrase *relativer Absolutismus*.

It was at this stage of the argument that Hendrik Kraemer launched on the world his first great book, *The Christian Message in a non-Christian World*, written in preparation for the International Missionary Conference held at Tambaram in 1938. Here he took up a position as different as possible from that of all the supporters of the comparative method. Speaking of the Gospel in terms of 'biblical realism', he argued that this story of the divine action in Christ is of its nature entirely different from anything to be found in any other religion. The comparative method had taken it for granted that all religions are commensurables—the possibility of comparison between them is self-evident. It was precisely this claim that Kraemer denied. The Gospel is in fact incommensurable with everything else; to attempt to bring it into such comparison with other faiths is at once to falsify it.

It is not necessary here to expound all Kraemer's views at length, or to go into the controversy provoked by his rather harsh and challenging way of putting them forth. Three points, however, may conveniently be made:

1. If we speak of 'religions', we imply at once that there is some general concept 'religion', under which all the particular forms of religion may be subsumed. But, in fact, every attempt to arrive at a satisfactory and agreed definition has proved fruitless. We all know roughly what we mean when we speak about religion; otherwise there would be no purpose in writing such a book as this; but, when we try to be precise, there is something that eludes us. This need not unduly disturb us. Do we not fall into almost precisely the same dilemma, when we try to say exactly what we mean by art?

2. Comparison can only be of ideas. We can work out more or less accurately the Christian idea of God, and compare this with the idea of God as it is found in Islam. If we are to put different religious traditions side by side at all, it is almost inevitable that we shall find ourselves doing something of this kind. But we must never forget that, when we do this, we are dealing with abstractions. In order to make comparison possible, we have detached certain ideas or theories or doctrines from the living experience which has given rise to them. In doing so we rob them of their life. Such study has the same value as the dissection of a specimen in the laboratory, and this must not be underestimated. But we must not be surprised if it tells us little about the living fabric of the religion from which the idea has been somewhat violently dissevered.

3. More and more we are coming to realize that faith is experienced as a whole, and cannot be experienced in any other way.

This has come home to us forcibly in recent years in ecumenical debate between adherents of different forms of the Christian creed. Even when we appear to agree on a doctrine or a certain form of words, our agreement is conditioned and limited by the rest of the system to which we adhere. The result is that emphases are different, perspectives are not the same, and even the apparent agreement is encompassed by the net of disagreement about other things. If this is true even within the varieties of Christian faith, how much more must it be true when we try to compare Christian faith in God with that which in some way comes near to it, the Muslim faith in God.

It has to be recognized that those things which are experienced as wholes are in fact not commensurable with one another, any more than one scent is really comparable with any other. Genetic or historical connexions may be traced; it is just the fact that a certain knowledge of the Bible and of Christian faith underlies certain parts of the Qur'an. An understanding of such connexions is useful in the study of religion as it is in the study of music. But, when we have said that the young Beethoven was at certain points influenced by Mozart, we have not really said anything very important about either of them; the music of each has to be felt and appreciated in terms of itself and of nothing else. Even when, as can happen, one musician has actually stolen a phrase or a melody from another, what he does with it is so idiosyncratic that the connexion has little more importance than that of a historic accident. The greater the composer, the less is it possible to think or speak of him in terms other than those of his own achievement.

The musical parallel is perhaps that which will help us most to understand the shift that has taken place in the modern approach to the study of religions. The only method which promises results is that of self-exposure, as complete as possible, to the impact of a religion as a whole. The attitude is not that of *theoria*, the dispassionate contemplation which was the ideal of the Greek, and which leads to nothing more fruitful than intellectual analysis. The new approach is that of engagement, personal involvement in something which is of deep concern to us because it is of deep concern to millions of our fellow human beings.

This is an exacting, indeed almost a terrifying, approach. Can one launch oneself into the heart and spirit of another religion without disloyalty to one's own? Does not such an approach involve such a measure of detachment as is incompatible with deep adherence to any system of religious belief at all? Oddly enough, experience seems to show that the last anxiety is groundless. It is those who have the deepest and most confident faith themselves who have the courage to launch out on this adventure of the human spirit; and their own commitment renders them more, not less, sensitive to the commitment of others whose faith finds a different object and a different form of expression. This way does call for sympathy and discrimination. It does demand patience and a willingness to suspend judgement. It does not involve indifference to truth or the abandonment of all objective criteria of judgement.

These criteria, however, will not be found lying ready to hand. Each religion, as we study it, will be found to be one expression of man's reaction to the total human situation within which he has to live. Our question concerning each will relate to its adequacy in the context of that total situation. Does it take account of everything, literally everything, in the human situation? Or are there certain areas that are disregarded and ignored? What needs of the human spirit does this system meet? Are there legitimate needs of the human spirit that it disregards or denies? To what extent does it serve man in the fullest development of what he has it in him to be? Is it related to the concept of community, of the city in which man can dwell at peace and in harmony with all his neighbours? Does it point to a fulfilment beyond the limits of time and space?

It may be objected that this is a man-centred way of looking at things, that many of the terms we use need closer definition, and so on. These are valid criticisms. The only answer that we can give at this stage of our study is that we must start somewhere, and, if there is to be any study of the whole field of what man calls his religions, we must establish certain areas of common concern by means of which we shall relate the study of one system to that of another. But we are postponing for the moment the central question of *truth*. Provisionally, we may be permitted to hold that the correspondence of a system to what we know of man's situation may be at least useful as a thermometer for the measurement of its objective truth. But it may prove that, when we have reached the ultimate question, we have to turn back to reconsider and perhaps to reject a number of earlier judgements.

We are engaging in this study frankly as Christians. We do not pretend to stand on any Olympian height of detachment from which we can survey all forms of human religion with splendid impartiality. We know now that that cannot be done. In all investigation—even in the most austere researches of the nuclear physicist—the personal equation is involved. In the study of religion the personal equation is at its highest, and it would be unscientific to pretend that this is not so. We shall speak and question as those who live within one particular system, one particular understanding of the world. But this does not necessarily mean that our approach will be prejudiced, and that we shall distort everything we see by looking at it through our own spectacles, though this is a danger that must be borne in mind. It does mean that our study can be carried on only by way of dialogue. We shall question others as to their beliefs. But this means that we must expose ourselves, honestly and without protection, to the questions that they may ask of us.

The willingness to take this attitude corresponds to one reality of the present situation. To go back again for a moment to the report of the Liverpool Conference of 1860, we can read there the passionate plea that 'native agents' of the Church should be kept away from the English language! A vain hope; it was already much too late, and the Churches could no more turn back the unrestrained eagerness of the Asian and African peoples for Western knowledge than Mrs. Partington could turn back the waves of the sea with her broom. Except for one chapter of this book, we shall be encountering in our studies those who are perfectly prepared to meet us on our own level. In earlier times dialogue was difficult, because the Westerner and the Christian usually had the advantage in knowledge and prestige. Now this is no longer so. Leading representatives of the ancient religions have deeply studied the Christian faith and have rejected it. We may at certain points find that we wish to ask them to think again; but we are not speaking to those who do not know.

We have further to reckon with this new factor in the situation— that several of the ancient religions of the world have entered into a missionary phase of their existence. They will have their questions to ask of us, and some of these may prove highly embarrassing. The comparative study of religions to-day is not for those who have timid spirits and queasy stomachs. It is a stern and relentless business. But, if it is our incomparable privilege to stand within the truth, we shall have everything to gain and nothing to lose by exposing ourselves to questioning. The questions should help to elucidate our faith, to open up aspects of it that were previously hidden from us, perhaps to rid us of some illusions, and in the end to strengthen our hold on that which, or rather him whom, we have believed.

It is time to set forth, in brief outline, the ground from which we make our approach to the other faiths of the world. This is not the place for a treatise on Christian theology. We must, however, begin with certain agreements among ourselves as to the kind of way in which Christians think, as to the kind of questions they believe must be raised if we are to talk of religion at all, and as to the area within which they believe that the answers are to be found.

To start with, then, we may lay down three categories, within which Christians find themselves thinking all the time, and without the use of which they cannot think as Christians at all. These are not yet beliefs or doctrines; they lie behind all doctrines and make possible the formulation of doctrines, when the time for that comes.

1. The first is the principle of contingency, or contingent being. Human thought has swayed over the centuries between the extreme of realism, the belief that the visible world is all that exists, and the extreme of idealism, the belief that the visible world does not really exist at all except in so far as our minds give it a certain brief and illusory reality. Christian thought rejects both these extremes. The world, and man within it, has reality, has existence. But this is a wholly dependent reality and existence. Nothing in the world, and least of all man himself, can be explained in terms of forces and principles solely within this world. There is a beyond, in dependence on which the world exists and man can find his freedom. If we wish to go a step further and put the matter theologically, we cannot think as Christians at all without the concept of creation; we take our stand on the first verse of the Bible: 'In the beginning God created the heavens and the earth.'

2. Secondly, we can think only in terms of purpose. The most significant thing about human beings is that they are creatures which can form purposes. It is probably true that man alone among living beings has the capacity for conceptual thought—his universal use of articulate speech suggests it; but we know so little of the mental processes of animals that this is hard to prove. We do see traces of purpose even among the animals. But these are

rudimentary, and seem to depend more on instinctive response than on conscious planning. Man has the faculty of forming purposes, such as the purpose of writing a book, which may involve years of effort, the co-ordination of innumerable subsidiary purposes, the co-operation of a great many other minds, which can be adhered to in the face of frustration, disappointment and partial failure, and in the carrying out of which a man feels that he is most truly living.

The purpose of God is one of the postulates of Christian thinking. This is very different from the old argument from design. That argument was too simple; it broke down in face of the all too evident fact that the universe considered as a machine does not work nearly so well as a machine designed by infinite intelligence and maintained by infinite power ought to do. It took far too little account of imperfection, failure and tragedy. Very different from this is the idea of purpose. We are accustomed to working out our own purposes slowly, patiently, and by the use of materials that are always more or less refractory. An observer might find it extremely difficult to guess what the purpose is, as he sees an author sitting surrounded by an apparently shapeless and hopeless chaos of notes. But, given the necessary resolution, conviction and patience, the shape of the purpose will eventually emerge. If, then, there is a divine purpose in the universe, and if it emerges only slowly, through many set-backs and apparent failures, if at times it is evident to faith rather than to sight, we shall be neither surprised nor disturbed. Such a method cannot be stigmatized as either irrational or unworthy of a God who is prepared to respect the freedom of the human creatures with whom he has to deal.

3. The third conviction is that events really happen. History is the medium in which we have to operate and in which God is also prepared to operate. Now history is always the scene of the unpredictable and the unexpected. History and prophecy move in different worlds. The forces that make up history are so diverse and complex that action is always accompanied by hazard. Human decisions count and really affect the future. If there is a predetermined plan, as in the Marxist understanding of history, then nothing really new emerges—history is merely the unfolding of a pattern that was there from the beginning, and then it is no longer history. History is the field in which the genuinely new emerges. Furthermore, it is the field in which nothing ever happens twice. History never repeats itself, though it may manifest certain recurrent

patterns. The Greeks thought in terms of the endless cycle, in which all things come back to that which they were in the beginning. Not so the Christian. To him the future is a world of glorious possibilities, influenced indeed but not predetermined by the past.

All this should prepare us to recognize that <u>man is extremely important in the Christian scheme of things.</u> It is an exaggeration, but perhaps a helpful exaggeration, to say that Christian doctrine can be reduced to a doctrine of man.[4] But, of course, this means man in dependence on God, and no sense at all can be made of Christian thought unless full attention is paid to both poles of the ellipse.

More than perhaps any other form of religion or philosophy Christian faith takes the human situation very seriously. It never doubts for a moment that it is a great and glorious thing to be a man. It can find a place, though not without criticism, for all the wonderful achievements of man in society, in culture, in art, even in the somewhat tarnished glories of his technical civilization. But at the same time it looks with wide-open and dispassionate eyes on the squalor, the contradictions, the self-destroying absurdity of human existence. Man by his ingenuity has built up a brave new world of his own invention, and now, like a child tired of its toys, he seems to be set on destroying it, and with it the whole race of which he is a part. In vision and aspiration his head touches the heavens; but his feet still stand firmly in the ooze and slime of primeval chaos. As Pascal saw so clearly long ago, we cannot understand man unless we consider him in both his greatness and his misery. But, having made an exhaustive inventory of the misery, Christian faith still affirms that it is a good thing to be a man.

This being so, it should come as no surprise that Christianity is the religion of a Man. We shall encounter other religions which have historical founders; but in none of them is the relation between the adherent of that religion and its founder in the least like that which the Christian believer supposes to exist between himself and Christ. The old saying 'Christianity is Christ' is almost exactly true The historical figure of Jesus of Nazareth is the criterion by which every Christian affirmation has to be judged, and in the light of which it stands or falls.

[4] As for instance, Rudolf Bultmann maintains that St. Paul's anthropology is the centre of all his thinking, and that it is only in the light of this that his theology as a whole can be understood. *Theologie des neuen Testaments* (ed. 4, 1961, p. 192; Eng. trans. p. 191).

Jesus came to show what the life of a man really is. The characteristic dimension of human existence is freedom. On this narrow sand-bank between existence and non-existence, between coercion and chaos, God has withdrawn his hand so far as to make a space in which man can be really, though not unconditionally, free. In Jesus we see what a free man looks like. We could hardly have guessed in advance that this is what the picture would be.

The first paradox in this freedom is that it means complete acceptance of a situation as it is given without man's own choice. Jesus was born a Jew and lived under the Roman oppression. At no point does he show any resentment against this situation or regard it as a hindrance to the fulfilment of his task. These are the raw materials given him by God; with these materials and no others is he to work out the perfect pattern of human liberty. What is true of him is true also of us all. Within the limits of the given material a great variety of choices is open to us; but there are certain unalterable structures of our life; if we resent these or kick against them, we merely reduce our capacity to make the best of what may in itself be a rather unpromising situation.

The second paradox is that this freedom can be lived out only in a state of total dependence upon God. This element in the life of Jesus is made plain in all the Gospels. At first sight surprisingly, it is more deeply stressed in the Fourth Gospel, the Gospel of the glory of Christ, than in the other three. Again and again in this Gospel Jesus affirms that of himself he can do nothing, that he does only what he sees the Father doing, that he speaks only the words that the Father has given him to speak. He cannot act until his hour has come—and this means always the *kairos*, the moment appointed by the Father. To the lusty spirit of independence which is characteristic of our highly independent age, such dependence might seem to resemble slavery rather than freedom. It is not immediately self-evident that the richest freedom is enjoyed in perfect co-operation, as when pianist and violinist finds each his perfect complement in the playing of the other.

It is plain that this freedom can be exercised only in suffering. The free man accepts his situation, but he cannot be conformed to it. He will always be the critic, judging all things by a standard external to the things themselves. This means that he will always draw down on himself the hatred of those who are pledged to the *status quo*, and of all those who through laziness or self-interest are unwilling to listen to a new voice. But, paradoxically, when they have taken away the last vestige of his liberty and nailed him to a cross, he still remains sovereign in his freedom; he, and not they, is master of the situation; he has affirmed his mastery across the ages.

The purpose of this life of freedom was to restore to all men the possibility of true human life as from the beginning it was intended to be. Life as we know it is full of contradictions, and contradictions lead to frustration and weakness. Here is life without inner contradiction, and therefore peerless in its strength.

The miracles of Jesus are to serve as signs of the breaking in of the new order. Almost every one of them is concerned with the restoration of the being of man to its normal working—the withered hand is quickened with new life, the paralytic takes up his bed and walks, not without a reminder that the paralysis of sin is a graver matter than the paralysis of arms and legs. Even the saying that the poor have the Gospel preached to them is to be interpreted under this rubric of restoration. The 'poor' are not simply the poor in this world's goods, though this is also included; they are those who in their helplessness have looked up to God in hope and expectation. To them the word is now given that their prayer has been heard—God himself is bringing in his own new order; 'The world's great age begins anew.'

But this renewal cannot be through regression to an imagined past of primitive innocence. Man has eaten of the tree of the knowledge of good and evil, and he cannot go back to the garden of Eden. He can only go forward to a new relatedness to God. Jesus is the last Adam; he too is tempted, in just the same way as the first Adam, to assert his independence of God and so to fall away from the true reality of human life. He is accepted, because the victory over temptation has been won, and human nature has been maintained in perfect fellowship with God up to the point of death and beyond it. No other man can be accepted in this way. For every other man the renewal of fellowship can take only the form of forgiveness, and for this reason the affirmation of the forgiveness of sins is the heart of the proclamation of the message of Christ. That is why the new order brought in by Christ is spoken of as the new creation. Forgiveness is always creative; it brings into being a new world, a totally new situation, in which division has been taken away and has been replaced by a new and firmer fellowship. This is true even of human forgiveness. Much more is it true of the forgiveness

of God. Forgiveness is always a movement in one direction—from
the one who has been wronged to the one who has done wrong. It
can never spring from any other motive than sheer goodwill, un-
caused by anything other than the spontaneous generosity of the one
who is prepared to forgive. God created one universe in the beginning by the word of his power; now he has created another by the
word of his grace declared in Jesus Christ.

We can no longer avoid the simple and primary question—Who
is God? We usually assume that we know. But the Christian answer
is that we do not know until we have seen Jesus Christ. 'He that
hath seen me hath seen the Father.' The converse is also true—'He
that hath not seen me hath not seen the Father.'
   The greater part of Christian theology has been unwilling to
take this tremendous affirmation as seriously as it is taken in the New
Testament. If, when we see Jesus Christ, we see God, then any
previous idea we may have had of God must undergo a reconstruction which amounts to rebuilding from the basement to the coping-
stone. We need not deny the value of the Old Testament and of all
that we can learn from it, in order to recognize that even the Old
Testament is a preface that gives only hints and glimpses of the
glory that is to follow. For, if we see God in Jesus Christ, what is the
principal thing that we learn about him? It is that God is a servant,
and that, when he most fully makes himself the servant of all, the
glory of his power finds its fullest self-expression.
   No other interpretation of the being of God is possible, if we
take seriously what has been said about freedom as the dimension
of the true life of man. One who respects the freedom of another in
a very real sense makes himself the servant of that other. And God
respects the freedom of man. He exercises no coercion. When men
reject and repudiate his good purposes, apparently he allows himself
to be frustrated, he gives himself, as it were, helpless into their
hands, just as Jesus suffered himself to be helpless in the hands of
those who could do him the utmost wrong. How else can we explain
the age-long history of wrong and sorrow on the earth?
   For it is a mistake to imagine that this aspect of the being of God
dates only from the incarnation. It is true that the Son of God took
upon him the form of a servant. It is true that, though he was rich,
for our sakes he became poor. But this could only come about
because what was seen in Jesus was there in God from the beginning.

The greatest act of God's self-emptying was the creation of a universe on which he would confer existence in a measure independent of himself. God was and nothing else was. He was unrelated to anything except himself. And then of his own free will he chose to be related to a world existing in space and time. He exchanged his liberty for the servitude of being bound to the created world that he had brought into being. Having made the world he would not forsake it; he had bound himself to the world, to its sorrow and its sin.

All too often the coming of God into the world in Jesus Christ is spoken of·almost as though it were a kind of trick, a desperate remedy adopted to put right an almost desperate situation. This travesty of theology can be avoided only if we take seriously the revelation that Jesus has given of the Father. The incarnation was inevitable because God is what he is. Love leads to redemptive action. Love entered into time and redeemed time. Love entered into the human race as one of us, and by doing so made all things new.

Jesus Christ is a figure of history. In him is seen the action of God at a particular point of space and in a particular epoch of time. But the writers of the New Testament were right in seeing that this action in history cannot be understood, unless we look both before and after it.

'The same was in the beginning with God.' The doctrine of the pre-existence of Christ is not a theological puzzle intended to make faith difficult; it is our assurance that the mercy which was manifest in Jesus was there from the beginning. What we touch in him is the unchanging love of God our servant.

And he shall come to be our judge. God has committed all judgement to him because he is the Son of man. So it is that, while the New Testament looks forward to that day of triumph when the nature of the new creation will finally be revealed, at the same time it tells us that the judgement is going forward day by day. The verdict of the day of judgement will not be some arbitrary sentence imposed upon us from without; it will simply be the manifestation of what we have made of ourselves, and the standard and criterion of judgement will be what we have done with Jesus Christ. Every man is faced with the alternatives of coming to the light, in so far as light has been given to him, or turning from the light and choosing to remain in darkness. In a very real sense we are our own judges; we pass sentence on ourselves by what we are and do.

The Christian outlook on the future is never separated from Jesus and the continuing reality of what he is. The details of the narratives of the resurrection of Jesus Christ may cause us some perplexity; as to the central truth that they are intended to express there can be no doubt. The most striking feature of the narratives is their homeliness; here is no magnificent theophany in power, but a familiar figure who is prepared to eat a piece of a honeycomb, and to stand on the shore of the lake cooking breakfast for his hungry friends. The risen Jesus whom the astonished disciples meet is the same Jesus whom they have known. If we may so put it, the manner of his being is changed, but *he* is not changed. He is the same yesterday, to-day and for ever. He has not been re-absorbed into God from whom he came; he is for ever Jesus, and no eternity can touch the reality of the mysterious 'taking of the manhood into God'.

This is decisive for all Christian thinking about the future of the individual and the Church. We too shall be changed, but we shall still be ourselves. That is why the Creed speaks of the resurrection of the body and not of the immortality of the soul. As recently as the time of John Donne, Christians thought of a literal resuscitation of the flesh, in which God will gather together every seed-pearl that has been scattered through his wide universe. Lately we have come to understand that the word 'body' in the New Testament comes as near as any word available to those ancient writers to what we mean to-day by personality. We may join with William Temple, who once arrived panting at the top of a steep ascent in the Lake District with the words, 'I am glad that I don't believe in the resurrection of the flesh.' But we are encouraged to believe that, just as Jesus is Jesus for evermore, so it is I myself who will be raised to new life in that other world.

The Bible is the story of God's care for the individual. He holds all the universe in the hollow of his hand; yet the word of God comes to Moses, to Isaiah, to this man and to that. It is by God's particular care for us that we are held in life. There is no reason to suppose that the love of God for you and me is affected by so small an accident as physical death. But, if there is love, there must needs be a lover and a loved one. The mystic may think of the total absorption of the self into God, so that there is no longer any distinction between I and Thou. This is not the Christian picture. God called the I into being, and gave it room to stand over against himself, in

order that this relationship might become eternal and find its fulfilment in a world that is exempt from change and chance.

The reality of the individual is in his relatedness to God. But
this is never thought of out of connexion with the complementary
relatedness to other selves. Once again, to the mystic the presence
of other selves may seem irrelevant or even a disturbing nuisance.
The Christian, whether he likes it or not, is bound by the profession
of his faith to accept his brother, the brother whom without his
choosing God has given him in the Church. This is only common
sense. If we are destined to live with one another for ever and ever,
we had better begin to learn to live with one another now. Thus in
Christian faith there is nothing whatever of that 'flight of the alone to
the alone,' made famous by the closing phrase of the *Enneads* of Plotinus. Every picture, every image, of life in the beyond given to us in
Scripture is strictly social in character. The book of Revelation
culminates in the vision of the city. The mind of the reader who
knows the Old Testament goes back to such phrases as 'Jerusalem
is built as a city that is at unity within itself' (Psalm 122.3), and to
countless other words which speak of the earthly Jerusalem as a
community of responsible men bound together by loyalty to one
another and to their God. This is the ideal which finds its consummation and its perfection in the Christian hope for the individual
and the Church. We find the reality of our being not in our loneliness, not in 'what we do with our solitariness', as A. N. Whitehead
supposed, but in the fullness of relatedness to other human spirits in
whom also God dwells.

Christians have never been able to explain to themselves or
others the nature of eternal life as this is experienced by finite
spirits. We naturally tend to think of it merely as the prolongation
of chronological time without end, without the natural limit of
death. The ancient myth of Tithonus warns us that this would be a
frightful prospect. Time without end would seem to be also time
of endless boredom. On the other hand the Greek concept of a
timeless eternity in which nothing happens does not fit well into
Christian categories of thinking. The only God we know is God in
action; that the same God is also God in repose we may well believe,
but it is beyond the possibilities of our understanding to bring
together the two aspects of his being. This means that, if we speak
at all of the other world, we can do so only in terms of apparent
paradox and contradiction, and this will always be an offence to

those who like everything to fit into the tidy categories of philosophic thought.

The aim of this section of our study has not been to give in tabloid form an outline of Christian doctrine. Its purpose has been to indicate certain perspectives, or perhaps we should call them dimensions, without the use of which it is not possible to speak of Christian faith at all. We have found it necessary to make use of such terms as creation, history, personal being, responsibility, forgiveness, relatedness, resurrection. It has to be recognized from the start that many of these dimensions are not found in other great religions, and some are found only in order to be violently repudiated. Hence the difficulty of comparative study. What is it that we are really comparing? We shall not insist at every point on these Christian categories while looking at other religions in their contemporary form. But we must constantly bear them in mind; otherwise our study is in danger of being unrealistic, and of leading to apparent reconciliations which are in fact no more than empty and irresponsible truces.

And yet, with all these qualities that distinguish it so sharply from every other form of human religious experience or ideal, Christian faith claims for itself that it is the only form of faith for men; by its own claim to truth it casts the shadow of falsehood, or at least of imperfect truth, on every other system. This Christian claim is naturally offensive to the adherents of every other religious system. It is almost as offensive to modern man, brought up in the atmosphere of relativism, in which tolerance is regarded almost as the highest of the virtues. But we must not suppose that this claim to universal validity is something that can quietly be removed from the Gospel without changing it into something entirely different from what it is. The mission of Jesus was limited to the Jews and did not look immediately beyond them; but his life, his methods and his message do not make sense, unless they are interpreted in the light of his own conviction that he was in fact the final and decisive word of God to men.

Attempts to demonstrate the 'absoluteness' of Christian faith on rational or philosophic grounds cannot be said to have been entirely successful. As long as faith is interpreted in terms of *understanding*, it is always possible that understanding might be reached in some other way than that of the Gospel of Jesus Christ—indeed that some other form of understanding might prove in the light of modern knowledge to be more complete and more logically self-consistent. It is better, perhaps, to speak rather of the uniqueness of Christianity than of its absolute validity.

Here we are on safer ground. For the Christian Gospel is rooted in event and not in idea. Now every event in history is in itself unique and unrepeatable. It is possible to find parallels to almost every saying of Jesus in the books of the Rabbis; that does not alter in the slightest the fact that each human life is distinct from every other, and that any system of religious faith which is not centrally concerned with Jesus Christ cannot be in the least like a system which is so centrally concerned.

Simply as history the event of Jesus Christ is unique. Christian faith goes a great deal further in its interpretation of that event. It maintains that in Jesus the one thing that needed to happen has happened in such a way that it need never happen again in the same way. The universe has been reconciled to its God. Through the perfect obedience of one man a new and permanent relationship has been established between God and the whole human race. The bridge has been built. There is room on it for all the needed traffic in both directions, from God to man and from man to God. Why look for any other?

Christian faith is prepared to submit itself to the most radical tests as to its relevance to the life of man now and at all other times. It maintains that in Jesus account has been taken of the whole human situation in every aspect of it; nothing has been overlooked or ignored. No situation can ever arise in the future which cannot be interpreted in the light of the central event of human history— though the interpretation may demand more sensitiveness, patience and humility than Christians are able always to command.

Making such claims, Christians are bound to affirm that all men need the Gospel. For the human sickness there is one specific remedy, and this is it. There is no other. Therefore the Gospel must be proclaimed to the ends of the earth and to the end of time. The Church cannot compromise on its missionary task without ceasing to be the Church. If it fails to see and to accept this responsibility, it is changing the Gospel into something other than itself.

Naturally to the non-Christian hearer this must sound like crazy megalomania and religious imperialism of the very worst kind. We must recognize the dangers; Christians have on many occasions fallen into both of them. But we are driven back ultimately on the question of truth. It is not crazy megalomania for the science of chemistry to affirm that the physical universe has been built up in one way and not in another; the atomic weights of the various elements have been worked out and are printed in a table—that is the way things are and no amount of wishing will make them any different from what they are. It is true that new discoveries are being made all the time, and that the physical universe proves to be far more subtly constructed and flexible than we had at one time supposed. This does not invalidate the earlier results, which still stand. The Christian claim is very close to the claim of the chemist. It states quite simply that the universe under all its aspects has been made in one way and not in another, and that the way in which it has been made has been once for all declared in Jesus Christ. When Jesus stated that he *was* the truth (John 14.6), he did not mean that he was stating a number of good and true ideas; he meant that in him the total structure of the universe was for the first time and for ever disclosed. But since this truth is set forth not in propositions, to which intellectual assent would be the right response, but in personal form, what it demands is not so much understanding as surrender. The man who has seen Jesus as the truth of God is thereby pledged to 'do the truth', in a self-commitment which must become ever more intelligent and ever more complete until it reaches its consummation beyond the limits of space and time.

On all this the Christian cannot compromise. Yet his approach to the other forms of human faith must be marked by the deepest humility. He must endeavour to meet them at their highest, and not cheaply to score points off them by comparing the best he knows with their weaknesses, weaknesses such as are present also in the Christian scheme as it is lived out by very imperfect Christians. He must, as far as imagination will permit, expose himself to the full force of these other faiths in all that they have that is most convincing and most alluring. He must rejoice in everything that they possess of beauty and high aspiration. He must put himself to school with them, in readiness to believe that they may have something to teach him that he has not yet learned. He must sympathize with their earnest efforts to relate themselves to the needs of men in the modern world. He must listen with respectful patience to every criticism that they have to make both of Christian thought and Christian practice.

All this can be done, if the Christian is really humble. Self-assertion is always a sign of lack of inner confidence. If the Christian has really trusted in Christ, he can open himself without fear to any wind that blows from any quarter of the heavens. If by chance some of those winds should blow to him unexpected treasures, he will be convinced that Christ's store-houses are wide enough to gather in those treasures too, in order that in the last day nothing may be lost.

CHAPTER II

THE KING OF THE JEWS

A GREAT many people have read the notable novel to which the *Prix Goncourt* for 1959 was awarded—*Le Dernier des Justes* by André Schwarz-Bart, translated as *The Last of the Just*.

This is a story of Jewish life. Its first scene is that of the famous massacre at York on 11 March 1185, when the Archbishop of the day proclaimed a pogrom against the Jews in the name of the God of the Christians. Most of the Jews were caught and killed immediately. But a number, with Rabbi Yom Tov Levy, took refuge in a deserted tower, where they were besieged for seven days. On the seventh morning the Rabbi said to his companions: 'Brethren, God has given us life; let us ourselves give it back to him.' So each in turn the Jews drew near to the Rabbi, to receive from one hand the benediction of God and from the other the knife; and last of all the Rabbi turned the knife against his own throat.

Later there grew up a legend among the Jews that God had revealed to Solomon the son of Rabbi Yom Tov Levy, who had been miraculously saved from the massacre, that in each generation there would be born in his family a righteous man, who would receive in his own heart the sorrows and sufferings of the whole race. This would be a terrible vocation; but to the end of time the race of the Righteous would not fail.

This legend is not totally meaningless, expressing as it does the profound conviction in the heart of the Jew that though God seems to have forgotten he has not really forgotten; he is still there. In the words of the old chronicler, 'Companions in our age-long exile, as the waves flow into the sea so all our tears flow back into the heart of God.' This accounts for the panic of the small boy, called though he does not know it to be one of the Righteous, when he is first brought face to face with the possibility that God may not exist: 'Oh my God, if you do not exist, what becomes of all the suffering? It is just lost, just lost.'

It would be hard to imagine a more dramatic manner of presenting the tragic history of the Jews. Again and again through history the Christian sword has been drawn against them. Edward I drove them out of England; Ferdinand and Isabella drove them out of Spain. No Christian nation can claim that in this matter it is free of guilt. And now in our own day we have seen the latest and most terrible manifestation of this fury carried to the point of the extermination of the hated race. No one knows exactly how many Jews perished in Hitler's Germany and in the conquered countries; sober estimates put the figure at six million and probably this is not an exaggeration. There has never been any crime like it in history.

And yet the Jew survives. Alone among the ancient races of the world he has retained his separate and distinguishable existence.[1] It is hard to say what it is that has kept the Jews together. There has certainly been considerable mixing of the blood. The Jewish people has been scattered over the face of the earth. Jews have become loyal citizens of a variety of countries, and have fought heroically against one another in the alien conflicts of the Christians. The law and the synagogue have done much to hold them together. But many Jews have abandoned both law and synagogue without losing their Jewishness. Hatred, massacre, exile, forcible conversion, have reduced their numbers—and yet there they still are, in almost every country of the world, a mystery and a problem to their neighbours. Is it perhaps the fact that we Christians have created Jewry? That strange and evil plant anti-Semitism keeps rearing its ugly head; even in civilized societies, where one would have believed such things to be completely impossible, the Jew seems destined to be pointed out as the inevitable victim. Is it this that holds them together? Is it that every Jew knows in his heart of hearts that he has been appointed for suffering, and that every Jew carries somewhere deep within him the heart of a martyr? Hundreds of witnesses have described the astonishing dignity with which Jews of both sexes stripped themselves of their garments, leaving even these poor spoils to their enemies, lay down in Hitler's trenches, and waited for the machine-gun bullets that would add them to the endless roll of Jewish martyrs.

There they are. To the world they are a political or a social problem—or menace, as the interpretation may go. To the Christian they are also a theological problem. If there is any providence in the world, why has God kept his ancient people in being as a people?

[1] We should perhaps add the Armenians as a parallel example of survival from ancient times.

This was the problem with which Paul had to wrestle in chapters 9 to 11 of his Epistle to the Romans. It has been the habit of commentators to concentrate on the first eight chapters of the Epistle as a great exposition of the foundations of the Christian faith—and such indeed they are—and to pass rather lightly over the other eight chapters. For instance, Bishop Anders Nygren in his deservedly celebrated Commentary on the Epistle takes 355 pages for the exposition of the first eight chapters, and only 101 for the whole of the rest of the Epistle. In particular there is a tendency to regard the three chapters, 9, 10 and 11, as an intrusive body, a parenthesis, which can be neglected by the reader without serious loss.

In reality these three chapters form the very heart of the argument. Older expositors tended to treat the Epistle as a theological treatise—here at last, in contrast to the other Epistles, Paul has consented to set out in systematic form the essentials of his theology. More recent study has come back to chapters 14 and 15 as the clue to the interpretation of the whole, and has recognized that here as elsewhere Paul writes his letter in response to problems in the Christian life that simply must be faced. It is true that, as is his way, in order to find an answer to immediately practical questions he has to sound all the depths of the mysteries of God. But it is the practical question that sets him loose on his theological quest. What then was the question put to him by fellow-Christians in Rome, whom he did not yet know face to face?[2]

There were three groups in this little Church of Rome, probably as yet unvisited by any apostle—the Jewish Christians, who had been circumcised and naturally kept certain parts of the Jewish law; Gentile Christians who had agreed to be circumcised; and Gentile Christians of the Pauline tradition, who had not been circumcised and did not recognize any obligation to keep the law. And then there was the further problem of the Jews who were still outside the New Covenant and walked in the way of the fathers. How could three such disparate groups live together in real fellowship? Was there real equality, or could the Christians of the circumcision claim a superiority in view of the election of Israel? And how were they to solve the endless problems in social life that arise for a Christian minority living surrounded by an immense non-Christian majority?

[2] There is a good discussion of this problem by Günther Harder in *Theologia Viatorum, 1954–1958* (Berlin, 1959), pp. 13–24.

Finally, what were they to think of the continued existence of Jewry around them? Was the old covenant with Abraham and Moses still in some sense valid, or had all its validity been absorbed in the new covenant in Christ?

To consider in detail the exegesis of these three difficult chapters would carry us far beyond the limits of what is relevant to our present study. It is sufficient to note that Paul has here brought us face to face with what is still a living problem of theology for Christians, and that to-day as in the past Christians tend to take divergent views as to the solution of the problem.

The first and simplest view is that Christ, as the end of the law, is the end also of the history of Israel. In its crudest form this finds expression in the bitter traditional attitude that the Jews rejected Jesus and that therefore God has rejected the Jews—a view which runs directly contrary to Paul's affirmation that God has not cast off his people. In more theological form, it has been maintained that the Church, as the new Israel, is the heir to all the promises made of old to Israel after the flesh. This is now the only true Israel and there is none other. The survival of the Jews is merely a historical accident, perhaps a warning. Jewry is a sociological phenomenon. But from the point of view of revelation and of the Word of God its day is at an end.

A careful student of the New Testament is almost bound to admit the truth, though perhaps not the exclusive truth, of this understanding of the situation. Again and again Paul addresses Christians in terms which make no sense unless they are in very truth the Israel of God. He assures them that they are heirs through faith of the promises made to Abraham. The whole concept of 'the people of God', with the remarkable transference in 1 Pet. 2.9 of all the characteristics of the old Israel to the new, strengthens this view. It is through the Church that the manifold wisdom of God is to be made manifest to the whole creation. It is within the Church that the Creator Spirit is at work and that the living Word of God is now spoken.

In sharp contrast to this is the view held by some that the old Israel and the new are both in a real sense the people of God, and that they co-exist for the fulfilment of separate but significant purposes of God. We shall consider later some Jewish expressions of this point of view. In the Christian camp Dr. James Parkes has probably gone further than anyone else in affirming the continuing validity of the synagogue alongside the Church.[3] 'Judaism', he writes, 'was obviously not an incomplete Christianity but a *different kind* of religion. It is almost true to say that every strength in Christianity is a weakness in Judaism, and *vice versa*. Christianity is an orthodoxy and Judaism is an orthopraxis, and each has the special quality of its character . . . Judaism spoke to man as a social being; Christianity to man as a person, as an ultimate end in himself.'[4]

It is not likely that many Christians will go as far as Dr. Parkes in such an understanding of the relation between Judaism and Christianity, but obviously this is a point of view that must not be forgotten. And even those who do not share it may well go so far as to believe that the great schism within the Church took place not at the Reformation, but when church and synagogue at the end of the first century irremediably separated themselves from one another. By this separation the Church was inevitably cast into the arms of the Hellenistic world, and ever since that time has continued to think in terms which are mainly of Greek and not of Hebraic origin. This may have been a necessary step in the evangelization of the Graeco-Roman world; some scholars regard it as the moment of the theological downfall of the Church. To-day we are laboriously learning from our Old Testament experts the meaning of the Hebrew categories and of the Semitic approach to life, which are the background of the Gospel; it may be that we shall not recover the fullness of our inheritance until the Jews come back to be our teachers within a restored fellowship of the people of God.

This reflection leads us on to the third main view that has been held among Christians. Many have believed that the Jews have been preserved as a people through all their trials because God has still some great purpose for them, to be fulfilled at the end of the days. God has not cast off his people. Paul foresees them brought back into fellowship with the new Israel in an experience which he can describe only as life from the dead. In the nineteenth century there was a great revival of the study of 'unfulfilled prophecy', much of it based on unscientific methods of Bible study and leading to fantastic conclusions. But, if there was one point on which those who pursued this study were agreed, it was that Israel would be brought back to

---

[3] See *Frontier*, winter 1959, pp. 271–7; but also a whole series of books, notably *Judaism and Christianity* (Chicago, 1948); especially chapter 5, 'The Rediscovery that Jews are a Living People and Judaism a Living Religion'.

[4] loc. cit. p. 273.

Palestine 'in unbelief'. All through the nineteenth century small groups of Jews had been finding their way back to Palestine, and had begun in their colonies to make the desert blossom as the rose. But, until the beginning of the First World War, the prospects for a national return of the Jews to Palestine seemed as bleak and improbable as anything in the world of imagination.

Nothing in recent history is stranger than the story of the contacts between Arthur James Balfour and Chaim Weizmann, the great prophet of Zionism. Balfour was cool and calm in temperament, a philosopher with a sceptical tinge to his thinking, and next to Mr. Asquith the most experienced politician in England. It seemed most unlikely that he would yield to the dreams and fantasies of a Jewish enthusiast. Yet so it came about. The white-hot passion of Weizmann so worked on Balfour that he came to agree that Jerusalem is as much Jewish as Manchester is British.[5] The British government, surely with a very imperfect understanding of what it was doing, committed itself to the Balfour Declaration in favour of the establishment of a national home for the Jews in Palestine. To-day Israel is a nation. For the first time since the destruction of Jerusalem in A.D. 70, the Jews have again a country, a state and a national existence.

The creation of the state of Israel has thrust upon the world a whole range of political and religious problems.

There are, first, the internal problems of Israel itself. That little country has now within it every kind of Jew, from the extreme conservatives who will not consider the alteration of a single letter in the Rabbinic tradition to the Jews of the modern generation who are at home in the boulevards and cafés of Tel-Aviv, who are prepared to accept Judaism as an element of cultural value in the life of the nation but can see in it little if any religious significance. How are these diverse elements to be brought together in any real national unity? After years of division, Jerusalem, including the ancient holy places is now united and in the possession of the Jews. For the moment the new owners have left things very much as they were; but sooner or later they will have to decide what to do with the Dome of the Rock, the site of Solomon's Temple. Will they rebuild the Temple just as it stood of old time? Will they introduce

---

[5] This was an expression actually used by Weizmann in conversation with Balfour. It must not be forgotten that Weizmann, a brilliant chemist, had made contributions to the Allied cause during the war, for which he may have thought himself entitled to a recompense.

the daily sacrifices, as they were observed in the days of our Lord? Or will they consent to that gigantic inner revolution in the Jewish faith which would be involved in admitting that sacrifice and all the ritual connected with it are now things of the past? The Christian, instructed by the Epistle to the Hebrews, can give good reason for his understanding of the end of sacrifice; the Jew would be confronted by a different and perhaps more complex theological problem.

In the world of international politics the very existence of the state of Israel is a running sore. The whole Muslim world speaks and thinks only in terms of 'the crime of Israel'.[6] The Jew thinks of the Jewish return to Israel in terms simply of coming home; this has always been his home. To the Arab it presents itself in plain terms as armed robbery and aggression. Probably a great number, perhaps even the majority, of the Arab refugees from Palestine could by now have been settled elsewhere. But they will not be settled. To them Palestine is still home, and home they are determined to return. The Muslims may claim that in the past they have on the whole treated Jews better than the Christians have done. As regards Muslim-Jewish relationships, however, the future is dark and lowering. The Jews are building up for themselves a treasury of hatred throughout the whole Islamic world.

With these political problems we are not here specially concerned. And the time has hardly come when Christians can begin to think theologically about the state of Israel and the part that it may be called to play in the fulfilment of as yet undisclosed purposes of God. Nevertheless, the recovery of Jewry as a power in the world has brought home to a great many Christians the existence of a problem that they had been inclined to overlook. What do we think of the Jews, of Judaism, and of the Christian's duty in relation to them?

The simplest answer would be to say that we will let them go their own way, and have as little to do with them as possible, except in the way of personal friendship if we happen to meet them. This is an attitude which would undoubtedly commend itself to a great many Jews, who only want to be left alone. It has received unexpected

---

[6] The Arabs 'feel that they have been betrayed and deceived by the West again and again, and that promises made by the British and French and Americans are a mockery. ... They claim that the existence of the State of Israel can be justified upon no grounds at all, save those of expediency, and even then only by expediency at their expense'. Denis Baly, *Multitudes in the Valley* (1958), p. 82.

encouragement from one of the most famous of living Christian teachers.

Professor Reinhold Niebuhr has included in his book *Pious and Secular America* an essay on 'Christians and Jews in Western Civilization'. In the course of this essay he puts forward the view that Christians are wrong in attempting to convert Jews to the Christian way:

Our analysis assumes that these activities are wrong not only because they are futile and have little fruit to boast for their exertions. They are wrong because the two faiths despite differences are sufficiently alike for the Jew to find God more easily in terms of his own religious heritage than by subjecting himself to the hazards of guilty feeling involved in conversion to a faith which, whatever its excellencies, must appear to him as a symbol of an oppressive majority culture. . . . Practically nothing can purify the symbol of Christ as the image of God in the imagination of the Jew from the taint with which ages of Christian oppression in the name of Christ have tainted it.[7]

Here is a challenge expressed in plain and forceful language. It has not been difficult for those who know the situation intimately to point out that Christian missions to Jews have not been quite so infructuous as Professor Niebuhr imagines.[8] All the older generation of preachers was brought up on Edersheim's *Life and Times of Jesus the Messiah*, a book which could hardly have been written except by one who was himself a convert from Rabbinic Judaism to the faith of the Gospel. The Bishop of Liverpool, Dr. C. A. Martin, preaching at the 150th anniversary of the Church's Ministry among the Jews, referred from his own experience to a remarkable case in which a whole Jewish family, first the son, then the mother, and finally the father, had been brought to living faith in Christ, and had settled down happily to be servants of the Church and witnesses to Jews and Christians alike concerning their new-found faith.[9] Almost all of us could give parallels from our own experience.

The significance of Professor Niebuhr's challenge lies elsewhere. Taken as it stands, it would rule out almost every Christian attempt anywhere to win any adherent of another religion to faith in Christ. Especially in these days of inflamed national feeling, any

[7] R. Niebuhr, *Pious and Secular America* (Scribner's, 1958), p. 108.

[8] For instance by the Rev. G. H. Stevens, Secretary of the Church's Ministry among the Jews, in the *International Review of Missions*, October 1959, pp. 427–32.

[9] See *The Church Times*, 4 December 1959, p. 11.

Hindu or Buddhist or Muslim convert is likely to be branded as a traitor by his co-religionists; he has to take the risk of suffering from guilt-feelings for having abandoned what was so precious to his fathers. He too has to accept a faith associated with traditions of colonialism and oppression which are detestable to him. He has to learn to make a new home in a strange land. In such circumstances has the Christian any right whatever to attempt to make converts? The answer has been given succinctly by Bishop Hassan Dehqani, himself a convert from Islam. Of course conversion to the Christian faith involves carrying the cross; but why should Christians try to put obstacles in the way of the Muslim, if he feels himself called by God to carry that particular cross?[10]

Professor Niebuhr's dictum lands us in a yet deeper theological perplexity. What does he mean by the expression 'to find God'? Is this something that can be achieved in a variety of different ways? If so, are we not at once landed in that relativism which later we shall find so ardently propagated by the contemporary Hindu? If the Jew can as satisfactorily find his way to God through Judaism, and the Hindu through Hinduism, without the traumatic experience of separation from culture and traditional ways of living, what have Christians to preach, and why should they preach? The Christian mission springs from the conviction that Christ is *the* Word of God, and that to have encountered God revealed in the face of Jesus Christ is to have entered into an experience wholly different from anything else that life can offer.

If the Christian holds this view, he cannot do otherwise than wish to share his experience with all men, Jew and Gentile alike.

This does not rule out the possibility that the nature of his approach may have to be carefully thought out afresh in relation to new situations. The old term 'Missions to Jews' has fallen under the displeasure that now attaches almost everywhere to the terms 'mission' and 'missionary'. To the Jew of to-day the word seems to speak of that time when Jews were weak and poor and Christians were rich and strong; of patronage, and of charity in the bad sense of the term. A better formulation was reached when the International Missionary Council sponsored the International Committee on the Christian Approach to Israel. Yet even here there is a certain onesidedness—a certain suggestion that the Christians are the givers and the Jews the destined receivers. In our day we have to

---

[10] H. Dehqani-Tafti, *Design of my World* (Lutterworth Press, 1958), p. 60.

move forward a step further; we can think and speak only in terms of the dialogue between Jewry and the Church, between the old Israel and the new.

This formulation, however, at once gives rise to some further considerations. In what circumstances does genuine dialogue become possible? Dialogue is not the same thing as dispassionate and academic discussion; it implies an element of engagement, of rival claims to certain common territory, of perhaps unexpressed hostility, of the desire to win. All this of course can be carried through in the truest spirit of friendship and mutual respect, as it is for the most part in the dialogues of Plato. But it is the inner tension that gives life and vitality to the discussion; this is a life and death struggle in which the prize of victory is the truth. Now religions which have no common frontier and do not wish to have one can go on for ever in isolation, or in the calm climate of purely academic study; no confrontation and no decision are involved. If Christianity lives within the Church and Judaism within the synagogue, peaceful co-existence presents no problems—neither need be vitally concerned with the other. True dialogue between religions would seem to be possible only when each makes some claim to universality. This is a point to which we shall have occasion to recur again and again in dealing with the ancient religions of Asia. The claim to universality can be maintained in a spirit of narrow and bitter aggressiveness; but it can equally well lead on to genuine dialogue, in which sincerity and integrity on one side are matched by sincerity and integrity on the other.

Our first question, then, to our friends within the synagogue relates precisely to this question of universality. Is Judaism something which exists for the Jews alone? Or is it something which they hold in trust for the whole of mankind? If the latter, how do they understand their universal mission, and in what terms would they wish to exercise it in relation to the rest of the world? There is a strain of universalism in the Old Testament—the expectation that all nations will come up to Mount Zion to receive the word of the Lord and his law. Is this something that is still present in Judaism as it is to-day?

Our second question to our Jewish friends must relate to their willingness or unwillingness to take another look at Jesus of Nazareth.

In a very real sense, since the day of Calvary the Jews as a people have never looked at Jesus Christ:

The Jews encountered Christ once at a single moment in history, encountered him as a people, and as a people acquiesced in the rejection of him by their leaders. From that moment in history onward, all that concerned Christ was carefully withheld from the following generations, as parents withhold a painful and terrible secret from their children. Generation after generation united in an unspoken pledge of silence: the painful and terrible secret must be kept from the children. Of course 'the children' were living in the world and news of this 'secret' was bound to reach them, and reach them it did, not as good news, but as 'bad news', not as a message of love, but all too often as a message of hate. In this way, for hundreds of years generations grew up encountering Christ only as an 'excuse' for the neighbours to despise or destroy them which of course was not an encounter with Christ at all, rather with the devil.[11]

This statement has overtones of poetry; yet it is not far from literal truth. It is unusual for Jewish books on the history of Israel to contain such simple factual information about Jesus of Nazareth as will be included on David and Hezekiah. The Jew is brought up to approach the subject with a closed mind.

But to-day all that seems to be changing. From the Jewish side there are remarkable evidences of a new openness, a willingness to consider the story of Jesus of Nazareth objectively, even perhaps to re-instate him as one of the greatest of Jewish teachers[12] instead of rejecting him as that apostate who is alluded to but never mentioned by name in the Jewish Mishnah.[13]

British scholars have long been familiar with the work of Dr. C. G. Montefiore. Montefiore was the leader of liberal Judaism in Britain, and believed that it was possible, while remaining a Jew, to absorb all that was best in the traditions of Christian culture. His *Commentary on the Synoptic Gospels* (2nd edn. 1927) is the classic expression of this liberal synthesis, and was welcomed by

[11] Cornelia and Irving Süssman, 'Marc Chagall, Painter of the Crucified', in *The Bridge*, ed. John M. Oesterreicher (New York, Pantheon Books, 1955), p. 107. The whole of this fascinating study needs to be read.

[12] Note a remarkable passage, quoted from John Cournos, *Hear, O Israel*, in Hans Kosmala and Robert Smith, *The Jew in the Christian World* (1942): 'I have repeatedly stated that Jesus stands at the very apex of Jewish culture. Can any Jew who has honestly studied the sayings and parables of Jesus deny this? And can he honestly reject him, exclude him from the hierarchy of Jewish prophets, of whom he is the logical culmination? For reasons already stated Jews must remain Jews. Yet to remain Jews, they must take up their culture where they left off nineteen centuries ago. They must resume where they broke off the thread of their living tradition.'

[13] It is striking that in the Fourth Gospel the Jews never refer to Jesus by name, but only as 'this man'. This is the way in which later Judaism would refer to an excommunicate person.

Christian scholars for the light that it cast on the Gospels from an unfamiliar angle.

In more recent times Mr. Victor Gollancz in his letters to Timothy his grandson has poured out his interest in the Christian faith.[14] 'I am desperately anxious', he writes, 'that you should understand Christianity, for that, when it comes to it, is what this letter is about; and there are things in Christianity, I feel certain, that can be better understood for a previous understanding of Orthodox Judaism.'[15] Mr. Gollancz goes on to write movingly of his own spiritual pilgrimage—'I was on the way to the adoration of Christ.' He writes in terms that could hardly be bettered by a Christian: 'He lives and reigns for me eternally; and whether or not I should hesitate to call Him Lord, I can assuredly call Him Master.' Amid the perplexities of this frightful world, there is for him only one answer, the answer of the Sermon on the Mount, and this must be accepted absolutely.

Why, then, having gone so far, has Mr. Gollancz never seen his way to acceptance not only of Christ but also of his Church? The answer is without doubt to be found in his attitude to the resurrection. As an undergraduate at Oxford, 'In the physical resurrection I was hardly interested at all . . . I am of the opinion . . . that no educated man genuinely "believes in" it now. . . . But the spiritual Resurrection is another matter: this is an undeniable fact, and of supreme importance.'[16] We shall meet in another context the significance for faith of the physical resurrection of Christ. It is clear that for Mr. Gollancz Christ is not alive and reigning in the sense in which Christians understand those words; he has evaded the Christian challenge at a central point, and therefore it is natural that he should have rejected also the appeal of those beggarly elements of the Body of Christ which are the Church.

Jews who have gone so far in their recognition of the significance of Jesus are faced by a difficult problem—how are we to understand the co-existence of synagogue and Church? Various attempts have been made to suggest that each has an equal and contemporary validity.

The source of most of this understanding of the situation is the teaching of Franz Rosenzweig (1886–1929), one of the few

---

[14] Victor Gollancz, *My Dear Timothy* (London, 1952).
[15] op. cit. p. 111.   [16] op. cit. pp. 394, 402, 403.

original thinkers in the Judaism of the past century. Rosenzweig had very nearly become a Christian, and then at the last moment turned back to Judaism. His interpretation of the situation is that Judaism and Christianity both have a legitimate existence. The Word of God to the Jews was the final and ultimate revelation; but Jesus Christ is the one through whom this revelation could be made accessible to the heathen, and through whom the heathen could be brought back to the place in which the Jews already are:

Judaism and Christianity are religions of the same revealed reality and should not only tolerate but champion each other, for each complements the other. Judaism is 'the eternal fire' and Christianity is 'the eternal rays'. Judaism faces *inward* and stays with God. Christianity faces *outward* to the Gentile peoples, constantly marching for God to conquer the un-redeemed world for him. . . . The Jew is born a member of the eternal people who in order to remain eternal must forswear any part in the life of the world. Moreover, Christianity needs Judaism and shall to the end of history, for Judaism is the eternal fire, and is a perpetual witness to the God to whom Christianity calls the Gentiles. Judaism is already at the goal to which Christianity is drawing the peoples of the world. Judaism is, therefore, the 'eternal life', to which Christianity is the 'eternal way'.[17]

A position a little like that of Rosenzweig has been maintained by Will Herberg. Dr. Herberg has as wide, calm and unprejudiced a knowledge of religions as any man now living, and in addition a deep practical concern for the peaceful co-existence of the various religions in the United States of America. He has returned to this theme again and again in a stream of books and articles.

For Herberg the centre of everything is the covenant. There is no immediate access of man to God—it is only through a covenant that man can be brought into relationship with God. The covenant with Israel is an eternal covenant; there is a new covenant in Jesus, but this is not to be understood as in any way annulling the covenant with Israel—it merely extends it, so that the Gentiles can enter into the same covenant relationship with God. The Jew fulfils his voca-tion simply by being a Jew—he cannot alter or evade the fact that he is a witness to God. The Christian fulfils his vocation by going out into the world. But this is a perilous vocation—the Christian is always in danger of being assimilated by those whom he goes out to win. Therefore he needs the Jew, who by staying with God

[17] Edmund Perry, *The Gospel in Dispute* (New York, Doubleday, 1958), p. 125. Dr. Perry is here summarizing Rosenzweig's thought, referring specially to Nahum Glatzer's *Franz Rosenzweig: His Life and Thought* (New York, 1953).

remains as the unchanging witness to that which the Christian also in his vocation ought to be. Neither Jew nor Gentile can say that his vocation is complete and perfect without the other; they are to be understood as complementary; there can therefore be no question of conversion from one to the other as the result of the Christian-Jewish dialogue.[18]

No Jewish thinker has ever pondered more deeply the meaning of Jesus than Martin Buber. It is impossible to weave into a simple pattern Buber's many and not always entirely consistent utterances. But it seems that for him the central problem is that of messiahship, in the sense of the final deliverance and reconciliation of man. Buber is prepared to go far in recognizing Jesus as one who stood within the tradition and the vocation of messiahship, but he refuses to recognize in him the One who was to come, and whose coming makes both impossible and unnecessary any other coming:

I firmly believe that the Jewish community, in the course of its renaissance, will recognize Jesus; and not merely as a great figure in its religious history, but also in the organic context of a messianic development extending over millennia, whose final goal is the Redemption of Israel and of the world. But I believe equally firmly that we will never recognize Jesus as the Messiah Come for this would contradict the deepest meaning of our Messianic passion. . . . In our view, redemption occurs for ever, and none has yet occurred. Standing bound and shackled in the pillory of mankind we demonstrate with the bloody body of our people the unredeemedness of the world.[19]

It is this unredeemedness of the world that has made the deepest impression on Buber's mind. Jesus believed and claimed that in him redemption has come. If it had really come, the Jew would be ready, indeed would be bound, to receive him. But the whole of history bears witness to the truth that no redemption has taken place:

The Jew as part of the world, experiences, perhaps more intensely than any other part, the world's lack of redemption. He feels this lack of redemption against his skin, he tastes it on his tongue, the burden of the unredeemed world lies on him. Because of this almost physical knowledge

[18] Dr. Herberg has written many articles and books on this theme, notably *Judaism and Modern Man* (New York, Farrar and Straus, 1951); *Catholic, Protestant and Jew* (New York, 1956); and briefly and conveniently 'Judaism and Christianity: their Unity and Difference', in *Journal of Bible and Religion*, XXI, 2 April 1953.

[19] Martin Buber: *Pointing the Way* (trans. and ed. Maurice Friedman, New York, Harper, 1957), p. 18; quoted in *The Bridge*, Vol. iii, p. 218.

of his, he cannot concede that the redemption has taken place; he knows that it has not.[20]

Clearly this judgement rests on the assumption, common to Martin Buber and the Jews of the time of Jesus, that we know what redemption is, or ought to be, on this earth. It is that paradisal state symbolized in the ancient Scriptures by the picture of every man sitting in peace under his own vine and his own fig-tree. Dr. Buber is not prepared to concede that Jesus might have an understanding of redemption so revolutionary as to be irreconcilable with those ideas of it which we have formed in our own minds. For to the Christian, resting as he believes on the words and the example of his Lord, to be redeemed means to be called to take up daily the Cross of Christ and to suffer with him until the world's end.

This falls outside the limits of Dr. Buber's understanding, and he is therefore left with an unsolved problem. How could it come about that one to whom Buber is prepared to accord such reverence as man and teacher could be so fatally deluded? Buber's answer is deeply interesting and revealing. Messiahship is something that accomplishes itself through long aeons; until the moment appointed by God for redemption, the one who is privileged to live within the secret process of messiahship must remain hidden as the arrow which is concealed within the quiver. The error of Jesus was that he was not prepared so to remain hidden and claimed messiahship for himself:

Jesus is the first in the series of men who stepped forth from the seclusion of the servants of God, forth from the real 'messianic secret', and in their hearts and in their speech attributed messiahship to themselves. . . . That this first one . . . was incomparably the purest, most legitimate of them all, the one most endowed with real messianic power, does not alter the fact of his firstness, rather does it belong to it, belong to the awful and pathetic reality of that entire series of self-appointed Messiahs.[21]

So Christians who believe in Jesus share in his error, they are under the same delusion that redemption has already been accomplished, and that we live already in the new creation.

And yet, Professor Buber of his charity is prepared to admit that Christians and Jews have many things in common, and in many things can work together:

---

[20] Martin Buber, *Israel and the World* (New York, Schwaber, 1948), p. 40.
[21] Martin Buber, *Hasidism* (New York: Philosophical Library, 1948), p. 114.

To you the book is a forecourt; to us it is the sanctuary. But in this place we can dwell together, and together listen to the voice that speaks here. . . . Your expectation is directed toward a second coming, ours to a coming which has not been anticipated by a first. To you the phrasing of world history is determined by one absolute midpoint, the year nought; to us it is an unbroken flow of tones following each other without a pause from their origin to their consummation. But we can wait for the advent of the One together, and there are moments when we may prepare the way before him together.[22]

This is a beautifully eirenic utterance, and we must welcome the spirit that has prompted it. Does this alter the fact that the chasm between Jews and Christians is far wider and deeper than any of these conciliatory spirits is prepared to admit? Either the Messiah has come, or he has not; either God's last word to man has been spoken or it has not. We do no service either to truth or to one another if we refuse to look this stark alternative in the face.

Perhaps the whole idea of messiahship has become problematic to the Jews through these long centuries of waiting. Many and varied interpretations of the idea would seem to be current among different schools of thought in Judaism to-day. There are the Orthodox, who still look for the appearing of that one single figure who will at the appointed moment bring the age-long process of messiahship out of its hiddenness and proclaim it to all the world. Many liberal Jews have without doubt abandoned the whole idea of individual messiahship as historically conditioned and no more than symbolic, just as a great many Christians have abandoned the idea of the second coming of Christ in the sense of a literal and physical re-appearance on earth at the end of time. Some few, thinking more in political than in religious categories, may accord to messiahship no more transcendent meaning than the reconstitution of Israel visibly as a nation. Perhaps the largest number of all identify Israel itself with the Messiah—it is the continued existence of Israel as the people of God that is God's unchanging act of messianic redemption for the world.

It is quite clear that Jesus Christ cannot be fitted into any of these messianic categories, any more than he could be fitted into any of the forms and shapes of messianic expectation that were current in the days of his sojourning on earth. Wherever he comes, he has to create his own dimension and his own form of speech, for no human formations of thought can hold him, and no ordinary human speech can express him. He is at all times the expression of the sovereign freedom of God, who will always do things in his own way, and whose ways are often as different as could be imagined from those that we would ourselves have chosen. The rightness of God's action can afterwards be discerned by faith; it can neither be foreseen, nor apprehended in the moment of God's acting.

In the days of Jesus, the Jews as a whole did not want that kind of Messiah, and so they rejected him. Is it unfair to say that to-day too the Jews neither feel the need of such a Messiah nor desire to have him? Jesus as Messiah is still to them a scandal and an offence.

One of the things that most impresses Christians in their contact with Jews is the Jewish sense of wholeness, of completeness. This sense has recently found very clear expression in the words of a French Jew:

Judaism *affirms* life, its nobility, its purity, its significance; it is not marked as for Christianity with a minus, it needs no redemption from without. Life is transfigured from within by the constructive effort of men who fulfil the law of God. Community of Law, Judaism entrusts the effort of obedience and edification to the global man. No rent in the nature of man, as Christianity has it; no mistrust of matter, of the flesh, of the letter. All holds together organically, and nothing is to be despised. All contributes to the same objective of sanctification. . . . Israel's role is not to bring the other peoples to itself but to God, whereas for Christianity men can come to God only through Christianity.[23]

We should probably wish to make some reservations with regard to the presentation of Christianity in these paragraphs; they do seem to set out in clear form something that is essential in the Jewish outlook, or rather in what the Jew feels on the deepest levels of his being. It is the feeling of being 'all right', in tune—at desperate odds, indeed, with a cruel and misunderstanding world, but free from inner self-contradiction and schism.

This is perhaps the spirit of the best Judaism of the end of the Old Testament period. Fifty years ago it was taken for granted that the period of the Law was a period of declension from that of the great witness of the prophets. In quite recent times Old Testament scholarship has done more justice to the period of the Law. The Law was not resented as a burden, it was felt rather to be a blessing,

[23] André Neher, 'Jews confront Christianity', in *The Student World*, 1959, No. 1, pp. 85-6.

the greatest blessing that God had given to his people. Such piety as is expressed in Psalm 19 and Psalm 119 is of a pure and deep type, the profound feeling of a people who have received a royal law and delight to keep it as the reasonable service of their God. No doubt seems to enter in as to whether this law can really be kept or not— it is taken for granted that the world is being saved by 'the constructive effort of men who keep the law'.

It is at this point that the Epistle to the Romans becomes painfully relevant. Is this the highest possible form of religion for man? Are we being serious with ourselves or with God, if we affirm that there is no rent in the nature of man? Paul was one of those who had kept the law and found himself blameless in conscience. And yet he was not at peace with God. For the keeping of the law had brought him into a situation of total despair. The man who fails to keep the law is judged in the sight of God. But the man who keeps the law tends to set himself up as a judge; he builds up a righteousness of his own on which he rests in the presence of God; by so doing he repeats the primal sin of Adam, who desired to make himself independent of God, and thus cuts himself off from that total dependence on God's grace which is the only form of true blessedness for man.[24]

The apocryphal book of *Wisdom* represents with considerable fidelity the calm confidence of the Jew in his standing in the sight of God. As Bishop Nygren has shown in his commentary on the Epistle, in chapter 2 Paul relentlessly takes up point by point exactly these grounds of confidence, and shows that they have no validity in the sight of God the righteous judge.[25] The virtuous Pharisee was of the opinion that there is no rent in the nature of man. Paul deliberately affirms that there is, and introduces this rent where it is not felt in order to lead man on to another dimension of religion, another order of blessedness. Is the Epistle to the Romans exactly the message that the Jew needs to-day?

Is it more than accidental that Buber, who shows so deep a respect and understanding for Jesus of Nazareth, has no words too hard to say about Paul?[26] In Jesus he recognizes one who practised *Emunah*, the type of faith which consists in a joyful and trustful

---

[24] On this see particularly Rudolf Bultmann in his essay on 'Christ the End of the Law' in *Glauben und Verstehen*, Vol. ii, pp. 32–58 (Eng. Trans. pp. 36–66).

[25] *Pauli brev till Romanna* (Stockholm, 1944), pp. 121–5.

[26] See *Two Types of Faith* (New York, Macmillan, 1951), especially pp. 7–12, 170–3.

self-commitment to a God recognized as good and merciful. It was the gnostically-minded Paul, he tells us, who corrupted everything by introducing a Greek concept of *pistis*, faith, in which through an act of intellectual consent God is received as an article of faith. Now what Buber is here affirming is simply untrue. *Pistis* in Paul means exactly what Buber means by *Emunah;* it *is* the trustful self-commitment of a man to God who is recognized as good and merciful. But there is a difference. Jesus is the true man, the one in whom in sober reality there is no rent in nature; therefore his faith in God is of a special kind without parallel. Paul is the man aware of the rent in his being, who knows that he can come to the peace of faith in God only by the tragic way of death and resurrection.

The law is holy and right and good. But, if a man is content with the limited perspectives that are offered by the law, the law serves as a barrier to keep him from heights and depths of experience that for the Christian are included in the word 'God'.

So the Christian has still a witness to bear to the Jew. His approach must be made with the utmost reverence and humility. Christendom as a whole has never adequately repented of what it has done to the Jews. The Christian who meets a Jew must in his own person incorporate that profound penitence which can never be fully expressed. At the same time he must be moved by deep respect for one who stands for that ageless and timeless faithfulness that finds expression in every synagogue service.[27] But still he has a duty —to ask the Jew to look once again at Jesus Christ, without hate and without prejudice, and to ask himself whether there are certain things in the picture that so far he has missed. The Jew is not without a sense of sin; every day in his prayers he asks for the forgiveness of God.[28] Yet he has been so much more sinned against than sinning that perhaps forgiveness and acceptance by God are too easily assumed. The rent can be healed, if once its existence is fully and honestly recognized. The only thing that reveals to man the rent in his being is the Cross of Jesus Christ, understood both as God's visible judgement on sin, and as the divine act of redemption and

---

[27] This is summed up in the first of the eighteen Benedictions of the Jewish Prayer Book: 'Blessed art thou, O Lord our God and God of our fathers, God of Abraham, God of Isaac, and God of Jacob, the great, mighty and revered God, the most high God, who bestowest loving kindnesses, and art master of all things: who rememberest the pious deeds of the patriarchs, and in love will bring a redeemer to their children's children, for thy name's sake.'

[28] In the fifth of the eighteen Benedictions.

mercy on behalf of men who cannot bring in the kingdom of God by their own constructive effort.

We have gone a long way round in the attempt to understand the purposes of God for his ancient people, and, when we have done our best, we must admit that much still remains dark to us. But we may rest in the absolute assurance that the faithfulness of Israel is precious in the sight of God, and will in time receive its reward. We can hardly add anything to what was written by Robert Browning a century ago:

> God spoke, and gave us the word to keep,
> Bade never fold the hands nor sleep
> 'Mid a faithless world—at watch and ward,
> Till Christ at the end relieve our guard.
> By his servant Moses the watch was set;
> Though near upon cock-crow, we keep it yet.
>
> Thou! if thou wast He, who at mid-watch came,
> By the starlight naming a dubious name!
> And if, too heavy with sleep—too rash
> With fear—O Thou, if that martyr-gash
> Fell on Thee coming to take thine own,
> And we gave the Cross, when we owed the Throne,
>
> Thou art the Judge. We are bruised thus.
> But, the Judgment over, join sides with us.[29]

CHAPTER III

ISLAM IN CRISIS

AMONG the great religions of the world Islam is unique in that it came into existence later than Christianity, and in some sense is dependent upon it. Like Christianity, from very early times if not absolutely from the beginning, it has laid claim to universality. Because of its assertion that it is the final revelation, the last word of God to man, it must stand in opposition to Christian faith; it must deny its claims and attempt to discredit its credentials.

The word Islam means 'surrender'. The Muslim is the one who is surrendered to the will of God. But Christians frequently misinterpret this term, as though it meant a quietistic and fatalistic acceptance of whatever happens as the will of God; its truer and original meaning is 'an acceptance of His pleasure, a dynamic readiness to give oneself to carrying out what ought to happen.'[1] What ought to happen? The Muslim does not make the same kind of distinction as Western man between the sacred and the secular, between religion and other concerns of men. He does not think of one community which is the Church and another community which is the state. On his view God through Muhammad revealed a total pattern for the life of man, in which politics, ethics, economics, social order, are bound together in an indissoluble totality by the will of God, which is the transcendental element in the compound. This is the way in which men ought to live. This is human society as it should be. The Muslim is the man who is committed to bringing to realization, by his devotion and his efforts, this society as God has willed it to exist to the ends of the earth.[2]

This means that the Muslim, like the Christian and the Marxist, is interested in history. History is the sphere in which the purpose of God is to be carried out. God is omnipotent and sovereign. And since the Muslim as such identifies his own existence with the will of God, he must expect to see in history, progressively and over ever-widening stretches of the earth, the establishment of the divine

[1] W. Cantwell Smith, *Islam in Modern History* (1957), p. 16, n. 10.
[2] Sir Muhammad Iqbal summed up the nature of Islam as a social polity whose purpose is to 'realize the spiritual in a human organization'. Quoted in *Modern Trends in World Religions* (ed. Joseph M. Kitagawa, 1959), p. 24.

society as he has understood it. The crisis of Islam to-day is that, from this point of view, history seems to have gone wrong.

The Christian can well understand this perplexity, since in a measure he shares it. He too believes that the divine community must spread to every part of the earth; he too believes that it is only through the effort and witness of Christians that the community can be extended. But for him the problem of disappointed expectations can never be quite so agonizing as it is for the Muslim.

Let us put it quite crudely. Jesus was a failure and Muhammad was a success. The Gospel was from the start a story of victory arising out of defeat. For centuries the Christians were a minority of insignificant and persecuted people; they saw the miracle of progress as the direct act of God who uses the weak things of the world to confound the strong. The time came, indeed, when the Christians were strong and took over the rule of the Empire; they fell into the disastrous error of using force against the unbeliever, and even of turning the Christian sword against the Christian. But they never officially accepted as part of their faith the error of identifying political success with the progress of the kingdom.[3] If they had been tempted to do so, they would have been put on the right track by one of the greatest of all monuments of Christian thinking, Augustine on *The City of God*. Here it was made plain for ever that the City of God cannot be identified with any human city.

This being so, it is possible for the Christian, though saddened by Christian reverses, to take them on the whole fairly calmly. He may look out on the contemporary world with troubled eyes, seeing the Christian cause so weak and threatened where we had believed it to be strong; but he will not be tempted to identify temporary setbacks with final defeat or extinction. We have not been promised any kind of a success story. The Church will be to the end of time a persecuted Church; the purpose of God will be fulfilled slowly and obscurely, through many disasters and defeats. Accepting weakness and frustration as part of its earthly destiny, the Church does not expect to see the glory until the final manifestation of the Son of man.

Very different is the outlook of the Muslim. He has been brought up on a success story. Muhammad was a great leader of men. Finding the Arab tribes of the eighth century weak, divided and

[3] There was, of course, in the nineteenth century, a very real danger that Christians might fall into the error of identifying Christian progress with the increasing dominance of the Western nations over the rest of the world.

purposeless, through the force of his personality and his creed he knit them into a unity, gave them a social organization, and launched them on an astonishing career of conquest. Looking back we can see that the victories of the Muslims were due rather to the weaknesses of their enemies than to their own skill; all the ancient kingdoms had been eaten away internally by corruption, love of ease or the debility of old age. Still, the story is astonishing. Within a century of the death of the Prophet the Muslims had taken over Persia, Mesopotamia, Syria, Egypt, North Africa and the greater part of Spain. They were driven out of France only by the victory of Charles Martel at Tours in 732. Later centuries did not quite come up to the surging vigour of the first advance. Yet Islam continued to make progress for more than a thousand years.

The great threat of the Crusades, in which the whole weight of resurgent Europe was thrown against Islam and seemed to threaten its very heart, had been thrown back after two centuries of intermittent warfare.[4] India was entered and penetrated, and in course of time passed in great part under the dominion of a Muslim dynasty. In 1453 the greatest Christian city in the world, Constantinople, fell before the invaders; the great Church of the Holy Wisdom was turned into a mosque and the Christian Empire of more than a thousand years was brought to an end. Islam continued to press forward. The chief centres of the ancient civilization fell into Islamic hands. In 1683 the Turks were at the gates of Vienna—it was the pressure of the Turks on the eastern frontier which more than anything else saved the Reformation from that threat of extermination, which seemed to be always hanging over its head.[5] By the middle of the nineteenth century there were millions of Muslims in China, in Indonesia and in tropical Africa. There had been set-backs; but the Muslim, looking back on history, might well feel that his faith was justified; here was a great and solid unity, stretching unbroken across the great land mass from the Atlantic almost to the Pacific Ocean.

It was only in the nineteenth century that things began to go seriously wrong. In the Middle Ages Islam had been expelled from

[4] Jerusalem was captured by the Crusaders in 1099; Acre, their last stronghold, was finally lost in 1291.

[5] In 1526 the Turkish victory at Mohacs laid Hungary open to invasion. The inveterate tendency of the Christian King of France to ally himself with the Paynim against the Christian Emperor did more perhaps than anything else to save Protestantism for Europe. It was the Turkish danger that compelled Charles V to listen to the Protestant princes at the Diet of Augsburg in 1530.

Spain, but that loss had quickly been made up by other gains. Now, however, began a steady crumbling of the political power and influence of Islam. The liberation of Greece in 1821 was the portent. This was followed by the gradual detachment of the Balkans from the Turkish Empire. But the withdrawal became a débâcle only when Turkey chose the wrong side in the First World War, and suffered all the consequences of the defeat of Germany in that war. The Empire of Turkey, ramshackle, incompetent and reactionary, had stretched from Morocco to the borders of Persia, from the Adriatic to the upper waters of the Nile. The Sultan as Khalif had exercised a shadowy authority as the political, and in a measure also as the spiritual, centre of the whole Islamic world. Now all this was no more. The Turkish Empire collapsed and broke up into a large number of separate fragments.

No doubt to many Muslims liberation from the Turkish yoke brought a certain satisfaction. But it was not immediately clear that king stork was better than king log. Turkish rule had been slovenly and ineffectual, but at least it was Islamic. Now, in a way never experienced even in the time of the Crusades, the destinies of the whole Muslim world seemed to be controlled by alien and Christian powers. There were the French newly installed in Syria; the British in Palestine and Egypt; the Italians in Libya. The recently created Arab kingdoms were nominally independent; but in fact Britain exercised a great deal of control over Jordania, and under treaty was the dominant power in Iraq. Further East the British continued to rule serenely in India, the Dutch in what is now Indonesia. Christian dominion had been carried into the very heart of the Arab and Islamic world.

It is not surprising that the Islamic world has caught the fever of nationalism that is raging everywhere among the peoples of Asia and Africa. The special intensity and vigour of Islamic, and especially Arab, nationalism springs from a complex of causes—memories of past splendour, resentment over Muslim weakness and Christian strength, above all that obscure sense of malaise, the feeling that in some way history has gone awry, that somehow the purposes of God are not being fulfilled as the Muslim has a right to expect.

The achievements of the post-war period have been considerable. Egyptian self-assertion has made the Middle East one of the chief problem areas in the world. Libya became independent after the war. Morocco and Tunis have since won their independence.

In Algeria the story of detachment from France was long and painful. But here too, in 1962, the goal of total independence was attained. And so the story goes on.

And yet the dominant mood throughout the Islamic world seems to be anxiety, the sense of a crisis that is not being resolved and perhaps cannot be resolved:

For many Arabs the problem is no longer that the Islamic dream is unrealized. Religions can live with their dreams unrealized; this is part of the religious genius. . . . One may live a straitened life and feel that in His good time God will actualize the ideal community, will make the dream come true. One may awake to a strenuous life and with one's fellows strive to actualize it, with God's favour to make it come true oneself. But it is harsh to wake to the fact that aliens, without that favour, have in some way actualized it while one slept. The challenge is no longer simply that the dream is unrealized. The new challenge to the Arab world is in the fear of the recognition that the dream may be invalid. . . . the fear that Islam itself even in its ideal form, even if implemented, would—the very idea is blasphemous—be too weak in the world of today.[6]

If this diagnosis is correct, a piquant contrast exists between that which first strikes an observer of Islam, its cohesion and its strength, and this agonizing experience of inner uncertainty.

For, though the success of Islam may not have been as great as the Muslim thinks it should be, it still is impressive simply as a historical phenomenon. Muslims number more than four hundred million. This means that they out-number the adherents of the much older religions of Hinduism and Buddhism. Islam has adapted itself to different regions and varying types of background. For all its own inner tensions, sects and heresies, it is held together by the very simplicity of its creed, proclaimed every day from countless minarets and repeated endlessly by every pious Muslim— the affirmation that there is no God but Allah, and that Muhammad is the prophet of Allah. The Muslim feels himself to be a member of a great brotherhood in which, as he is not slow to point out, barriers of race and colour have been far more successfully overcome than in that Christian fellowship which also proclaims itself to be the universal brotherhood. The Muslim who succeeds in making the pilgrimage to Mecca goes through an overwhelming emotional experience. Many of the regulations may seem to Westerners

---

[6] W. Cantwell Smith, *Islam in Modern History*, p. 112.

survivals of barbarism, many of the ceremonies trivial. But just the acceptance of a common discipline, the carrying out of these time-less rites in company with an immense crowd gathered from almost every country in the world, catches the worshipper up into the inmost sanctuary of faith, impresses on him the might and unchang-ing power of Islam, and sends him back humbled and more deeply convinced than ever that this is the true revelation of God. A few may be put off by the rabid commercialism of the modern town of Mecca or by some of the attendant circumstances of the pilgrimage; the majority appears to take all these things in its stride, and to feel only the spiritual glory of the experience.

And yet, with all this, anxiety will not be dispelled. From end to end the Islamic world is in crisis, wrestling with new and un-familiar political problems which drive the Muslim back on many kinds of intellectual questioning, and this in the end drives him back to look again at his religion and to ask how it can manifest itself as adequate, as he is sure that it is, to all the needs of the faithful Muslim, and ultimately to the needs of all men, in the perplexities of the modern world. The nature of this anxiety can be elucidated by considering briefly the emotional situation of four of the main blocks of Muslims in the world today.

The Muslim world is not the same as the Arab world. Yet the origins of Islam in Arabia are still deeply stamped upon it, and the Arab, or Arabic-speaking, lands are the heart-lands of Islam and always will be so.

This is partly a matter of the language. Islam has performed the remarkable feat of imposing not merely a civilization but a language over a vast area where other languages have been displaced. In Egypt Coptic survives only as the liturgical language of an oppressed Christian minority; in some other areas local languages have completely disappeared. In part this is due to the splendour and flexibility of the Arabic language itself; in part it is due to the central place played by the Qur'an in what more than any other religion is the religion of the Book:

The medium in which the aesthetic feeling of the Arabs is mainly (though not exclusively) expressed is that of words and language—the most seductive, it may be, and certainly the most unstable and even dangerous of all the arts. . . . We know something of the effect of the spoken and written word upon ourselves. But upon the Arab mind the impact of artistic speech is immediate; the words passing through no filter of logic or reflection which might weaken or deaden their effect go straight to the head. It is easy, therefore, to understand why Arabs, to whom the noble use of speech is the supreme art—and other Muslims also, to whom by long familiarity the Arab sensitivity to its language has become second nature—should see in the Koran a work of super-human origin and a veritable miracle.[7]

Here is one of the great bonds of unity in the Islamic world. No other language may be used in worship. Until recently no translation of the Qur'an into any other language was permitted. In quite recent times the authorities of the al-Azhar University in Cairo have taken the view that the use of translations of the Qur'an by non-Arab Muslims is legitimate. But this extends only to non-liturgical use; for all purposes of worship, public and private alike, the Arabic language stands unchallenged and supreme.[8] This one fact secures for the Arabic-speaking lands their permanent position as the centre of the world of Islam.

It is interesting to note, however, that the policy of promoting Arabic as the one language of the religion was not everywhere successful. Some cultures have proved resistant to the pressure of centuries. In Persia, for example, Islam performed the remarkable feat of imposing a script planned to meet the needs of a Semitic language on an Indo-European form of speech with an ancient history and a great literature of its own; yet the language of Iran today is Persian and not Arabic. In India, in that elegant hybrid Urdu, it accepted the basic Indo-European structure, but together with the script transformed almost the entire vocabulary by the introduction of Arabic and Persian words. Something of the same process has gone on in Swahili, the *lingua franca* of East Africa. But in many parts of tropical Africa, as in Indonesia and China, Arabic has made no headway at all except for purely religious purposes. The diversity of language serves to some extent as a clue to the variety of crises that the Islamic peoples are called to face in these days, though all the crises spring ultimately from the one central crisis of faith in the modern world.

For the Arabic-speaking countries the burning issue is that of unity. Where is leadership to be found? Can the Arab League be turned into something more than a debating club in which members are free to disagree on every issue that comes before them? President

[7] H. A. R. Gibb, *Modern Trends in Islam* (Chicago, 1947), p. 5.
[8] op. cit. p. 131, n. 1.

Nasser has made a tremendous attempt to bring about Arab unity under Egyptian leadership. It is clear that this leadership is unacceptable to the more strictly Arab peoples of the Middle East. The common sentiment of hatred against Israel helps forward the cause of unity; but this rather negative feeling has not succeeded in producing any form of close political organization as its effective expression.

Turkey does not fit easily into any familiar pattern. Its revolution in the years after 1918 was secular, almost secularist, in tone and manner. In a few years Turkey leaped out of the Middle Ages into the modern world, and the process involved the abandonment of almost everything which had been traditionally maintained by Islam. An amendment to the constitution established 'laicism', or what in English we would more commonly call secularism, as one of the cardinal principles of the state. The old Islamic law, the *Shari'ah*, had already in 1926 been replaced by Western legal codes.

Had Turkey ceased altogether to be a Muslim country? This was not the feeling of the Turks themselves. They had dissolved the connexion between 'Church' and 'State', but they believed themselves to have done so on the best Islamic principles. Islam is a religion without a priesthood; where it falls under the control of a priesthood, so the Turks maintained, it is distorted and every kind of evil results. In its nature progressive, it had become bogged down in meaningless and out-of-date tradition:

Turkey simply took the to-day necessary, salutary reforming step of making religion what it should be, an individual personal matter, a thing of the conscience, a matter of private faith. The religious feeling is much too strongly imbedded in the human soul for religion to be abolished. We have simply freed it.[9]

It is in accordance with this understanding of the Turkish revolution that certain startling changes have recently been brought about. In 1946 a proposal to introduce Islamic teaching in state schools was favourably received. In 1948 instruction for religious functionaries was established with state support. In 1949 a Faculty of Theology was set up in the University of Ankara.[10]

[9] W. Cantwell Smith, op. cit. p. 177. Dr. Smith is here giving in his own words a summary of many conversations with Turkish Muslims.

[10] *The Times* of 23 February 1960 carried a valuable and most interesting article under the title 'Turks turn again to Religion'. Note especially the sentences, 'This figure of 5,000 new mosques built in the ten years since 1950 is, by a curious coincidence, not

Islam is making its way back into Turkish life. But clearly this will be a kind of Islam very different from anything known before. The Turk believes himself to be at the head of progress, putting back movement into a great religious tradition that had lost it. To the Orthodox Muslim, however, Islam as interpreted in Turkey does not seem to be Islam at all.

Pakistan is also facing a revolutionary situation. But, whereas Turkey chose the secular path, Pakistan at the start declared itself to be an Islamic state. The only reason for the existence of Pakistan was the determination of Muslims not to live under what they believed would be Hindu domination. One of the first resolutions adopted by the Constituent Assembly affirmed that Pakistan would be a state 'wherein the Muslims shall be enabled to order their lives in individual and collective spheres in accord with the teachings and requirements of Islam as set out in the Holy Qur'an and the Sunnah'. In introducing the resolution, the Prime Minister, Liyaqat Ali Khan, affirmed that 'the State is not to play the part of a neutral observer . . . the State will create such conditions as are conducive to the building up of a truly Islamic Society, which means that the State will have to play a positive part in this effort'.

Had the leaders who made these declarations considered all that was involved in them? Can non-Muslims be citizens with full rights in an Islamic state? The tradition clearly excludes this possibility. As we have seen, the aim of Islam is to bring into being on earth the perfect community according to the will of God revealed in the Qur'an. This can be accomplished only by the *mukallaf*, the man who has accepted in full the obligation of carrying out the behests of God. In return for this acceptance of the will of God, the *mukallaf* acquires certain rights and privileges, the status, as we in the West would express it, of a citizen. But the one who is not so pledged to carry out the will of God cannot acquire either rights or privileges, because by his choice he has made himself incapable of contributing to the building up of the true community—all that he can do is to pay taxes.

From the start Pakistan had to wrestle with a disharmony in its own soul. How does one create an Islamic state in the modern world?

far from the figure which is given by the Ministry of Education for the number of new schools built during the same period. This silent struggle for scarce resources between mosques and schools seems highly symbolic of the greater struggle between the forces of secularism and Islam in Turkey.'

Most of those who came forward to take up leadership in the country had studied in the West. Under British rule they had become acquainted with the traditions of English liberalism and had absorbed a great many Western political ideas. Are such ideas ultimately compatible with Islam, as the older generation would wish to interpret it in the strict categories of the law and the traditions? It may be that the leaders themselves had not enough faith in Islam, or a deep enough understanding of it, to be able to answer the question. For the moment the country seems to have abandoned the problem as insoluble. In October 1958 a *coup d'état* established a military dictatorship. The constitution, which declared Pakistan an Islamic state and provided that no law should be valid which was repugnant to the Holy Qur'an or the Sunnah, has been abrogated. The orders of the new régime speak of the country simply as 'The Republic of Pakistan'. Its attitude is determinedly secular, though not anti-religious. As in Turkey the present view appears to be that religion is a matter of individual decision and no concern of the state. It would hardly be possible to imagine a more dramatic illustration of the Islamic dilemma in the world to-day.

The most disturbing problems in the whole of the Islamic world are those of the Muslims who have remained in India. The Muslims of Pakistan managed to create the most populous Muslim state in the world, but this was very far from gathering into itself all the Muslims in the Indian sub-continent. In fact India with forty million Muslims now represents the third largest aggregate of Muslim citizens. If problems elsewhere are acute, those of the Indian Muslim are agonizing. India has declared itself to be a secular democratic republic. As has been explained by Indian leaders, this is not to be taken as implying an attitude hostile to religion or a disregard of the significance of religion in human life. It means simply the total separation of religion from politics; the two fields are to be regarded as independent though co-existent. As we shall see later, not all Hindus are by any means satisfied with this definition of the policy of their country; but, to the credit of India as a whole and of the first Prime Minister in particular, it must be said that the policy of religious neutrality has been firmly maintained.

Nevertheless, the plight of the Indian Muslim is painful. The very principle of the totality of life, of the inseparability of its various compartments, by which he lives has been officially denied. He knows that he can never be anything but a member of a minority. In this world of heightened passions, no religious minority anywhere feels quite safe. What is he to do?

It has to be admitted that on the whole the Indian Muslim has made the worst of the situation. He has tended to regard Pakistan as his real home, an attitude sedulously fostered by Pakistan, and himself merely as a sojourner in an alien world. Some of the strongest Muslim leaders in India have left their homes to seek a new career in Pakistan. The situation is a little like that of the Protestant minority in the Republic of Ireland, when the independence of the Free State was first proclaimed. It was open to the Protestants to continue to regard themselves as the English colony in Ireland; the great majority took the other point of view, and determined to accept the position of loyal citizens of the new country—a position which would involve them in a number of hitherto unknown problems but would also open before them the possibilities of useful service.

Which of the possible attitudes will the Indian Muslims take up? The answer is not yet clear and there are few precedents to guide them. Muslims have known what it was to dominate, and to determine the life of the countries in which they lived. They have known what it was to live under a Christian oppressor and to bide their time. They have had experience of the impartial rule of colonial powers, which gave them religious liberty with no political advantage. (It is part of the Indian mythology that Britain in India deliberately favoured the Muslims as against the Hindus on the principle *divide et impera*, but no evidence in favour of this contention has yet been produced.) But now the Indian Muslim is face to face with a new situation. He is called neither to rule nor to submit but to share political power with others in a democratic state, where he will be in a minority and can therefore never hope for the realization of an Islamic society in the traditional pattern, but where he can hope to make his own contribution to a rich and varied national life. Will he rise to the opportunity?

One group which is thinking constructively in this situation has gone back for a precedent to the earliest years of the Prophet in Medina, when he was not yet in sole control of the situation, and had to accept the relationship of *muᶜahadah*, mutual contract, with the Jews in that city. The way in which this group conceive of the possibilities of their situation is summarized by Dr. Cantwell Smith in the following terms:

The specifically Islamic duty of the community within India now, in their eyes, is to keep loyalty to the Constitution and to work out within the national life, as an acknowledged minority within the larger society, such personal and social aspects of the total Islamic pattern as can be directly implemented in this situation, and such socio-economic-administrative aspects as they can democratically persuade the whole nation to adopt.[11]

This is far from the Islamic ideal of the great days; it may be the practical and constructive ideal for a changed situation.

It could be maintained that all the problems we have been discussing are primarily political in character. But this would be to misunderstand them from the Muslim point of view. We must insist again on the totalitarian understanding of human life which is characteristic of all Islamic thought. This is to be a community totally related to God and His revelation; law, ethics, government, the habits of daily life, religion, worship—all these things are covered, and the right answer to all questions relating to them has been unalterably revealed. Traditionally an Islamic government cannot be neutral. And our Western separation of politics and religion, which for us too is a very recent thing, is to the traditionally-minded Muslim unintelligible and unacceptable. Anything which touches any part of his life touches his religion as well. The whole Islamic world is in ferment and living through a period of crisis. Inevitably, part of this crisis is recognized as a challenge to take up the reconsideration and re-statement of Islam as religious faith.

Situations are varied and complex. It may, however, be said with some confidence that in the background of them all stands the sinister figure of 'the West'. To the Muslim this means the Christian West, a mixture of political and material power with religious intolerance, and at the same time a subtle, penetrating influence, which wherever it comes can have no effect other than that of detaching the Muslim from his own supreme loyalty to the demands of God. The Islamic world is becoming increasingly aware of the other great factor in world politics, the communist regimes. It is at times tempted to flirt with them as a counterpoise to Western influence, though as the experience of a very few years in Egypt and Iraq has shown the wooing of communist favour is likely to be followed in a very short time by a sharp anti-communist reaction. In any case, the working out of this relationship is for the future;

[11] W. Cantwell Smith, *Islam in Modern History*, p. 285.

for the moment it is the West which constitutes the major factor in the Islamic problem.

In so complex a situation Islamic attitudes have naturally varied. Some have welcomed the West with open arms, and have believed that a Muslim, without disloyalty to his faith, can turn himself into a variant form of *homo occidentalis*. Others have said a firm No to the West and all its ways, and have withdrawn into the seclusion of traditionalist existence. But perhaps the most characteristic attitude and perplexity is that of the combination of love and hatred, attraction and repulsion. This has been acutely analyzed by Dr. Cantwell Smith in the case of the Egyptian leader and publicist Muhammad Farid Wajdi (1875-1954):

This simultaneous repulsion and attraction in relation to the modern West is profound, and can be seen to underlie and to explain much of Wajdi's writing. It indicates that he and his readers are sufficiently involved in a community lack of self-confidence that the good opinion of Europe is a matter of deep concern to them. Yet that very lack of self-confidence is nourished by, or even stems from, an apparent adoption of the standards on which Europe supposedly forms opinions. At a more basic level it stems from an inability to form, and live by, genuine value judgments of one's own.[12]

It would be hard to imagine a more painful and exacting dilemma than this.

From the political dilemma the Muslim is cast back on the religious. We may distinguish three main tendencies, with a foot-note to one of them, in the attempt to make Islam viable in the modern world.

1. The first is the attitude of unbending Qur'anic orthodoxy, to be met with, for example, in the *ulemas*, the religious teachers of Pakistan, who claimed that Pakistan should live up to its professions and become a thoroughly Islamic state.

It is difficult for Christians to understand the role which the Qur'an plays in the world of Islam. The instinctive tendency is to compare it with the Bible, and this at once leads to misunderstandings in both directions. The Muslim, confronted with the Bible and with modern Christian explanations of it, cannot understand how Christians can possibly regard it as a holy book. Throughout it is the work of men. Even the Gospels are not the word of Jesus Christ but only words about him, with an element of distortion which is

---

[12] W. Cantwell Smith, op. cit. p. 141.

evident in the variant forms in which even the words of Christ are put forward. The most rigid Christian fundamentalist admits some human element in Scripture. The Muslim does not admit any human element at all in the Qur'an; it is the Word of God himself, existent with him from the beginning; it is a word addressed *to* Muhammad, and in no sense at all a word *of* Muhammad. It has rightly been maintained by a number of Christian scholars that, if we wish to understand the Muslim attitude to the Qur'an, the true parallel is not between Qur'an and Bible, but between Qur'an and the Word made flesh in Jesus Christ. The Bible is much closer to what the Muslim calls *ḥadith*, the inspired tradition. It is impossible altogether to avoid comparison of Qur'an and Bible; the comparison as commonly made involves us only in confusion and mutual irritation.

The strictly orthodox Muslim, holding the view indicated in the preceding paragraph, is convinced that everything that man can possibly need to know about God and the meaning of human life is to be found in the pages of the Qur'an and nowhere else. This has not always been the view of all Muslims. In history there have been three pillars of Muslim faith—the Word, the traditions, and 'consensus', *ijmā*. The traditions include a vast mass of material relating to what the prophet did or said in a variety of circumstances. The sifting and the classification of these traditions has been one main pre-occupation of Islamic theology. The *ijmā* is the consensus of the community, 'demonstrated by the slowly accumulating pressure of opinion over a long period of time'.[13] Now the *ijmā*, however strictly controlled, could become a principle of movement in Islam; therefore the tendency among the strictly Orthodox has been either to reject it altogether as a pillar of the faith, or to limit it to the first generation of Muslims, who were nearer to the great events of the origins and therefore in a position to elucidate what had not become clear in the words of the Qur'an itself.

2. If Islam has its fundamentalists, it also has its modernists, those who would rethink the faith courageously in the light of modern demands and needs. To their rescue comes another principle, that of *ijtihād*, 'exercise of judgment'. The meaning of this term is defined for us by Professor Gibb as follows:

It in no way implies, as some modernists would like us to believe, 'freedom of judgment'. The word literally means 'exerting oneself', in the

[13] H. A. R. Gibb, op. cit. p. 11. The basis of *ijma* is a tradition in which are ascribed to the Prophet the words 'My community will never agree on an error.'

sense of striving to discover the true application of the teachings of Koran and tradition to a particular situation, and it must not go against the plain sense of these teachings.[14]

Naturally the orthodox doctors have always disliked this principle, since it might seem to open the way to all kinds of innovations. *Ijtihād*, on their view, is ineffective without *ijmā*. In the course of centuries, all the gaps in revelation have been filled in, and therefore the door of *ijtihād* has been closed for ever.

It is this doctrine of *ijtihād*, however, which the Islamic modernists have taken up, sometimes with what one can only call a ruthless determination to rethink the whole of Islam in relation to the needs and claims of the modern world. The most notable of these new interpreters was Sir Muhammad Iqbal, distinguished as a poet in several languages and spiritually one of the founders of Pakistan. His approach to the problem, particularly in the domain of law, is trenchantly set forth in one of his lectures on *The Reconstruction of Religious Thought in Islam*:

I know the Ulema of Islam claim finality for the popular schools of Mohammedan Law . . . but since things have changed and the world of Islam is today confronted and affected by new forces set free by the extraordinary development of human thought in all its directions, I see no reason why this attitude should be maintained any longer. Did the founders of our schools ever claim finality for their reasonings and interpretations? Never. The claim of the present generation of Muslim liberals to reinterpret the foundational legal principles, in the light of their own experience and the altered conditions of modern life, is in my opinion perfectly justified.[15]

Things have changed in the world, and therefore the religion must change with it. Such is always and everywhere the argument of the liberal and the modernist. God has not changed, replies the fundamentalist, and therefore the religion which depends on his word cannot change in any particular. The old-time religion was good enough for grandpa and grandma, and it's good enough for me.

3. There is a third attitude, which is more difficult to define, and which is perhaps hardly as yet articulate. We may approach it with the question, 'To what is the loyalty of the Muslim directed? Is it to Islam, as it has evolved, with its multiplicity of doctrines and precepts? Or is it to the God who revealed Himself in the original

[14] op. cit. pp. 12–13.
[15] op. cit. pp. 159–60, quoted by H. A. R. Gibb, op. cit. p. 101.

Islam?' We must recognize that for the orthodox this question is meaningless—such a distinction cannot be drawn. The Christian is perhaps entitled to ask it, because he claims the right to ask just this question in relation to his own faith, to his Church and to its claims upon him.

On this understanding of it, Islam would be not so much a creed or a set of rules as an attitude, an approach, a willingness to listen. It would be hard to find a better expression of this understanding than the words with which Dr. Cantwell Smith closes his remarkable book *Islam in Modern History*:

One may perhaps not be overly bold in surmising that the creative development of Islam as a religion on earth lies rather in the hands of those Muslims whose concern for the forms and institutions evolved in Islamic history is subordinate to their lively sense of the living, active God who stands behind the religion, and to their passionate but rational pursuit of that social justice that was once the dominant note of the faith and the dominant goal of its forms and institutions. . . . The Islam that was given by God is not the elaboration of practices and doctrines and forms that outsiders call Islam, but rather the vivid and personal summons to individuals to live their lives always in His presence and to treat their fellow men always under His judgement.[16]

There has been in Islam from the beginning a mystical tradition; the human spirit cannot rest entirely satisfied with the arid scholasticism into which much of Islamic tradition has dried up. If Sufism can quote nothing in the Qur'an itself in support of this other approach, it can at least rely on a venerable tradition in which God is represented as saying, 'My servant draws near to me by works of supererogation, and I love him; and when I love him, I am his ear, so that he hears by me, and his eye so that he sees by me, and his tongue so that he speaks by me, and his hand so that he takes by me'. From such sources, and no doubt also from Christian influences, spring the many Sufi utterances that have so startlingly Christian a sound in Christian ears, as for instance in the famous prayer uttered by Hallaj at his execution in A.D. 922:

And thy servants who are gathered to slay me in zeal for thy religion and in desire to win thy favour, forgive them, O Lord, and have mercy upon them; for verily if thou hadst revealed to them what thou hast revealed to me, they would not have done that which they have done; and if thou hadst hidden from me that which thou hast hidden from them, I should not have

---

[16] op. cit. p. 308.

suffered this tribulation. Glory unto thee in whatsoever thou doest, and glory unto thee in whatsoever thou willest.[17]

No doubt this strain persists and will persist within the world of Islam. But this yearning for mystical oneness with God is not the approach of which Dr. Cantwell Smith is thinking. For mysticism, in Islam as elsewhere, concerns itself directly with individual salvation and only indirectly with secondary consequences that may accrue to others; whereas in the quotation given above our attention is rightly directed to that which was and ought to be always central in Islamic thinking—the sense of social justice not simply on the level of human concern, but as a result of the total submission of all creatures to the will of God.

It is clear that, if such an approach is accepted by and acceptable to Muslim leaders, a new element of flexibility is introduced into the picture. This might involve far more than mere adjustment and adaptation to changing circumstance within a firmly fixed framework of custom and belief; it might make possible genuinely new discovery, and a reformation within Islam that would be parallel in its extent and its consequences to the Reformation that broke on the Christian Church in the sixteenth century. On this only a Muslim scholar could pronounce; and even such a scholar would probably be hesitant to commit himself to any definite view of consequences that at present lie entirely hidden in the womb of the future.

The Christian reader may by this time have become aware that, in all the crises by which the Islamic world is confronted and in all the varying approaches from the Muslim side, there is one fundamental and underlying question:

The question for the future is whether Islam will remain, what it has been in the past, a comprehensive culture based on a religion, or become a 'church', a religious institution accepted by larger or smaller bodies of adherents within the framework of a secular civilization.[18]

There it is in a nutshell. Professor Gibb is thinking particularly in terms of law, and the challenge presented to the traditional *Shari'ah* by codes of law set forth on the authority of governments and on other than Islamic principles. But we have seen the

[17] Quoted by R. A. Nicholson in *The Legacy of Islam* (1931), p. 217.
[18] H. A. R. Gibb in *The Concise Encyclopedia of Living Faiths* (ed. R. C. Zaehner (1959), p. 208.

same problem arising in Pakistan in connexion with politics, and in India in relation to the participation by Muslims in the institutions and life of a non-Islamic state. And, for all the emphasis on social justice present in the quotation from Professor Cantwell Smith given above, he too is thinking in terms of 'the vivid and personal summons to individuals', rather than in the context of a complete society ordered in every part by the revelation given to man through the prophet Muhammad.

Christians ought to be able to sympathize most profoundly with Muslims in this time of transition and perplexity. For during the last few centuries we ourselves have been passing through similar crises, and as yet with highly indeterminate results. The ideal of the Middle Ages, both in Byzantium and in Rome, was that of a community in which Church and state were not distinct entities, or rather in which, though they were distinguishable entities, there was no point at which the life of man was not touched by the authority of the Church and the teaching of the Gospel. When Henry VIII launched the English Reformation, he did so on the legal basis that the English nation was one people, which could be considered under two aspects, either as commonweal or as spiritualty, with one head over both, the Christian Prince. The history of the four centuries since the Reformation has been the history of the gradual disintegration of the Christian body politic as it was conceived by all parties, except the Anabaptists, in the sixteenth century. Church and state co-exist in a complex variety of relationships in all the countries of the once Christian West; in no country, with the possible exception of Spain, is there any approximation to the medieval ideal, and even in Spain there are signs that the 'state' is not prepared to submit to being regarded as less than an independent power in its own right.

What, then, is the Christian Church? What is the Christian people? Where, if anywhere, are we to look for the *Corpus Christianum*? When we consider the difficulty that Christians experience in finding answers to such questions, we ought to be ready to recognize that these are precisely the problems with which the Muslim is also wrestling. 'The Holy Spirit shall guide you into all truth', said Jesus. Where is that truth now located? 'My community will not agree in error' is the utterance of the Muslim tradition. What sense is to be given to the words 'my community' in the world to-day? Such considerations should predispose the Christian

C

to a most sympathetic approach to Islam in its varied manifestations and its perplexities in the modern world.

The Christian attitude must be marked not merely by sympathy; it must be marked by penitence. We have already spoken of the tension between the *Dar-al-Islam*, the world of Islam, and the Christian West, which has been one of the dominant factors in world history for a thousand years. There have been faults on both sides and these we can leave to the judgement of God. What is essential is that we should understand the dark shadow which has been cast everywhere on the Muslim mind by the sense of the wanton aggressiveness of the West. Like the Jew, the Muslim may forget his own faults in the contemplation of ours; we may leave him to this occupation, and welcome only the service that he has rendered in calling our attention to our own. Memories are long in the East. To us the Crusades are very ancient history; to the Muslim they are as though they had happened yesterday.

It may be profitable at this point to cite two estimates of the Crusades by two Western scholars approaching the subject from very diverse points of view. Professor Ernest Barker writes:

If we regard their larger scope, and the long after-swell which followed the original impulse, we shall not regard the Crusades as a failure. . . . They defended Western Christianity during the crucial period of the growth of Western civilisation in the Middle Ages; they saved it from any self-centred localism; they gave it breadth—and a vision. 'The people that hath no vision perisheth'; and to the peoples of the Middle Ages the vision of the Crusade—seldom steadily seen, perhaps never seen whole—was none the less a saving ideal.[19]

From a purely Western point of view this is unexceptionable. But what did it look like from the other side? Here we can cite the judgement of Sir Steven Runciman, who has an incomparable knowledge of the Byzantine and Eastern authorities of the period. The third volume of his great *History of the Crusades* ends with a melancholy chapter, entitled 'The Summing Up', of the force of which brief quotation can give only a very imperfect impression:

The Crusades were launched to save Eastern Christendom from the Moslems. When they ended the whole of Eastern Christendom was under Moslem rule. . . . Seen in the perspective of history the whole Crusading Movement was a vast fiasco. . . . The triumphs of the Crusade were the triumphs of faith. But faith without wisdom is a dangerous thing. . . . In

[19] In *The Legacy of Islam*, pp. 76-7.

the long sequence of interaction and fusion between Orient and Occident out of which our civilization has grown, the Crusades were a tragic and destructive episode. The historian as he gazes back across the centuries at their gallant story must find his admiration overcast by sorrow at the witness that it bears to the limitations of human nature. There was so much courage and so little honour, so much devotion and so little understanding. High ideals were besmirched by cruelty and greed, enterprise and endurance by a blind and narrow self-righteousness; and the Holy War itself was nothing more than a long act of intolerance in the name of God, which is the sin against the Holy Ghost.[20]

These are hard words. But they may well be pondered by those who would enter the mind and the heart of the Muslim to-day.

Christian approaches to the Muslim, with certain notable exceptions, have been carried out on the basis and in the spirit of polemic. It is hard to deny that controversy may have its place in such meetings; but here, once again, we may well be persuaded that dialogue represents the better way. This is the approach that is commended to us by our Christian guides in the field of Islamics to-day.

This attitude is not quite so fresh and new as is sometimes imagined by those who are introduced to it for the first time. Many of us learned something of it more than a generation ago from a great scholar in this field, Duncan Black Macdonald. Macdonald describes for us his perplexity, when he first travelled in the East, as to the way in which he should approach the tombs of Muslim saints, access to which had been opened to him by the authorities, and the decision that he made:

The course that I followed . . . was to visit them frankly in reverence, and I found that the fact that I did so—that I behaved, as my Eastern friends would say, like a religious-minded man and a gentleman—helped me indefinitely in my intercourse with Muslims. There is one usage, for example, that is of rule when visiting the tombs of Muslim saints. You advance to the railing that surrounds the tomb, you hold it in your right hand . . . and you recite the *Fatiha*, the first chapter of the Koran, which holds pretty much the place with the Muslim that the Lord's Prayer does with us.

I do not know whether any one of those standing there were especially spiritually benefited by it. I do know, however, that I was benefited by feeling the nearness of the spiritual kindred of all that call upon the Lord,

[20] Steven Runciman, *A History of the Crusades*, Vol. iii, *The Kingdom of Acre* (1954), pp. 469, 480.

and I know too that those Muslims who saw me do this or who knew that I did it, felt that here was a spiritual unity, that this man, Christian though he might be, reverenced their saint and knew what it meant to recognize holiness and the life hid in God.[21]

I have always liked this picture of the reverence of a Christian man in a place which to the believers of another faith was holy ground. We shall understand at once why a much more recent expositor of Islam, Canon Kenneth Cragg, has called one of his books *Sandals at the Mosque*. In the East you enter a temple, a mosque, or a church barefoot. Canon Cragg is teaching us that, unless we approach that which to others is holy, even though it may not in the same sense be holy to us, in that spirit of humility and reverence, we shall find all the doors barred and bolted against us. We may attain to intellectual knowledge; but that is far removed from the inner understanding which it ought to be our desire as Christians to attain.

In all his writing Canon Cragg lays stress on the truth that, if we wish to understand the Muslim, we must approach him by way of his worship. Dr. Macdonald referred to the *Fatiha*, the first chapter of the Qur'an, which every Muslim repeats many times a day. Here are the words of it:

In the Name of Allah, the Merciful, the Compassionate. Praise belongeth unto Allah, the Lord of the worlds, the King of the day of Doom. Thee do we serve, of thee do we ask aid. Guide us in the straight path, the path of those to whom thou hast been gracious, not of those with whom thou art angered or of those who stray.

Later we may find many points at which our convictions differ from those of the Muslim; but it is clear, at a first reading, that this is a prayer which every Christian could use, given only liberty to read into it certain meanings which may not have been there in the prayer as originally given.

Five times a day the Muslim is supposed to say his prayers, with the necessary ritual—the prostrations and so forth. Both' words and forms are rigidly fixed, and to Christians accustomed to more flexible and variable forms of prayer it may seem that this monotonous iteration represents a certain ossification of the spirit of religion. Yet it cannot be doubted that this prayer, by the very fact that it is endlessly repeated from day to day, impresses on the Muslim soul a

[21] D. B. Macdonald, *Aspects of Islam*, (1911), pp 24–6.

certain pattern, a certain temper. And what is it that the Muslim says?

God is most great. God is most great. I bear witness that Muhammad is the apostle of God. God is most great. In the name of God, the merciful Lord of mercy. Praise be to God the Lord of the worlds, the merciful Lord of mercy, Sovereign of the day of judgment. Thee alone it is we worship; Thee alone we implore to help. Guide us in the straight path, the path of those to whom thou art gracious, who are not the incurrers of thine anger, nor wanderers in error. God is most great, God is most great. . . . I bear witness that Muhammad is the apostle of God. . . . May God send down blessing upon him and preserve him in peace. Peace rest upon you and the mercy of God.[22]

Even a cursory reading of this prayer must surely suggest to the Christian that Islam and the Gospel are concerned about the same things. They are concerned about the reality, the oneness and the sovereignty of God, about revelation and mercy, about the responsibility of man, about eternal life and destiny, about God's call to submission and obedience, about the need for decision on the part of man. Here would seem to be all the elements needed for fruitful dialogue; and many distinguished Christian expositors of Islam in recent years have gone as far as Christian faith permits to make this dialogue possible.

But it takes two to make dialogue; the most disappointing factor in the present situation is the almost total failure so far of the Muslim scholar to approach Christianity with that reverence and open-mindedness which he rightly demands of the Christian scholar in his approach to Islam. 'There isn't a single Moslem scholar in all history, so far as I know, who has written an authentic essay on Christianity.' This is the opinion of one singularly well qualified to judge, Dr. Charles Malik, one of the most distinguished scholars of the Arabic-speaking Orthodox Churches, and for many years representative of the republic of Lebanon at the United Nations.[23] This lamentable judgement is echoed by Dr. Cantwell Smith, another scholar who cannot be accused of lack of sympathy for Islam:

The present writer knows no book by a Muslim showing any 'feel' for the Christian position; nor indeed any clear endeavour to deal with, let

---

[22] It will be noticed that this prayer includes the *Fatiha* in a rather different translation from that quoted above. I have left the two side by side, as an illustration of the extreme difficulty of conveying in English the significance of Arabic words, in which sound and sense are so closely linked together. A third rendering will be found in N. J. Dawood, *The Koran* (Penguin Classics, 1956), p. 15.

[23] In an essay, 'The Near East: the Search for Truth', in *Foreign Affairs*, 1952, p. 258.

alone understand, the central doctrines. The usual Muslim attitude is not to take the central doctrines seriously at all. That is, they do not recognise that Christians take them seriously; and that however absurd they might seem to outsiders (to Muslims they appear both stupid and blasphemous) the Trinity, the Deity and Sonship and Crucifixion of Christ, and the like are affirmations deeply meaningful and precious and utterly integral to the Christian's faith.[24]

I do not think that anyone who has ever attempted to discuss questions of faith with Muslims would regard this judgement as too severe. We are still a very long way from the possibility of dialogue.

We must note one partial exception to the sweeping statements quoted above. *City of Wrong—a Friday in Jerusalem* by Kamel Hussain[25] is a remarkable study by a convinced and educated Muslim of the events of Good Friday. Kamel Hussain remains just within the borders of Islamic orthodoxy; but he has read the Gospels carefully, and has tried to understand what it was in the teaching of Jesus that impelled men so fiercely to be rid of him. Many fundamental questions are not raised, much less answered. Yet here seems to be a voice such as had not previously been heard from the world of orthodox Islam.[26]

For the most part we still live in the twilight of misunderstanding. From the point of view of the possibility of dialogue, what the ordinary Muslim believes and thinks is more significant than the abstract categories of truth. And this brings us to the consideration of the categorical Muslim denials of many of the central articles of the Christian faith. Most serious of all is the denial by the Muslim of that on which everything else in Christianity hangs, a historic fact—that Jesus of Nazareth was crucified and died in or about the year A.D. 29 in Jerusalem. Christianity is not a religion of ideas, it is a religion of facts and happenings. If these should be disproved or discredited, the religion ceases to be itself.

Here is the Muslim denial in the words of the Qur'an itself:

> (The Jews) said boastfully,
> 'We killed Christ Jesus

[24] W. Cantwell Smith, *Islam in Modern History*, p. 104, n. 1.
[25] Translated by Kenneth Cragg (Djambatan, Amsterdam 1959).
[26] Even more understanding utterances can be quoted from the books of the Sufis; but these represent a tradition alien from the main current of Islamic thought. On Kamel Hussain's book, see a number of very pertinent observations by M. A. C. Warren in *C.M.S. Newsletter*, no. 221, November 1959, p. 6.

The Son of Mary,
the Apostle of God'.
But they did not kill him,
Nor did they crucify him.
But it was made to appear
that way to them. . . .
For of a surety
They did not kill him.[27]

In recent times attempts have been made with great ingenuity
and learning, both by Professor R. C. Zaehner,[28] and by the editor
of *Operation Reach*, the valuable series of booklets sent out by the
Near East Christian Council with the aim of helping Christians
towards sympathetic and understanding dialogue with Islam, to
show that these words do not necessarily mean what they appear
to mean, and that the denial is not as absolute as both Christians
and Muslims have supposed. I cannot say that I have found the
argumentation convincing in either case. But even if it were, we are
faced by the undoubted fact that Muslims to a man believe to-day
that Jesus was never crucified. If there was no death, naturally
there could be no redemption through that death, and Christianity
as Gospel ceases to exist.

It has been noted earlier that all the ancient religions of the East,
awaking from long somnolence, or stirring themselves out of the
defensive attitude to which they had been reduced by the first shock
of the encounter with the West, are now taking the initiative and
sending out their own missionaries into the Western lands. On the
Islamic side, the spear-point of missionary work in the West is the
Ahmadiyya movement. And naturally the starting-point of the
Muslim campaign is the denial, in the name of truth, of those things
which Christians most firmly believe.

The Muslim starts with certain preconceived ideas, and into these
everything has to be fitted. Anything which cannot be fitted into
this framework must be rejected as invention or sheer falsehood.
Here let us note especially two of these preconceptions. The first is
that the Qur'an is the Word of God and is truth. It is the standard

---

[27] Sura IV, 157.
[28] R. C. Zaehner, *At Sundry Times* (1958), Appendix, 'The Qur'an and Christ',
pp. 195–217. Especially p. 212: 'It is roundly asserted that the *Jews* neither slew nor
crucified the Messiah, Jesus, Son of Mary, but that God raised Him up to Himself—
the implication being that it was God Himself who slew and crucified Jesus. The Jews
took the credit for what was really God's own initiative.'

by which everything else is to be judged. The second is that all the prophets from the beginning have proclaimed the same religion, the faith of Abraham; this has often been forgotten and obscured, but has now blazed forth in full glory in the revelation given to Muhammad. Once again, this revelation is the criterion by which everything else must be judged. If anything in other faiths is discrepant, that must be false, an unauthorized addition to the teaching of the Prophet, which is assumed to be true at every point and in every respect.

It is well known that at many points the Qur'an does not agree with the Jewish and Christian Scriptures. Therefore, from the Muslim point of view, it follows of necessity that these Scriptures must have been corrupted. Historical evidence makes no impression on the crushing force of the syllogism. So it is, and it can be no other way. The Muslim controversialist feels no need to study evidence in detail. The only valid picture of Jesus Christ is that which is to be found in the pages of the Qur'an.

A prophet can speak only the truth. It is impossible, so it is argued, that a prophet should ever fall into the ignorance and blasphemy of claiming for himself divine prerogatives. Jesus was a prophet. Therefore he can never have made any such claim. In point of fact he does not make such claims in the Gospels, even in the form in which Christians have preserved them. Therefore it is clear that the whole of this section of the Christian Creed is due simply to misunderstandings and exaggerations on the part of the followers of Jesus. What he was concerned about was the proclamation of the kingdom of God. This shows that he himself stood in the line of the prophetic faith and proclamation and did not depart from it.

The Islamic missionary claims, then, that his task is to show to Christians what it really means to be a Christian. The defect in Christianity as it is to-day is its failure to make use of reason. If Christians will only read their own Gospels with the eyes of reason, they will see that they can cast away the complex absurdities of later Christian doctrine, and come back to the simple prophetic faith in God of Jesus himself. If they will take one step forward they will find that this is the same as the faith of Muhammad, except that in this latter form the faith is still further stripped of idealistic fancies, and brought within the compass of the man of the world who has to live and earn his daily bread. There is no doubt that such a presentation makes its appeal to nominal Christians in the West, who have never come to an understanding of the meaning of Christian doctrine, and are inclined to agree with the Muslim that most of what they hear from the pulpit is merely unnecessary mystification and complication of something that in itself ought to be simple.

Dr. Guillaume has very conveniently set out for us the extent of agreement and disagreement between Christian and Muslim in terms of the Apostles Creed.[29] The words in italics are rejected by Islam:

> I believe in God
> *the Father*
> Almighty, Maker of heaven and earth:
> And in Jesus Christ
> *His only Son our Lord*
> Who was conceived of the Holy Ghost
> Born of the Virgin Mary
> *Suffered under Pontius Pilate*
> *Was crucified*
> (Dead)[30] *and buried*
> *He descended into Hell*
> *The third day he rose again from the dead*
> He ascended into heaven
> *And sitteth on the right hand of God the Father Almighty*
> From thence he shall come
> *To judge the quick and the dead*
> I believe in the Holy Ghost
> *The Holy Catholic Church*
> *The Communion of Saints*
> The Forgiveness of sins
> The Resurrection of the body
> And the life everlasting.

The agreements are impressive. Yet the Christian must ask himself whether the nature of the massive denials is not such that by their existence they change even the agreements into disagreements. Even when we use the same words, do we not use them in totally different senses?

If so, is any progress towards understanding really possible? It is hard, but we must not despair. Christians must persist in their

---

[29] A. Guillaume, *Islam* (1954), p. 192. Dr. Guillaume follows this paradigmatic statement with a useful comment on each clause of the Creed, pp. 193-7.

[30] Muhammad believed, of course, that Jesus ultimately died, but not that he died on the Cross.

earnest invitation to true dialogue; they must exercise endless patience and refuse to be discouraged. And the burden of all their invitation must be, 'Consider Jesus'. If the Muslim is prepared to admit, even hypothetically, that the Christian Gospels represent more or less accurately the life and teaching of the prophet Jesus (without entering for the moment into the controversial question of his death), he may find open certain perspectives of understanding that at present are closed to him.

It is perfectly true that the central concern of Jesus was with the kingdom of God. But everything depends on the meaning that is put into the word 'God'. Here is perhaps the very heart of our differences. Islam conceives the possible relationship of man to God in one way, and the Gospel in another.

While God was the exclusive source of the revelation to Muhammad, God himself is not the content of the revelation. Revelation in Islamic theology does not mean God disclosing himself. It is revelation *from* God, not revelation *of* God. God is remote. He is inscrutable and utterly inaccessible to human knowledge. . . . Even though we are his creatures whose every breath is dependent upon him, it is not in inter-personal relationship with him that we receive guidance from him.[31]

At this central point the teaching of Jesus diverges from what the Muslim believes to be the essential prophetic witness. His God is a God who cares for his creatures, who is prepared to enter into fellowship with them, and is concerned that they should love him in response to his love. Under the law man was in the position of a slave; now under the Gospel he is called to freedom, to the freedom of grown-up sons in their Father's house. The Qur'an never uses the word 'Father' of God. Jesus taught his disciples to address him as 'Our Father'. The whole of the Gospel is summed up in these two words.

This is a point of special difficulty. Muhammad himself seems to have been determined to use the word 'father' only in the grossest physical sense, and to refuse to recognize that it could be used in any other sense. If this were the only sense in which it could be used, Christians of course would equally refuse to use it. But in the New Testament the words 'Our Father' stand for trustful affection, confidence in a higher wisdom, understanding, rational obedience, intelligent co-operation. Such an attitude is reasonable only if there

[31] Edmund Perry, *The Gospel in Dispute*, (1958), pp. 155, 157.

is a God in relation to whom such terms have meaning. It is the affirmation of the prophet Jesus that there is such a God.

If the possibility is admitted that God might be such as Jesus declared him to be, the incarnation presents itself no longer as a blasphemous and irrational impossibility, but as something that appears even appropriate, in the light of this new perception of what the fatherhood of God might be.

The death of Christ at the hands of the Jews is rejected by Muslims on *a priori* grounds, which are absolutely convincing if the major premiss is admitted. It is impossible that God should so desert a prophet in the fulfilment of his mission. It would be contrary to His justice to permit the suffering of an innocent man on behalf of others. It would be contrary to His omnipotence not to be able to rescue a prophet in danger. Therefore Jesus cannot have been left helpless in the hands of his enemies.

Within this syllogistic framework argument is fruitless. If we know exactly what God is like, since he has revealed the truth about himself, we can predict exactly what God will do in any circumstances and there can be no exceptions. The Christian cannot feel himself tied down by any such certainty. The biblical emphasis is on the freedom of God, a God 'afar off', who cannot be tied down by any human understanding or expectation. His action is unpredictable and may go far beyond the limits of the highest and best imaginations of men. The Muslim starts from the assumption that God will not fail one of his prophets. The more flexible Christian approach leaves open the possibility that, for good reason, God might do just that. The Muslim feels that the Christian is denying or prejudicing the omnipotence of God; the Christian might answer that, in his doctrine of the death and suffering of Jesus Christ, the omnipotence of God is the very thing that he is trying to defend.

Here we must recognize that we come to one of the points in the Muslim-Christian dialogue where progress seems to be impossible. We ask the Muslim to read the story of Jesus of Nazareth without prejudice, and to consider whether there may not be here a revelation of the being of God which goes beyond that to be found in the Qur'an. But this is precisely what the good Muslim, *qua* Muslim, finds it almost impossible to do.

Popular Muslim thought, which has affected even some of the most ancient traditions, ascribes to Muhammad miraculous and almost divine powers. Evidences of Christian influence are not lacking, and the impression is left on the mind that, whatever Jesus did, Muhammad must be shown to have gone one better and to have manifested in even higher degree all the powers that Christians claim for Jesus Christ. The educated Muslim will probably look with a critical eye on many of these tales. Yet this cannot alter the fact that Muhammad himself is ultimately responsible for his own quasi-deification in Muslim tradition. He did claim to be greater than Jesus of Nazareth; believing himself to be the last of the prophets, he claimed the right to supersede and to declare abrogated all that had gone before him in the way of revelation.[32]

The Muslim has accepted this claim as part of the meaning of that which he affirms in his creed, that Muhammad is the Apostle of God. It is this which makes it so extremely difficult for him to accept, even theoretically and hypothetically, the possibility that there might be something in Jesus and his message which is not already there in Muhammad and his message.

Moreover, that which we ask him to look for in Jesus is in itself a cause of grave offence to Muslim pride. We suggest—we cannot do otherwise—that he find a Saviour. The Muslim affirms that he has no need of any such thing. In modern Muslim propaganda in the West, nothing is more strongly emphasised than the feasibility, the viability, of Islam. Men can turn and obey, if they will. Islam makes only reasonable demands upon men. This is part of the mercy of God—he knows what men can do, and does not lay upon them burdens too heavy to be borne. A constant contrast is drawn between the unpractical idealism of Jesus, suitable perhaps for ascetics and those who can flee entirely from the world, and the practical down-to-earth regulations of Islam. And the Muslim objects strongly to Christian stress upon the sinfulness of man. This seems to him to be mere evasion. By pleading his weakness man tries to excuse his failure to obey, and so to withdraw himself from the just judgement of God on disobedience. Instead, he should gird himself to the not overwhelmingly difficult effort of obedience. It is not hard to understand why such teaching awakens echoes of approval and assent in the West to-day.

At the heart of the Muslim-Christian disagreement, we shall find a deep difference in the understanding of the nature of sin. It is not

---

[32] This point is made by Emmanuel Kellerhals, *Der Islam* (Basel, 1956), pp. 335–6, with reference to the earlier work of S. W. Koelle, *Mohammed and Mohammedanism critically considered* (London, 1889).

true to say that the Muslim has no sense of sin or of the need for forgiveness. He has both. But sin reveals its deadly nature only when it is seen in its effects on personal relationships; and such an understanding of it is almost necessarily excluded, as we have seen, by the Muslim's concept of the possible relationship between the believer and his God. The believer may sin against the law and the majesty of God, and if he does so he deserves to be punished. The idea that man by his sin might break the heart of God is not yet within the spectrum of the Muslim understanding of reality.

It is at this point that Canon Cragg, who has gone perhaps further than any other living student of Islam in the attempt to understand and sympathize, changes from expositor to evangelist; and, coming after 120 pages of profoundly sympathetic exposition, the change is all the more impressive:

Law informs our ignorance, and when the problem is but obduracy, this it will rebuke and condemn. Then the gulf widens and the righteousness of the law goes by the way of the law, ever further from our reach. If we acquiesce in this situation we are complacent sinners: if we deplore it we are despairing ones. The Gospel of grace is beyond this dilemma of the law. It assures us in the Cross that it reaches beyond our despair, while leaving us no ground for refuge in complacency.

Even where it is despised and rejected by the soul of man, the Cross stands majestically. It has a patience and a promise, beyond the competence of law. Its grace will never let us go, as at some point law necessarily must. If we are burdened by the length of human waywardness, as in our questions we confess to being, we shall find in the Cross alone a commensurate enterprise of God for its redemption.[33]

There is the message of the Christian faith for Muslims. Anyone who has had any dealings with them knows how hard it is to persuade them even to consider the possibility that they may have something yet to learn. But our task is to go on saying to the Muslim with infinite patience, 'Sir, consider Jesus.' We have no other message. In the words of Professor Perry, our task is the 'retrieval of the emasculated Jesus from the Qur'an'.[34] It is not the case that the Muslim has seen Jesus of Nazareth and has rejected him; he has never seen him, and the veil of misunderstanding and prejudice is still over his face. It may be that, if and when he sees him, he too will turn to the Lord.

[33] Kenneth Cragg, *Sandals at the Mosque* (1959), pp. 138–9.
[34] Edmund Perry, *The Gospel in Dispute*, p. 173.

CHAPTER IV

RENASCENT HINDUISM

At the end of the eighteenth century, when the tide of Western influence rose in full flood and covered Asia, Hinduism seemed less prepared than any other of the great religions to stand the shock. Political decay and confusion appeared to have been accompanied by a temporary paralysis of the Indian genius. In the south the great tradition of *bhakti*, the adoring worship of a single god, had died away in the eighteenth century in the moving but not very poetical utterances of the Tamil seer Tayumanavar. Elsewhere there were few signs of inspiration and renewal.

When Europeans, missionaries among them, began to concern themselves with the religion of their neighbours, their first encounters were almost invariably with what from the Western point of view was repellent and degrading—animal sacrifice at the Kalighat in Calcutta, the burning of sometimes unwilling widows on the funeral pyres of their husbands, and the undoubted presence of the harlots' houses around the temples as in the Ephesus of the days of St. Paul. Indian scholars had, of course, guarded the ancient tradition of learning; there was never a complete breach in the continuity of philosophic thought and contemplation. But little of this was apparent in Hinduism as it was understood by the ordinary worshipper; the content of his religious understanding seemed to be conditioned by late and not very edifying Puranic tales of the doings of the gods. For all these things a spiritualizing explanation can be found; the first impression left on the mind of the observer was not that of a deeply spiritual nation or religion.

The same problem encounters the missionary who is taking up work in India to-day. In the course of his training he will almost certainly have been introduced to the classical traditions of Hinduism. He will have started with the Rig Veda, one of the very oldest monuments of human literary skill. He will have ploughed his way through the Taittiriya and Chandogya Upanishads and made himself familiar with the lively beginnings of Indian speculation. He may have gained some acquaintance with the six systems of Indian philosophy, and become aware that that capacious religion

70

can make room within itself for theistic and atheistic understandings of the universe. He will certainly have read the Bhagavad Gita. But, when he sets to work, he will find that these things are outside the world of most of the people with whom he has to do. The vocabulary of the classics, even when adapted to the modern forms of Indian speech, is unfamiliar to them. The ideas of the ancient religion are not theirs. He begins to wonder whether those whom he encounters are Hindus at all, and if so, in what sense.

Part of his perplexity arises simply from the fact that, though urbanization is rapidly advancing in India as in every other part of the world, 75 per cent of the population of India still lives in villages. The religion of most villagers is that which it is convenient to call animism (though the term has in recent years fallen into a certain amount of disfavour), and which will be considered in another chapter. Every village has one shrine at least, and probably several—but the names of the gods, or more probably goddesses, worshipped at them are not those of the Hindu pantheon. Much that is very primitive has survived; all this is recognized by Hindus as standing in some relation to other forms of Hindu belief and practice, but derives little from the classical traditions set out in most of the Western books on Indian religion.[1]

Yet those who treat Hinduism as essentially a unity in itself, and as the bond which has created a measure of cultural and religious unity among the many races which inhabit the Indian sub-continent, have a good deal to be said on their side. There are perhaps three elements of the Hindu system that have penetrated to the remotest Hindu village and condition the minds of those who stand in any kind of relation to the Hindu system:

1. Every individual who has any claim to the Hindu name is a member of one of the innumerable castes into which society is divided, and by his membership is pledged to keep its rules. Each caste has its own traditions, its own way of living, and these lay their iron hand on every part of the life of man and woman—on what they

---

[1] There is now a considerable literature on this more popular Hinduism. The most striking work of recent years is certainly Carl Gustav Diehl, *Instrument and Purpose* (Lund, 1956), in which a full bibliography is provided. Dr. P. D. Devanandan raises the pertinent question whether the renaissance of Hinduism has produced any effect at all on this level of Hindu worship and apprehension: 'Local cults do not seem to be growing in importance . . . it cannot be claimed that there is any manifestation of new religious zeal where local cults of popular Hinduism are concerned.' *The Gospel and Renascent Hinduism* (1959), p. 11.

wear and what they eat, on the words they use, the gods they worship, and the manner in which they order their social relationships. In the cities the old ways are rapidly changing; in the village their sway has hardly been affected by the transformation of the times.

Western observers have in the main been impressed by the divisiveness and wastefulness of caste. Individual initiative is at a discount. A man's occupation is determined for him by his birth and not by his choice; and the exclusion of nearly a sixth of the population from social privilege and participation in the cultural heritage of the nation must involve not only the sufferers but the whole people in terrible national impoverishment.[2] The Indian sees the other side of the picture. This marvellously ingenious fabric has secured to Indian society a stability unknown for centuries in the West. Every man knows exactly what his place is in society, and unless he flagrantly breaks the rules is assured throughout his life of the support and help of a close-knit community. All have some kind of rights. All render some kind of service to the community, and for this there is reward. The rights of the outcaste may be so limited as to be almost invisible; but they are not non-existent and are maintained by the general good sense of the community. The process by which the casteless aboriginal peoples of the mountains and jungles are being absorbed into the caste system continues to the present day.

2. Almost everyone who belongs to any Hindu community is likely to have some idea of the law of retribution, by which life and fate in this world are determined. Every man must eat the fruit of ancient deeds until they are wholly consumed. If there has not been time in one life for the debt to be fully paid, then the man must be born again upon earth, and so on endlessly until the uttermost farthing has been paid. Here the Hindu finds the explanation of all inequality and misfortune in this earthly life, and to him the explanation is complete and logically irrefragable. 'One man is borne aloft in a litter', says the ancient classic; 'four men sweat at the pole. What can this be, other than the fruit of ancient deeds?' This is a fatalistic creed, yet not merely fatalistic, since there is always the hope that by acquiring merit in this life the Hindu may

---

[2] It is to be noted that untouchability has now been legally abolished in India. But it takes time for the effects of such beneficent legislation to permeate the whole life of a great country.

attain to a higher stage in the next existence, and ultimately to release from the *Samsāra*, the endless wheel of existence and change.

3. Everywhere in the Hindu world there is the all-pervading sense of the invisible and the supernatural. In this sense India is still a profoundly religious country. But some qualification of this statement is needed. The villager is well aware that he is surrounded by unseen powers; but only in rare instances does he regard these powers as beneficent. They are more likely to be cruel, capricious and vengeful. The idea of the great God is not wholly absent—but he is far away, and unlikely to concern himself about such insignificant creatures as the poor dwellers in Indian villages.

We shall have to bear in mind the extent to which this part of the world of Hinduism has proved resistant to the currents of change. But for the greater part of our exposition we shall be concerned with that educated tenth, and in particular that English-educated twentieth of the Indian people, which has been exposed in varying degrees of severity to the assault from the West.

Such an assault is bound to produce a variety of reactions.

The first was, naturally, the reaction of refusal. Those who by temperament or status were inclined to conservatism refused to have anything to do with the new ways. The old is better, sanctioned by immemorial custom. Any hand which is laid on any part of the structure must of necessity be a sacrilegious hand. Dr. Percival Spear has strikingly interpreted the Mutiny of 1857 in terms of emotional self-defence against a threat to the familiar world-order:

The supreme expression of the reactionary spirit was the Mutiny of 1857. In one tense and tragic moment all the country's love of its old way of life, regret for past glories, and distrust of and disgust at foreign innovations flared up in a violent explosion of emotional resentment. . . . So far from being the first war of independence or a national revolt in the modern sense, the Mutiny was the final convulsion of the old order goaded to desperation by the incessant pricks of modernity.[3]

A great deal of this sheer, emotional rather than intellectual, conservatism no doubt survives, especially perhaps among the Brahmans, the traditional guardians of the law and practice of Hinduism. It underlies one of the modern movements by which the Hindu scene is diversified.

[3] Percival Spear, *India, Pakistan, and the West* (4th ed. 1967), p. 115.

Dayananda Saraswati (1824–83) had become convinced that modern Hinduism is corrupt and therefore ineffective. To recover its vitality Hinduism must go back to its original sources, the Vedas, and everything subsequent to them must be discarded as mere tradition. We have encountered a similar 'fundamentalism' in Islam, and we know well that similar movements have recurrently appeared in the Christian world. Dayananda was prepared to ascribe to the Vedas literal and verbal inspiration, and in the light of his understanding of them to denounce even such venerable Hindu practices as idolatry and the caste system.

In 1875 Dayananda founded the Arya Samaj to propagate his ideas and to put into effect his ideals. The membership of this group has never been very large, but it has had considerable influence in shaping one section of contemporary Indian opinion. For this was an active and polemical movement. 'For the first time for centuries Hinduism took the offensive.'[4] Christianity and Islam, no less than corrupt modern Hinduism, were the objects of Dayananda's attack. One of the most characteristic activities of the Arya Samaj has been the movement for the reconversion of those, especially among the outcastes, who have forsworn the faith of their fathers for the Christian way.

Dayananda has his heirs in the political as well as in the religious sphere. India has chosen to be a *secular* democratic republic. Certain political groups, notably the Hindu Mahasabha and the Rashtriya Sevak Sangh, regard this as the basic error and betrayal. In sharp contrast to the international understanding of Hinduism to which we shall come later, such groups maintain that Hindustan must be the land of the Hindus and its whole life an expression of a certain spiritual ideal. This point of view can be carried to extremes, as will be evident from the following utterance of Shri Golwalkar, one of the leaders of the Rashtriya Sevak Sangh:

The non-Hindu peoples in Hindustan must either adopt Hindu culture and language, must learn to respect and hold in reverence the Hindu religion, must entertain no ideas but those of glorification of the Hindu race and culture, or may stay in the country wholly subordinate to the Hindu nation, claiming nothing, deserving no privileges, far less preferential treatment—not even citizenship rights. There is, at least there should be, no other course for them to adopt. We in Hindustan cannot give up religion in our national life as it would mean that we have turned faithless

---

[4] A. L. Basham, *Concise Encyclopaedia of Living Faiths*, p. 256.

to our Race Spirit, to the ideal and mission for which we have lived for ages.[5]

The second reaction was that of warm welcome to many of the new ideas and a deliberate attempt to work out a syncretistic faith in which a prominent place would be accorded to Christ and his teaching alongside the ancient traditions of the Hindu faith.

Here two great names are to be recorded. First in this field was Ram Mohan Roy (1770–1834), who in his own day 'was regarded as a marvel rather than a portent, as an occasional comet rather than as a rising sun',[6] but who restored to the thoughtful Hindu his confidence and his self-respect, in the belief that in faithfulness to the Scriptures of his own faith he could meet the West without shame and without fear. Keshub Chander Sen (1838–1884), less intellectual and more emotional than Ram Mohan Roy, could speak of Jesus Christ in terms of passionate devotion, and was thus able to make a profound impression on his Christian hearers. Dr. James Martineau, the Unitarian scholar, has recorded this impression of his meeting with Keshub Chander Sen:

The impression was so powerful upon most of us, at least in London, when we heard him preach, that I venture to say that few of us had ever been under a Christian preacher and been moved to so deep a sense of Christian conviction and of Christian humility. . . . It appears to me that the visit of Keshub Chander Sen was a demonstration that our churches are wrong in their definition of Christianity, and that the very essence of it lies, not in the doctrinal and historical machinery, but in the spirituality of which this machinery is the mere vehicle to our souls. If this be so, I think it a lesson of the deepest moment to our Christian churches.[7]

We need not here pursue the question of truth as against 'spirituality', posed by the quotation from Dr. Martineau; that will come before us later. History shows that syncretistic forms of religion do not ordinarily manifest strong vitality. The Brahmo Samaj, founded by Ram Mohan Roy in 1829, though distinguished intellectually, has always been small in numbers, and has lacked that

---

[5] Quoted in J. R. Chandran and M. M. Thomas, *Political Outlook in India* (Bangalore, 1956), pp. 112, 113.   [6] Percival Spear, op. cit. p. 188.

[7] Quoted by P. D. Devanandan, 'Hindu Missions to the West', in *International Review of Missions*, October 1959, p. 402, from P. K. Sen, *Biography of a New Faith*, Vol. ii, p. 49. Dr. Martineau must have heard Keshub Chander Sen preach some time in 1870.

dynamic originality without which religious movements do not long survive the initial impulse that gave them birth.[8] Yet the third of the Hindu reactions to the West would not be what it is to-day, without the work of the two pioneering leaders of the nineteenth century.

This third reaction is more difficult to define in a phrase. Hinduism has always been polymorphous. It has manifested through the centuries an astonishing capacity for taking into itself the most disparate elements and yet itself remaining essentially unchanged. Those who stand in this third tradition would perhaps maintain that Hinduism has within itself all needed truth, indeed the highest truth yet manifested to mankind; but that it needs to purify itself from the confusions and accumulations of the centuries by going back to its own earlier sources, and that it can be stimulated and even helped in this task by insights that have come to it through contact with other religions. To put the matter very briefly, Swami Vivekananda lighted the spiritual flame of this ideal; Mr. M. K. Gandhi interpreted it in terms of practical activity; and Dr. S. Radhakrishnan has restated it in terms of intellectual validity.

Behind Swami Vivekananda (Narendranath Datta, 1863–1902) lies the greater figure of Ramakrishna Paramahamsa (1834–86), the devotee whom modern Hindus constantly cite as the most notable example of a human being who attained in this life to perfect union with the divine. About 1871, Ramakrishna began to study other religions, very much in the spirit which has been commended to Christians in this book. For a certain period he would read only the Scriptures of the faith that he was studying, as far as was possible carrying out all the appointed prayers and rituals. At the end of several years of such study and experiment he reached the conclusion that all religions in their inmost content are one—they all lead back to the truth apprehended by the mystic of the unity of all things in the supreme and universal Spirit.

It was the task of Swami Vivekananda to carry this message to the West. One of the most striking events in modern religious history

---

[8] Of great importance in the history of the Brahmo Samaj was the adherence to it of the Tagore family. Rabindranath Tagore, the famous poet, was the son of the second leader of the Samaj, Debendra Nath Tagore. In his day, Rabindranath as an interpreter of Hinduism to the West rendered to an earlier generation much the same service as is being rendered by Dr. S. Radhakrishnan to-day. See Amiya Chakravarti, 'Rabindranath Tagore and the Renaissance of India's Spiritual Religion' in *Modern Trends in World Religions* (ed. Joseph M. Kitagawa, 1959), pp. 157–92.

was the appearance of the young Bengali at the Parliament of Religions held in Chicago in 1893.

In the earlier stages of his journey Vivekananda had been overwhelmed by the wealth and power of the West. What reply can the East make to the crushing weight of this power? Vivekananda's solution of the problem was brilliant and lasting in its effects; he invented the myth of the spiritual East and the material West. The myth disregards both the glorious spiritual history of the West and the earthy materialism that is to be found in the East as much as in any other part of the world. But, sedulously propagated by Eastern emissaries in all the countries of the West, the message has proved attractive in a period when the West has begun to be weary of its own material triumphs.

What Vivekananda set forth was a purely 'spiritual' religion. In a passionate outburst he inveighed against the idea that man could be called, or regarded as, a sinner. Enlightenment he may need, and that the great religions are there to supply; the idea of redemption is from the start excluded as an outworn fallacy.

Following out the conviction of his master Ramakrishna that all religions are in essence one, Vivekananda proclaimed a doctrine of enlightenment and goodwill free from any sectarian bias. Thus he disclaimed any intention of making converts: 'Do I wish that the Christian would become Hindu? God forbid! Do I wish that the Hindu or Buddhist would become Christian? God forbid. . . . Each religion must assimilate the spirit of the others and yet preserve its individuality and grow according to its own laws of growth.' There is no reason to doubt the sincerity of these words uttered at the final session of the Parliament of Religions. It did not seem to Vivekananda at all paradoxical that Christians should accept the principles of Hindu Vedanta and at the same time continue to be Christians. Such disregard of the law of contradiction is perpetually infuriating to the Western student who desires to understand modern Hindu thought; whereas an insistence that things which contradict one another cannot be the same thing is regarded by the Hindu simply as evidence of Western lack of subtlety or as Christian intolerance.

When Vivekananda made his famous appearance at Chicago, Mohandas Karamchand Gandhi was a young man of twenty-four (1869–1948), then recently settled, and engaged in the practice of law, in South Africa. Many years will have to pass before it is possible to pass anything like a balanced and definitive judgement on the thought of this enigmatic man. One of our greatest needs is a critical biography of Gandhi. A beginning has been made by Otto Wolff in his book *Mahatma und Christus*.[9] But much work will yet be needed before the picture of the real man emerges from the aura of hagiographical worship that has attended his memory, and from the veil of mystification with which he tended to surround himself during his life.

During his years of residence in South Africa Mr. Gandhi came under strong Christian influences and engaged in a careful study of the New Testament. But there is reason to think that many of his leading ideas came to him indirectly rather than directly from the New Testament itself. His view of social equality is related to that put forward by John Stuart Mill. His dislike of industrial development and his preference for the old simple ways of India show traces of the influence of Ruskin and William Morris. His characteristic doctrine of non-violence is nearer to the later views of Tolstoy than to anything that can be found in the New Testament.

Nor must it be forgotten that Mr. Gandhi even in periods of apparent retirement was an active and extremely astute politician consumed by the one over-mastering desire that within his lifetime India should become a wholly independent nation; and a publicist whose use and understanding of the press and of public opinion throughout the world can be compared only to those of President Franklin Roosevelt. To state this is not for a moment to question the absolute sincerity of Mr. Gandhi's own religious convictions; it is to recognize the action and reaction of political ideals and religious convictions, as each developed on what was in many respects an independent path.[10]

Religious conviction has in the past led to bitter strife and division, as in the religious wars in Europe. Therefore, as Gandhi taught his followers, India must learn that all religions are essentially the same; none must make such an exclusive claim as would justify it in setting up barriers in the way of national unity. So, in the regular

---

[9] Berlin (1955). As far as I know, no English translation of this useful book has yet appeared.

[10] I find myself at this point in agreement with Dr. P. D. Devanandan, *The Gospel and Renascent Hinduism* (1959), pp. 16–17. 'Gandhiji did not profess to be a theologian. His plea for religious tolerance was motivated primarily by the desire to achieve the goal of Indian independence. . . . The one dominant motive was nation-building.'

meetings for prayer in his *āshram*, he would read selections from the Scriptures of many faiths, and the adherents of all religions were encouraged to feel entirely at home in this atmosphere of tolerance and mutual respect.

The degradation of the depressed classes presented another grave problem. National unity cannot be achieved when a sixth of the population is excluded from social privilege and economic equality. Mr. Gandhi was also well aware of the success of Christian propaganda among the untouchables, and of the grave danger that the whole fifty millions of them, or at least a very large section, might be seduced into separation and the formation of yet another large non-Hindu community. So at all costs the untouchables must be taught to regard themselves as Hindus, and to believe that their future and their destiny were to be found in adherence to Hindu society. They must be called the Harijans, the people of God, and welcomed with open arms into the fellowship of the movement for national independence.

India was weak, when face to face with the strength of one of the greatest of Western powers. A virtue must be made of weakness, and a demonstration given of the superior efficacy of 'soul-force' as against the mere brute force available to the militarized power of the West. The idea of soul-force lies very deep in the Indian consciousness; this was the kind of force that the sages and wise men of old acquired by the tremendous penances that they imposed upon themselves. But the idea that all alike are required to practise complete non-violence is not to be derived from the Hindu Scriptures, and least of all from the Bhagavad Gita, that ancient classic in which Mr. Gandhi declared himself to find deeper truth than in the Sermon on the Mount. In this long and intense dialogue on the field of battle, Krishna, who has taken the form of Arjuna's charioteer, explains to Arjuna that the world is kept in being only if each performs with diligence the duty that is assigned to him by the caste in which he has been born. Arjuna is by birth a warrior; the business of a warrior is to fight. Let him then cast hesitation to the winds and do his duty manfully in the battle that lies before him.

The idea of non-violence, then, is of complex and in large part of non-Indian origin. But it is this that has made a deeper impression on India and on the world than any other part of Gandhian doctrine. India has not, indeed, remained altogether faithful to the principles set forth by Mr. Gandhi, nor was he himself entirely consistent in his application of the principles. For all its policy of disengagement, the proportion of the total income of India that is spent on military preparation is higher in independence than it was in the days of British rule. So far the policy of non-violence and soul-force has been tried out on a large scale only against a government which was actuated by the highest principles of justice, and which maintained an almost miraculous level of patience over many years of strain and provocation.[11] To be fully verified, both doctrine and practice would have to be tried out under conditions such as those of Hitler's Germany or of Soviet Russia. Nevertheless, what Mr. Gandhi gave to India, and this was his greatest legacy of all, was a sense of moral superiority to the West. Where Europeans and Christians have blundered over centuries, so the Gandhian doctrine runs, Asia has at last come to the rescue with a new principle of political action through which all the problems of men can be worked out to a peaceful solution.

Mr. Gandhi never pretended to be anything but a Hindu. His kindly remarks about other religions, and the evident parallels between some of his teachings and those of the Gospel, sometimes led his friends and admirers to think otherwise. But they were mistaken. Mr. Gandhi was a Hindu, and was in fact 'the real architect of the new Hinduism'.[12] Everything in existing Hinduism of which he disapproved, such as caste distinction, the idea of ritual pollution, animal sacrifice and so forth, he regarded as corruptions which had somehow slipped into the pure waters of Hinduism; and all these he was prepared ruthlessly to expel. Conservatives could not but be aware of what would happen to Hinduism if this teaching were widely accepted. The assassination of Mr. Gandhi in January 1948 by a young fanatic of the Hindu right wing came as a terrible shock to the world. Yet those who had closely watched the course of events were hardly surprised; the challenge presented by Mr. Gandhi to the whole of Hinduism as traditionally understood was so intense that the surprising thing, in that land of continual violence, was not that he died but that he lived so long.

[11] 'Non-violence to a Gujarati does not mean a Tolstoyan non-resistance to evil; it means using non-violent means to get your own way, with the emphasis on getting your own way. This explains much in the non-violent tactics of Congress in the past and why non-violence sometimes seemed to the outsider less morally attractive than a little old-fashioned physical force.' Percival Spear, *India, Pakistan and the West*, p. 50.

[12] A. L. Basham, *Concise Encyclopaedia of Living Faiths*, p. 259.

The leader can be killed, but his ideas live on. The modern Hinduism as fashioned by Mr. Gandhi is very much alive in the minds and lives of his disciples, and particularly of the most notable of those disciples, Vinoba Bhave (born 1895). Vinoba Bhave walks the length and breadth of India propagating the *Bhūdan* (giving of land) movement. Landlords are encouraged to give up some of their lands to their landless peasants, and thus to develop the spirit of equality and fellowship in the village. This is one part of the more general concept of *Sarvodaya*, universal service or benevolence. It is admitted that the idea of *Sarvodaya* was born in 1907, when Mr. Gandhi encountered Ruskin's *Unto This Last*. But Vinoba Bhave would probably contend that this Western influence was only the stimulus which led to the rediscovery of something that had been there in Hinduism from the beginning, with its basic ideas of equality and simplicity. He regards it as his task 'to establish a classless, casteless and conflictless society in which every individual and group will get opportunity and means for an all-round development.'[13]

This is the way in which men are *acting* in India. Social reform is in the air; appeals for service are being made, and seem to meet with a ready response. But is this what Hinduism really is? Are the springs of men's action to-day really the inherited beliefs to which with greater or less conviction they profess adherence? Or has a gap come into existence between the real religion of the modern Hindu, in the sense of the ideal to which he is committed, to which he will gladly render service, and the formal principles of the religion of which he is nominally an adherent?[14] Has Hinduism within itself the vitality to provide both the intellectual categories in which the new understanding of life can be expressed, and the spiritual power through which the exciting vision can be realized?

The way in which men act has changed. The change would seem to demand a restatement of the religious beliefs on which Hindu society rests. It is at this point that we encounter the third and in some ways the most important of the three great creators of modern Hinduism, Dr. Sarvepalli Radakrishnan.

[13] Quoted by P. D. Devanandan, op. cit. p. 19.
[14] Cf. P. D. Devanandan, *The Concept of Maya* (1950), p. 221: 'Every aspect of Hindu life is affected in an unprecedented way by the acceptance in practice of alien principles of conduct and life and outlook, which are subversive of the basic assumptions of the religious theory on which Hindu India's thought fabric is built.'

Dr. Radhakrishnan studied at the Madras Christian College, and thus at a very early age was brought into contact with the Christian faith as represented in men of stainless integrity and real intellectual power. He is typical of the present situation, and representative of one side of the Christian conflict in the world to-day. Formerly the Christian had the advantage that he knew well the faith that it was his purpose to teach, whereas his listeners were at best imperfectly acquainted with it. Now the situation is entirely different. The champions of the non-Christian religions have fully studied the Gospel, have weighed it, and have rejected it. Some of them have at one period of their life been Christians, and have turned back from the Christian way to the way of their national heritage. Dr. Radhakrishnan knows the Bible well.[15] Not merely so; he has an extensive acquaintance with contemporary Christian writing in the field of dogmatic theology, and can turn this knowledge to his advantage in contrasting the confusions and contradictions of Christian thinking based on the Bible with the lucidity and certainty of Eastern thinking based on the Vedanta.

In a whole series of books Dr. Radhakrishnan has set himself to commend Eastern wisdom to the materially-minded peoples of the West. With a perfect command of English and an attractive style he is almost the ideal showman for the purpose. Yet, for all the attitude of generous tolerance which Radhakrishnan assumes and attempts to maintain, the careful reader can hardly fail to receive the impression that much of what he writes is the expression of a dislike, amounting at times to a passionate hatred, of Christianity.[16] Christianity must not be allowed to score a single point; all the trumps must be in the hands of the Eastern thinker. Thus, for instance,

The emphasis on definite creeds and absolute dogmatism, with its consequences of intolerance, exclusiveness and confusion of piety with patriarchism are the striking features of Western Christianity.[17]

The implication is that the religion of the East is free from all these defects.

This attitude represents what is perhaps the final stage in the reaction of the East against the West. First, there was a period of

---

[15] He is not, however, always happy in his interpretation of it. For a curious and elementary misunderstanding of Romans 1.14, see *The Brahma Sūtra* (1960), pp. 250–1.

[16] This is the view of Dr. Hendrik Kraemer, *Religion and the Christian Faith* (London, 1956), pp. 99–136, with which I find myself in entire agreement.

[17] S. Radhakrishnan, *East and West in Religion* (1954), p. 58.

anxious withdrawal, anxious because the evident superiority of the West in physical strength might be regarded as in some way justifying its affirmation of the superiority of its religion. Then followed the period of Vivekananda, in which the East is asserting its claim to equality with the West. Now we advance one step further; although due respect is paid to all forms of human religion, at least the hint is given that the Eastern form of wisdom as communicated in the Hindu Vedanta is not merely superior to any other but will be found to be of universal significance.

It is a cardinal principle with Radhakrishnan that every form of religion is a manifestation of genuine human striving after God, and that none therefore may be condemned as false and useless. This is not to say that all religions are equally true or equally useful. And in fact Radhakrishnan himself seems prepared to classify religions in a descending scale of validity.

At the summit stands the perception that the Ultimate and Supreme as it is in itself is impersonal, for personality is a form of limitation such as may not be attributed to that which by definition is unlimited. This Supreme is unknown by man, and is in fact unknowable. This humility of approach is expressed, better than anywhere else, in the Upanishads and in Hindu wisdom generally.

Not all men can attain to this austere comprehension of reality. For those whose wings grow weary in this steep ascent there is the possibility of belief in a personal God. There is good authority in the Hindu tradition itself for this attitude. The man who needs a personal object of worship may choose for himself his *ishtadevatā*, his own preferred deity. Each should choose that deity which best corresponds to the image or reflection of Reality that he is able to grasp and that is most suitable to him at this level of being. In this category of faiths Radhakrishnan is clearly able to find a place for Judaism and for Islam.

On a lower level still are the believers in incarnations. One who stands so low in the level of spiritual perception as not to be able to apprehend the deity in itself, even in a personal form, may need the help of some human figure to which he may cling as the only means by which on this level the divine can penetrate his spirit. This is not wrong, though from the standpoint of Hinduism it is at a very long remove from the true nature of reality. Christians are not wrong in worshipping Christ or in considering him as a revelation of God; they are wrong only in supposing that the whole of truth could be incorporate in a single manifestation, in their failure to see that there are other realms of Spirit of which Christianity knows nothing, and in the intolerance of the demand that others to whom the Christian medium may be quite unsuited should adapt themselves to it.

Even lower come the worshippers of idols and spirits. Highest of all the man who has no need even of a mental image for the purposes of his worship. Lowest is he who cannot form a mental image and therefore needs the outward and visual image to help him form some concept of the divine. Yet even this level must not be despised; even here there are gleams of divine truth, and this too is to be taken as one of the roads that lead to God.

It is not maintained that all roads are equally direct or that all forms of worship are equally near to the truth. There is a higher and a lower, the highest level being represented by Hindu Vedanta in its purest form. It is not, therefore, impossible that a man might pass from one form of worship to another, or that a teacher might help a man to rise from one level to that which is above it. But this must not be understood as conversion from one religion to another—it is a process in the inner evolution of the Self, through which it can rise nearer to the understanding of the basic Vedantic truth of the unity of all particular and empirical selves with the unchanging unity of the universe.

All this is set forth in terms of the most candid and engaging tolerance. Hinduism is a broad and all-embracing sea: 'As a result of this tolerant attitude, Hinduism itself has become a mosaic of almost all the types and stages of religious aspirations and endeavour.'[18]

'For a true Hindu there are few places dedicated to God in which he may not silently worship, few prayers in which he may not reverently join.'[19] Dr. Radhakrishnan in practice lives up to his theory; it is in this spirit that he has been known to read the lessons at Christian worship in the chapel of All Souls' College, Oxford.

This tolerance is possible only because of the underlying conviction of the relativity of all religion and all human religious experience. The truth is essentially unknowable, and all our approaches to it are marked by imperfection and error. The recognition of our weakness should lead us to gentleness and tolerance with one another:

[18] S. Radhakrishnan, *Eastern Religions and Western Thought* (1939), p. 313.
[19] *ibid.*

The truth which is the kernel of every religion is one and the same; doctrines, however, differ considerably since they are the applications of the truth to the human situation. . . . Rites, ceremonies, systems and dogmas lead beyond themselves to a region of utter clarity and so have only relative truth. They are valid so long as they are assigned their proper place. They are not to be mistaken for absolute truth. They are used to communicate the shadow of what has been realized. Every word, every concept is a pointer which points beyond itself. The sign should not be mistaken for the thing signified. The signpost is not the destination.[20]

The principle of *sarvāgamaprāmānya*, the truth and authority of all religions, is at the root and basis of Hindu conviction; thus it can serve as a unifying factor for them all, since it calls all to work together, and to find the unity of religion, 'not in a common creed, but in a common quest'.[21]

Such doctrine, sedulously propagated in charming English over many years, has undoubtedly exercised deep influence on many Western minds. The sense of mystery which to so large an extent has been lost in pragmatic Western religion, the call to the freedom of a quest in place of the inhibiting reliance on dogma, the broad genial tolerance which is prepared to find a place for everything, the respect for the individual which encourages him to find his own spiritual way—all these correspond to certain moods and tendencies which are widespread in the West of the twentieth century. Dr. Radhakrishnan is not alone in his advocacy. Dr. Bouquet quotes a passage from Professor Murti of the Hindu University at Benares, in which much the same ideas are set forth, though with a slightly more evident anti-Christian bias than is usually to be found on the surface of Dr. Radhakrishnan's writings:

There is something inherently secular and unspiritual in any organization. It tends to create vested interests and to breed corruption. In stifling freedom of expression and setting up a norm of dogmas to which the votaries are required to conform, organised religion (the Church) succeeds only in antagonising other religious groups and creating schisms and heresies within its own fold. What we need is the realisation of the spiritual, which is the bedrock of all our endeavour. Only mystical religion, which eminently combines the unity of Ultimate Being with the freedom of different paths for realising it, can hope to unite the world.[22]

[20] S. Radhakrishnan, *East and West, the End of Their Separation* (New York, Harper, 1954).   [21] S. Radhakrishnan, *The Hindu View of Life* (1927), pp. 20, 58.
[22] A. C. Bouquet, *Christian Faith and non-Christian Religions* (1958), p. 275. For an interesting exposition of a similar position from a Western point of view, see V. H. Mottram, *The Physical Basis of Personality* (Penguin Books, 2nd edn. 1952), pp. 148-61.

By such expositions of the Hindu faith as this it has been possible to restore Hindu self-respect, to enable the Hindu to feel that he can meet the West at least on terms of equality, perhaps even of superiority. But this does not answer some of the burning questions that must arise with the changed attitude and situation of India today. 'Reform in social *practices* required a restatement of corresponding underlying religious *beliefs*.'[23]

Hinduism has traditionally been a world-renouncing religion, a religion of destiny and submission. The pious Hindu is called to fulfil the duties of human life, as student and as householder. But, when he has seen the face of his grandson and ensured the perpetuity of his race, he has carried out his obligations and may seek release. The higher way is that of the *Sannyāsi*, who has renounced all things, and even broken the sacred thread, the sign of his dignity as a member of one of the higher castes. Moreover, as we have seen, one of the unchanging elements in Hindu faith has been the belief in *karma*; the laws of the universe cannot be broken, and a man's destiny is written on his brow at birth. So it was fated to happen and so it will happen; nothing can change it, since destiny has been irrevocably settled by the accumulated debts and merits of countless previous existences.

The modern Hindu is not prepared to lie down under this fatalism. He believes that, within limits at least, man's destiny is in his own hands and that he must strive and do. Dr. Radhakrishnan comes to his aid with no uncertain sound:

Man is not at the mercy of inexorable fate. If he *wills*, he can improve on his past record. There is no inevitability in history. To assume that we are helpless creatures caught in the current which is sweeping us into the final abyss is to embrace a philosophy of despair, of nihilism.[24]

This is fine bracing doctrine. But where did Dr. Radhakrishnan learn it? Did he find it in the Upanishads, or have we here as a matter of fact an echo of Carlyle's *Sartor Resartus*?

The heaviest blow at the traditional doctrine of *karma* was dealt by Mr. Gandhi, not by his teaching but by the manner of his death at the hand of an assassin. If all misfortune is the fruit of ancient deeds, then such a violent death should be evidence of a gravely sinful past. Confronted with the story of the Cross, no Hindu has ever in my hearing affirmed that the sufferings and death

[23] P. D. Devanandan, *The Gospel and Renascent Hinduism* (1959), p. 8.
[24] S. Radhakrishnan, *Recovery of Faith* (1956), p. 4.

of Jesus are to be understood as expiation for his own great sins in previous existences. But that is a tale of ancient times and belongs to an alien religious tradition; the Hindu may be excused if he does not immediately see its relevance to his own cherished beliefs. The death of Mr. Gandhi, on the contrary, happened only a few years ago and it happened near at hand. It has challenged the Hindu with something that he cannot interpret within the categories of his traditional thinking.

The Hindu of to-day believes that he is making history. The tempo of national life has quickened. Great plans for reconstruction are in hand. The Hindu believes that his country is called to play a great part in the life of the nations, and to help in leading mankind onward towards a better and more hopeful future. But what is history? And what place is there for it in the traditional Hindu scheme of things?

It is no accident that there is no indigenous tradition of history-writing in India. The Greeks, the Hebrews and the Muslims all had their understanding of history, and the sense that it was worth while to take the trouble to record it. In India the whole genius of the people seems to have been turned inwards to contemplation and the development of speculative thought. As a result whole centuries have perished without written memorial. The only definite landmark in early Indian history is Alexander's invasion; from that certain point of reference provided by alien incursion the historian moves cautiously backwards and forwards among a multiplicity of uncertainties. Traditionally the Hindu does not attach great importance to the events that occur in the three-dimensional world of space and time, or to the human beings that take part in them.

One of the great Hindu concepts that seems destined to undergo radical reconsideration in our time is that of *māyā*.[25] The term manifests a certain flexibility, as is to be expected in a word that has been in use over many centuries. But the sense generally attributed to it in Hinduism seems to be beyond question. *Maya* is not absolute nothingness. It has a certain minimal existence. But it seems closely to resemble the Greek concept of *hyle*, matter, at its lowest. *Hyle* is as near non-existence as could be; it is that potentiality on which form can for a brief space impress a partial and almost fictive reality.

---

[25] For a full study of this theme, the reader must turn to P. D. Devanandan, *The Concept of Māyā* (London, 1951), where every aspect of the subject is treated with knowledge and intelligence.

But it belongs irremediably to the realm of becoming and not to that of being. Much the same is the Hindu *māyā*. It resembles the clouds, which for a moment take the forms of splendid towers and castles and forthwith lose them again. Everything visible is insubstantial and transitory; everything that seems to be passes away into that which is not yet. Why, then, attach any importance to achievement in this realm of illusion and deceit? It is man's misfortune or his fault that he has been born into this realm of chance, of fantasy. His own separate existence is as much an illusion as the phantasmagoria by which he is surrounded. Blessedness consists in nothing other than as rapid an escape as may be from the world of the unreal into the real.

Now, if this view is taken of the physical universe, it is clear that there can be no incentive to constructive action within it, since such action itself is a sign of slavery and a means by which slavery can lay its hand upon the future. It is here that Dr. Radhakrishnan seems to be prepared to make the most radical reconstruction of the ancient Hindu ideas. His exposition is not free from ambiguity. But he would seem to come very near to the Christian idea of contingent existence, except that his doctrine does not include any valid idea of a Creator God. *Māyā* is not to be taken as sheer non-existence; it is partial and qualified existence. The only real achievement for man is still that illumination of the spirit, which sets him above all temporal goods and releases him into union with the source of all being. Yet *māyā* is still a field in which men can serve and in which genuine and real achievements are possible.[26]

But, if this is true, and accepted as true, may not the one who holds such views find that, perhaps all unaware, he has made a radical transformation of his theology, and that the results of such a transformation are more far-reaching than he is himself aware?

For, if history is a sphere in which achievement is possible, sooner or later we are driven back on the question of the relationship of this history, which is no longer the mere meaningless convolutions of *māyā*, to that other reality which lies behind it. The Hindu has in the past been inclined to take pride in the fact that Hinduism is a

[26] e.g. *The Brahma Sūtra* (1960), p. 140: 'Though the world has not absolute reality it is not to be compared with illusory experiences. . . . Embodiedness has positive value for the evolution of the soul and every form of life should be respected. . . . Our objective knowledge, though it apprehends an already degraded being, still reveals something of the reality despite its divorce from intimate, inward existence.'

religion of pure ideas, and in this respect to contrast Christianity unfavourably with it as a religion that is dependent on history. May the time have come when the Hindu will have to reconsider this classification of religions, and at least to weigh the possibility that an understanding of religion in historical terms may be something that he has to face?

If the Hindu is prepared to move in this direction, he will be following in steps that have already been taken in this century by some of his Christian brethren. When the liberal movement in Christianity was at its height, there was a tendency among Christians, following the traditions of the Enlightenment, to stress the value of the universal ideas and to depreciate history. The opposite point of view—that the incarnation of religious ideas in history is a benefit, and represents a higher stage of religious development—was expressed in 1915 by Dr. C. C. J. Webb in words which, since I cannot improve on them, I will venture to quote in full:

So far as by 'historical element in religion' we mean the element of sacred history, a belief in which forms an important element in some religions, it is a mark of higher development in a religion to emphasise this element. For in the recognition of such a sacred history religion comes to recognize itself as the most concrete and individual form of human experience, concerned not with mere abstract universals, but with concrete individuals, those and no others, in which, and not elsewhere, the universals with which we have to do are, as a matter of fact, particularized, and apart from which they possess no actual reality. A religion which involves as part of its essence a sacred history is, in this way, at a higher level than one which, while setting forth certain universal principles, moral or metaphysical, is ready to symbolize them by anything that comes to hand as it were, and is comparatively indifferent to the particular symbol chosen. Thus a religion which, having developed a theology, regards the narratives which are associated with it as mere illustrative stories, ranks below one which regards them as the actual forms which the universal principles have taken and could not but have taken in a world wherein reason is throughout immanent, and all must be rationally necessary, although we cannot always see into the necessity.[27]

So far we have considered reconstructions to which the Hindu may feel himself led by analysis of what he himself really believes to-day, and on the basis of which he acts in the world. We may now go on to a certain number of questions which the Christian may

[27] Clement C. J. Webb, *Studies in the History of Natural Theology* (1915), pp. 29-30.

D

respectfully present to him as relevant to the reconstruction in which he is engaged.

First, we may raise the question of personality. It is almost always assumed by the Hindu that the impersonal is by its very nature superior to the personal, and that the personal is a stage of religious experience which is, if possible, to be surmounted. But is there any evidence for this? Personality is the highest thing we know. In his remarkable book *The Phenomenon of Man*, P. Teilhard de Chardin concentrates attention on the immense forward step in evolution that was marked when sentient beings became personal by developing the power of *reflection*:

From our experimental point of view, reflection is, as the word indicates, the power acquired by a consciousness to turn in upon itself, to take possession of itself *as an object* endowed with its own particular consistence and values; no longer merely to know, but to know oneself; no longer merely to know but to know that one knows. By this individualization of himself in the depths of himself, the living element, which heretofore had been spread out and divided over a diffuse circle of perceptions and activities, was constituted for the first time as a *centre* in the form of a point at which all the impressions and experiences knit themselves together and fuse into a unity that is conscious of its own organization. . . . Because we are reflective, we are not only different but quite other. It is not a matter of change of degree, but of a change of nature resulting from a change of state.[28]

Is all this to be lost, as we move higher in the evolutionary scale? The characteristic of evolution seems to be that everything that is higher in the scale, at least in the sense of being more complex, retains within itself something of the whole history of the evolutionary process that has gone before. Man, the reflective being, may have to move out into far wider fields of relatedness, and, as religion teaches, to an indefinite enlargement of his reflective self by its apprehension of the whole. But would it not seem paradoxical, and contrary to everything that we know of ourselves and of the universe that we inhabit, to suppose that the most crucial thing that has yet appeared on this planet, individual awareness, is destined simply to vanish and to leave no trace in a total re-absorption into the impersonal? We may rightly look forward to a transcendence of personality, to a state that is as different from our present consciousness as that consciousness is from the consciousness of the animals.

[28] Pierre Teilhard de Chardin, *The Phenomenon of Man* (Eng. trans. 1959), pp. 165–6.

But it would be a stretch of the ordinary use of language to apply the term 'impersonal' to such a state.

We may believe that the Hindu, by returning to his own origins, may find himself nearer to Christians than at times he thinks.

Professor R. C. Zaehner of Oxford has analysed with great subtlety three kinds of mysticism, all of which are present in Hinduism in varying degree.[29] Any mystical experience is an experience of total absorption, in which for the time being individual existence is forgotten and the sense of identification is complete. Since such experiences, as described by those who know them from within, all seem to manifest the same 'feeling-tone', there is a tendency to assume that they are all in essence the same experience. But this is a simplification. We have to ask what it is with which the subject feels himself to be so wholly identified as to be unaware for a time of himself as a separate existence. Professor Zaehner identifies three distinct types or fields of mystical rapport.

The first may be called, for convenience, cosmic consciousness. This is most familiar to English readers in the nature mysticism of Wordsworth. Wordsworth finds peace in the sense of his identification with all other things. He loved to think of himself as 'clothed with the heavens and crowned with the stars';[30] and in two of the most familiar lines in all his writing he refers to himself as

> Rapt into still communion that transcends
> The imperfect offices of prayer and praise
> ('Excursion', book i, 214–15).

This experience, of course, is a genuine experience of one particular kind of reality. We are of the dust of the universe, and its smallest particle is of our kin. It is good that at times we should feel this kinship, and that the whole movement of all that is should for the time being deliver us from our restless gyrations in the pettiness of our own orbits.

Secondly, there is that experience in which a man finds himself at one with all the depths of his own being. A large number of Yoga techniques seem to be directed towards the liberation of the self into such an experience. The whole of modern psycho-analytic method rests on the belief that it is possible to bring into consciousness those deeper levels of human life, which may represent earlier

[29] *At Sundry Times* (1958), pp. 30–133.
[30] Basil Willey, *The Eighteenth Century Background* (1950), p. 287.

and forgotten stages of the individual's own pilgrimage, or, like some palaeozoic strata cast up from the depths of the sea, may represent the vestiges of some memory within him of the whole age-long pilgrimage of the human race. An experience very similar to this appears to have been produced by the drugs with which Mr. Aldous Huxley and his friends have been experimenting. This, too, is representative of a reality and a good. We are composed of many layers of being, and there is no limit to the depths of human personality. It is good that we should be aware of the whole of ourselves and reconciled to it. It is to be noted, however, that not all such experiences are marked by anything that could be called a specifically religious quality.

Thirdly, there are traces, even in Hinduism, of the possibility of ecstatic union, through love and devotion, to a god personally conceived. The greater part of the Bhagavad Gita consists of rather jejune argumentation, starting from the duty of Arjuna to engage in the battle with the Pandavas which is about to begin, and wandering through many questions of philosophy and psychology and ethics. Many European readers must have wondered why so flat a book has received such absorbed reverence from so many generations of Hindu readers, and why Mr. Gandhi declared that he found deeper revelations in it than in the pages of the New Testament. Then suddenly the tempo changes. Krishna, serving as the charioteer of Arjuna, is transformed before his eyes, and in a long passage of great rhetorical splendour reveals himself as the supreme reality, as the ultimate unity of all that is. 'The real message of the Gītā does not lie in its philosophy, but in its teaching that God is not a passionless Absolute but the love of man's soul, indeed love itself.'[31] Confronted with this manifestation of terror Arjuna cries out 'Bowing down and prostrating my body before thee. I implore thy grace adorable lord. Bear with me, I pray thee, as a father with his son friend with friend, lover with beloved.'[32]

Such theophany is hardly characteristic of the Hindu tradition in general. For the most part it has been overlaid by the later monism of Saṃkara, who, incidentally, in his commentary has a good deal of difficulty in explaining away the many things in the Gita that are really incompatible with his own philosophy. The *bhakti* tradition of later times does, of course, recognize vision and personal devotion; but a man's *ishṭadevatā*, that particular deity to whom he feels

[31] R. C. Zaehner, op. cit. p. 130.   [32] Bhagavad Gita, 11:44.

himself attracted and to whom he can give this kind of reverence, is held to be only a manifestation of the supreme, a lower reality which is to be transcended if a man can rise to the higher levels of religious experience. But is it certain that the monistic tradition is higher than the earlier and theistic? Without trying to teach the Hindus their own religion, has the Christian not the right very respectfully to ask the Hindu to go back to his own tradition, and to consider whether the revelation contained in this section of the Gita will not more truly set his feet on the way of understanding than the more abstract philosophy which has for so long been held out before him as the ideal to which he should attain?

In an entirely different realm also the Christian has his question to ask.

We have seen that one of the new things that has come into Hindu life has been an enriched sense of the value of the individual man. Social reform is in the air, and the aim of all these reforms is the removal of everything that hinders the individual from finding the fullness of his being. It must, of course, be said that the sense of community and of responsibility for the community is by no means lacking to-day. Yet there is a real and significant change of emphasis.

Why is the individual significant? In the past he has been regarded as little more than a link in the chain of being. On one hand, he is connected with the mysteries of birth and succession. He must marry and bring forth children, and so secure the continuity of existence and of human frames in which souls can take up their residence. On the other hand, he is merely the moment, the atom, in his own chain of endless existence, as he passes from birth to birth in the search of final release. So it has come about that traditionally the individual has been almost completely subordinated to the needs of the community and the race. The Hindu has acquiesced with comparative complacency in the sufferings of the outcaste and the untouchable on the ground that such things were necessary to the stability of society, and that too many tears need not be shed over any inconveniences incidental to a purely transitory stage of existence. Now all is changed; the individual is beginning to come into his own as having rights and deserving consideration for his own sake, and because he has an intrinsic value of his own. It is not merely that he is a voter who must be considered for secondary and interested reasons; he is coming to be seen as a fitting object for the serious concern of human beings other than himself.

But what gives him this value? On what intellectual or spiritual foundations does this new conviction rest? Here, once again, the challenge to the Hindu is to analyse and to become fully conscious of the principles that underlie his actions. To the Christian the answer to this question is obvious. The human individual is of value because he is the object of the unremitting care and interest of God. This the Hindu may not experience great difficulty in admitting, if it is squarely put to him. He may find it more difficult to proceed to the Christian corollary from this affirmation.

God is concerned with the individual as individual. What is of special interest about him is just those things that make him different from every other member of the human race. But, if that is true, will not his disappearance as individual, his re-absorption into the undifferentiated unity of the One, involve the whole universe in loss, in a diminution of the richness of its variety? Is the Christian belief in personal immortality necessarily to be considered as a form of selfishness, a desire for individual achievement and perfection? May it not be that God Himself delights in individuality, that he has deliberately made a universe in which it can exist, and that he intends it to continue, in other realms of being, as part of his delight in his chosen people and as part of the delight of his chosen people in him?

It will be interesting to see the extent to which Hinduism in the coming years is able to make clear to itself certain concepts that seem to be implicit in its present day practice. And, with the absorptive capacity of the Hindu tradition, all these ideas could be absorbed as ideas without disrupting the majestic fabric of Hinduism. The next Christian challenge, however, comes as a much more serious shock. The Christian believes that such ideas must find expression in a community which is appropriate to them, and that this must be a community of a particular kind. It must be a community, ultimately, of freedom, of choice and decision, of total loyalty and commitment, and therefore in certain directions necessarily intolerant since it cannot hold that all convictions are equally and indifferently of value. This is where the Hindu meets a challenge that he is not yet ready to face. The discussion between Hindus and Christians in India has been taking on sharper and less mellow tones in recent years. The stumbling-block for the Hindu is the Church.

The Hindu is accustomed to reckoning with two poles of religious existence.

He is perfectly familiar with the idea of 'the flight of the alone to the alone'. Ultimately every man has to find his way to God in splendid isolation. Ultimately he has to be responsible for his own salvation. There may be teachers and guides—there is as a matter of fact in Hinduism a magnificent tradition of spiritual teaching reaching right back to the time of the Upanishads. There can be intellectual discussion and even some exchange of spiritual experience. But, if the moment of enlightenment comes, it comes to the individual in his aloneness. There is in Hinduism no tradition of corporate worship or of the fellowship in the approach to God of which corporate worship is the expression.[33]

At the other end Hinduism is perfectly familiar with the *given* community, which is held together among other things by religious sanctions. Every Hindu is born a member of a caste and remains a member of that caste until his death. He will on occasion worship its gods, and every stage of his life is marked by the appropriate religious ceremonies. Even if he wished, there is no means by which he could transfer himself to another caste. Here everything is social, in contrast to that other field in which everything is individual. Here everything is determined by the iron law of custom as in that other field everything is free.

The one thing that the Hindu cannot understand is the idea of a community to which a man attaches himself of his own free-will and in permanence, to which he totally commits himself, in which he involves himself in a completely new set of responsibilities for his fellow-members, and by life within which his own character and being undergo extensive modification.

It is this that vitiates all discussion between Hindu and Christian on the subject of conversion. If conversion means the adoption of certain new and good ideas, the Hindu cannot see why this should involve leaving the community into which he has been born. Conversely, if anyone decides to leave his own traditional community, this is almost invariably interpreted to mean cultural betrayal, the abandonment of a precious part of India's heritage. Thus a distinguished contemporary Indian can write of missionaries, 'Their attempts, however honest, conscious or unconscious, at undermining the religious and cultural foundations of India through the varied means of proselytization were not worthy of them. Time

[33] Even at the great festivals, where crowds assemble round the shrine, there is no corporate worship as this is understood in Christianity and in Islam.

is ripe now when every civilized man must know that faith cometh out of the maturity of heart and fullness of understanding and not by ceremonial conversion, either this way or that way'.[34]

The Hindu is still very far from apprehending what conversion to Jesus Christ means to the Christian. In the Christian sense of the term, conversion involves commitment to a particular Person. On this follows self-dedication to a particular manner of life, in which every detail must be organized in relation to the central loyalty. Such a life can be lived only within a community every member of which ideally is inspired by equal loyalty to the divine Head. Thus we come to apprehend that the doctrine of the Church is not an appendage to the Gospel but an integral part of it. Such an idea is completely foreign to Hinduism.

The idea of the Church is essentially incongruous, and therefore repugnant, to the Hindu believer. The reason is obvious. Religious maturity in Hinduism is the result of individual achievement in self-discipline, towards which others like-minded can only help by the inspiration of example or through wise counsel. The idea of a transforming community is alien to the Hindu genius because of its basic belief about the nature of God as the eternal Brahman, and of the nature of man as essentially that of Brahman itself. There can, therefore, be no such community as the Church claims itself to be, where there is an inflow and outflow of personal influence which is transforming, because the real bond of fellowship therein is provided by the Holy Spirit which draws the members of the Church together in communion with God as revealed in Christ Jesus.[35]

The last point to which the Christian comes with his questions is the crucial one. The attentive reader cannot have failed to observe that the Hindu approach to religion has been constantly expressed in terms of 'enlightenment'. It is the man who knows who has been saved. Professor Radhakrishnan in his eloquent modern expositions of Hinduism again and again emphasises the truth that the ignorance which Hinduism identifies with darkness is to be understood in terms not of intellectual incapacity but of spiritual blindness. But the Christian must still come back with a question as to the nature of that darkness and that blindness. Must we not find a place in it for the corruption of the will? And, when the seeker has reached enlightenment, is he at once set free from all responsibility for the harm and injury that he has caused to others in the course of his pilgrimage?

[34] R. R. Diwakar, *Paramahamsa Sri Ramakrishna* (Bombay, 1956), p. 22.
[35] P. D. Devanandan, *The Gospel and Renascent Hinduism* (1959), p. 37.

Professor Radhakrishnan has published a notable edition of a Hindu classic, the *Brahma Sūtra*, with illustrations from the whole field of Western and Christian writing.[36] Is it without significance that the index does not contain the word 'forgiveness'? Radhakrishnan stresses that through the doctrine of *karma* the world is recognized as ethically and legally valid.[37] But are these the only two dimensions which have to be taken into consideration? If in fact Brahman and I are one, there is no one to be offended. Any offence that I commit is really committed against myself, and the retribution for it demanded under the law of *karma* may be regarded as adequate payment. If all other selves are in reality part of my own self, of the All, then as the Bhagavad Gita says, 'of a truth they slay not, neither are they slain'. But, if we should admit even for a moment, the possibility of duality, and of love, *agape*, as a factor in religious experience, do not all the categories of the Hindu at once reveal themselves as totally inadequate to the range of man's experience? 'Forgive us our trespasses' is at the very heart of the Christian Gospel. What man needs is not to be enlightened, but to be saved.

So in the twentieth century the two great forces of Hinduism and the Christian Gospel confront one another. Nor is it possible to foresee what the issue of the dialogue is likely to be. On the whole Hindus do not feel serious anxiety about the future, as they tended to do in the nineteenth century. 'Christian and Muslim propaganda is now no longer a serious threat', writes Mr. Basham.[38] Similarly, one of the most notable of modern Hindu apologists, Professor D. S. Sarma, writes:

It is obvious that we cannot absorb Islam or Christianity as we once more or less absorbed Buddhism. Our *Kabirs* and *Keshubs* must remain isolated phenomena and, at best, could give rise only to small sects. Therefore our policy should be not one of absorption but of fraternization. In this great country all of us have to live in peace, each community following its own *Dharma*.[39]

[36] London, 1959.
[37] 'The law of *karma* tells us that as in the physical world, in the mental and moral world also there is law. The world is an ordered cosmos. What we sow we will reap. . . . The universe is ethically sound. Even as the world would be a logical contradiction without the reign of law, it would be a moral chaos without the moral law.' op. cit. p. 194.   [38] *Concise Encyclopaedia of Living Faiths*, p. 260.
[39] D. S. Sarma, *Hinduism through the Ages* (Bombay, 1956), pp. 276-7.

The Christian must not be surprised if, between now and the end of this century, the work of Christian witness in India becomes more difficult than it has been for a century. He must be prepared to face the possibility that the greater part of his work must be from within Hinduism, in putting questions to the Hindu and helping him to understand himself better. But in doing so he will not be adapting himself to the Hindu ideal of what a missionary should be as 'one who, both by example and precept, helps the other to live his own faith more perfectly and not to forsake it for the missionary's faith'.[40] All the time he will be attempting to help the Hindu to see the radical unsatisfactoriness of all the answers that have been given to his questions, and so to point him to the One in Whom those questions can receive their all-sufficient answer, the Lord Jesus Christ.

---

[40] P. D. Mehta, *Early Indian Religious Thought* (1956), quoted in P. D. Devanandan, *The Gospel and Renascent Hinduism* (1959), p. 39.

CHAPTER V

THE DOCTRINE OF THE LOTUS

THERE can be no doubt that, of the ancient non-Christian religions of the world, Buddhism presents itself as the most attractive to the modern man of the West. Yet it is perhaps the hardest of all to understand, both because of the wide variety of forms in which it is to be found, and also because of the intricacy of the philosophical and psychological principles that the believer is expected to master.

At first sight there are a number of resemblances between Christianity and Buddhism.

1. Buddhism is quite clearly an offspring of Hinduism. It presupposes that ardent quest in search of reality, of an inner understanding of the truth of all things, which found expression in India between the eighth and the fifth centuries B.C. in the great series of the early Upanishads. But it differs from Hinduism and resembles Christianity in having one clearly identifiable founder. Gautama the Buddha is certainly an historical figure. Much careful historical criticism has to be exercised on the mass of legendary material that has accumulated above and around the primitive strata; but, when this preliminary work of excavation has been carried out, a real figure emerges, a figure which can be placed with a fair degree of certainty in its historical frame of reference.

Gautama was probably born (though the date is still contested by some) in 563 B.C. in Kapilavastu in the borderland between India and Nepal. He was of quasi-royal stock. All the traditions agree in affirming that up till the age of twenty-nine Gautama had lived the ordinary life of a Kshatriya prince, luxurious, sensual, though perhaps not to grave excess. Then, in a moment of crisis, there came to him the thought of the transience of all things; all that is grows old and feeble and dies. What lies behind the mystery of suffering? Impelled by the imperious necessity to know, at dead of night the young prince slipped out, leaving his sleeping wife and little son, to launch himself upon the pilgrimage of inquiry and asceticism.

In this he was not unique. The vividly written early Upanishads depict groups of seekers meeting in remote places to discuss the ultimate problems of reality. It is characteristic that many of those who join in these debates appear to be Kshatriyas, members of the noble and warrior caste. The Brahmans still maintained their priestly domination and their mastery of the secrets of the more ancient wisdom. But this had degenerated into concentration on the endless minutiae of not very interesting ceremonies, a pursuit that can hardly bring illumination to the minds of vigorous questing lay-men. It is perhaps not surprising that the initiative in philosophical speculation passed from the priest to the warrior.

But, if Gautama was not alone in the object of his quest, he was unique in the ardour of his pursuit and in the results that flowed from his achievement. For six years he seems to have followed the traditional methods of the ascetics—without finding that which he sought. He then withdrew to solitary meditation; and finally, as the crown of his endeavours, enlightenment came. From being a Boddhisattva, one on the way to enlightenment, he was now the Buddha, the Enlightened One, and as such the centre of human history. He had perceived that suffering is the dominant element in human existence. Whence comes suffering? It comes from desire, that eager grasping self that holds men chained to the wheel of in-substantial things. If desire can but be eliminated, release from suffering will be possible and then men's quest will be at an end. So the whole doctrine of the Buddha is centred on the radical elimination of desire. We note that this doctrine does not deal, like the Gospels, equally with joy and sorrow, with life in all its variegated complexity; it directs its attention principally to one side and aspect of life. This is a point to which later we shall have occasion to return.

2. What follows in the history is of almost unmatched beauty and charm. Once enlightened the Buddha did not keep his new knowledge to himself. He felt impelled to set out on a mission of proclamation, to pass on to other suffering mortals the message of peace that he had himself discovered. Then as now, in India the wandering ascetic who has something to communicate can be almost sure of finding an audience. It was not long before the Buddha, like Jesus, had gathered a band of disciples around him. In sharp con-trast, however, to Jesus, Gautama never lost an almost Manichean suspicion of women and of the harm that they could do, and it was only very hesitantly that women were admitted to the fellowship; but in the end Buddhism had its nuns as well as its monks. The next forty-five years were spent in a wandering ministry and in the

instruction of the disciples. Most of the earliest Buddhist records are in the form of dialogues between the Master and those who came to ask him questions. The death of the Buddha took place in or about the year 483 B.C. His last recorded words are, 'All forms of being are fleeting; strive without ceasing.'

The nearest parallel in literature to these early Buddhist Scriptures are perhaps the *Fioretti* of St. Francis. These later writings are clearly the product of perfect literary art, as well as of an inspired religious imagination. It is the somewhat dreary task of historical criticism to sift out the grain of the historical from the chaff of legendary and imaginative accretion; and the sober judgement of history may be that, when this has been done, not very much is left. But who, having read the *Fioretti*, does not feel that he has been in touch with the real spirit of the Little Poor Man of Assisi? He may not actually have spoken these words or done these things; he may not historically have converted the Wolf of Gubbio. But the man who created the greatest spiritual movement of the Middle Ages must have been not dissimilar to the man whom we encounter in these pages; what is given us is not photography but imaginative portraiture. It is much the same with the early Buddhist records. There is little of which we can say with absolute certainty that it is historical; most of the dialogues of the Buddha may have been invented by the pious meditations of later generations; but, as in the parallel case, we can say with confidence that such and no other must have been the man who created a religion that has survived more than two millenniums, and has laid its hold on some of the greatest countries of the world.

The first thing that strikes the reader who contemplates the character of the Teacher as here depicted is graciousness. This is a man filled with real concern for his fellow-men, fired with a passionate sense of mission, always calm, always reasonable, always gentle, not without a sense of humour. In him compassion breathes and takes form. Men are suffering and in darkness; it is the task of the Enlightened One to remain among them and to show them the Way to deliverance. As in the case of Jesus Christ, the decision to remain on earth for the service of mankind is set forth in the symbolic form of a narrative of temptation. As the Buddha he could now at once withdraw into the world of fulfilment and of bliss. But others have need of him, so he will remain and become their teacher: 'Lord, let the Blessed One preach the *Dhamma* [the rule of right]! May the

Perfect One preach the *Dhamma!* There are beings whose mental eyes are scarcely darkened by any dust; if they do not hear the *Dhamma*, they will perish. There will be some who will understand.'

3. In the third place, Buddhism like Christianity has been a missionary religion. Arising as a protest against the highly refined and intellectual Hinduism of the time, it was from the start filled with the conviction that this was the faith that must be preached to all the peoples. Since Judaism, though much older than Buddhism, failed on the whole to realize its missionary vocation, Buddhism must be regarded as the oldest of the missionary religions. It believed itself to be 'Good News'; and, like the Christian missionary of the early days, the Buddhist monk set out on all the ways of the world to pass his good news on to others.

Like Christianity, Buddhism has often found itself in alliance with the civil power. Asoka, one of the most remarkable rulers that the world has yet seen, in the third century B.C. spread his power over the greater part of the Indian peninsula, established Buddhism wherever he went, and set up here and there his great pillars as signs of his conquering advance. It was a son, or younger brother, of Asoka who introduced Buddhism into Ceylon, where for two thousand years it has continued to be the principal religion of the island, and has maintained itself in perhaps a purer form than anywhere else. By the seventh century Buddhism had begun to penetrate into Tibet, and was undergoing that strange northern transformation which has turned a system of thought which, if not atheistic at least has nothing to say about God, into a phantasmagoria of polytheistic worship.

Then begins the reversal of history. Hinduism experiences a great revival and Buddhism begins to die out in the land of its origin. The famous *Manimekhalai*, one of the great classical romances of Tamil literature which probably dates from the seventh century A.D., is full of echoes of Buddhism. Three centuries later hardly anything is left. Tradition says that this disappearance is to be accounted for by violent persecution on the part of the now militant Hindus. Whether this is true or not, the victory of Hinduism was complete.[1] We note here yet another curious parallel with Christianity, which also has been expelled from the country of its origin. In

---

[1] This victory seems, in point of fact, to be associated with that astonishing manifestation of Hindu piety, the *bhakti* movement, of which the purest expression is to be found in the Tamil poems of Manickavasagar.

the one case as in the other, loss in one area has been fully compensated by gain in another. Buddhism has penetrated China and deeply influenced its civilization. It has made itself the dominant, though not the exclusive, religion of Japan and Korea.

The centuries of the domination of the West have been for the most part centuries of quiescence for the Buddhist world. It has continued to exist, and to care for the faithful. Monks have been enrolled in the monasteries and have kept up the liturgies. In Burma and Siam it is customary for every boy, even the king himself, to spend part of his boyhood in a monastery, submitting to its discipline, going out on his rounds with his begging bowl and learning the Buddhist Scriptures.[2] But the faith seemed to have little in it but tradition. It lacked burning conviction, and was producing little in the way of new thoughts or convincing literature.[3] Accustomed as it was to depending a good deal on the ruling power, now that the ruling powers were for the most part Christian or indifferent the religion seemed to sink down into a certain torpor and unexciting acquiescence.

With the rise of Asian nationalism Buddhism like other religions of the East has been stirred into a new period of vigour and self-assertion. This is a phenomenon which ought not to excite any surprise. All human cultures known to us up to the twentieth century (we shall consider later the extent to which Marxist Russia and America can be regarded as exceptions to this rule) have been based on religious ideals. When the culture is flourishing, the religion also flourishes, being taken for granted as something that all good citizens observe, though they may not manifest any great enthusiasm in the observance. When the culture is dormant, the religion tends to be apathetic, though it plays a deeper part in the make-up of the race than is imagined by many observers. When the culture revives and begins to find expression in terms of national self-assertion, one of the first things that the national leaders strive

---

[2] For a vivid description of the initiation of a Buddhist monk, see George Appleton, *The Christian Approach to the Buddhist* (1958), pp. 15-16, quoting from Ananda Mettiya (an Englishman who had become a Buddhist monk): *The Religion of Burma*.

[3] 'The creative impulse of Buddhist thought came to a halt about 1500 years after the Buddha's Nirvana. During the last 1000 years no new school of any importance has sprung up, and the Buddhists have merely preserved, as best they could, the great heritage of the past. . . . The Dhamma cannot be heard in a world dominated by modern science and technical progress. A great deal of adaptation is needed, and a great change is bound to take place in the exposition of the doctrine'. E. Conze, quoted in *The Revolt in the Temple* (1953), p. 25.

to produce is a revival of religion as a spiritual undergirding of their purely political aims. In our time we have seen this most clearly in Ceylon and in Burma.

In Ceylon the Buddhist priesthood played a considerable part in securing the election of Mr. Solomon Bandaranaike as Prime Minister in 1960. As a reward for their co-operation they demanded the recognition of Buddhism as the national religion of Ceylon, and, as part of this, the recognition of Sinhalese as Ceylon's one national language. Tamil, they said, is the language of the Hindus and Muslims, English of the Christians. In a Buddhist country only the traditional language of Buddhism should claim official recognition as the language of the country. Naturally opposition on the part of the two million Tamil-speakers was intense, bitter, and prolonged. The supporters of the Buddhist claim went so far as to jeopardize the unity of their island in the religious cause.

In Burma matters have not gone quite so far. Article 20 of the Constitution is a guarantee of religious freedom; but Article 21 goes on to recognize the special position of Buddhism as the religion professed by the great majority of the Burmese people; and it is clearly understood that the protection of Buddhism, of its integrity and of its status, is one of the duties of the government. Thus a few years ago Mr. U. Nu, at that time Prime Minister of Burma, spoke on behalf of an act for the protection of Buddhism:

From certain quarters Lord Buddha's omniscience has been questioned and ridiculed. Worse than that some even go to the extent of declaring that Lord Buddha was a lesser man than Karl Marx. It will be one of the functions of this Buddhist organisation to combat such challenge in the intellectual field. Any doubt regarding the existence of omniscience must be promptly dispelled. We must be able to explain what omniscience really is. If any Marxist comes out with the statement that Karl Marx was a very wise man, it is not our concern to question it. But if he encroaches on our sphere and ridicules Lord Buddha whom we all adore and revere and if he has the effrontery to say that Marx was wiser than Lord Buddha, it is up to us to retaliate. It will be our duty to retort in no uncertain terms that the wisdom or knowledge that might be attributed to Karl Marx is less than one-tenth of a particle of dust that lies at the feet of our great Lord Buddha.[4]

It may be doubted whether the Prime Minister of Burma had thought out in full the philosophical implications of the term 'omni-

---

[4] Quoted in A. C. Bouquet, *Christian Faith and non-Christian Religions* (1959), p. 290.

science'; nevertheless his words must be taken as a clear and firm declaration that, as in Muslim countries any words which imply disrespect of the prophet Muhammad, so in Buddhist lands any word which seems to attribute less than perfection to the Buddha may land the incautious speaker in trouble with the authorities.

It is not surprising that, with this recovery of national pride in itself, Buddhism should at the same time have recovered its missionary impulse, and should be setting itself both to bring back those in Buddhist lands who have fallen away to Christianity and to extend its influence in the West.

Since the time of Schopenhauer in the middle of the nineteenth century a number of thinkers in the West have been attracted by Buddhism. It has seemed to offer a carefully worked out philosophical system, in which a number of the problems that have baffled the thinkers of the West have been brought near to at least a provisional solution. But the number of Western Buddhists has so far been extremely small. It is only in quite recent times that efforts have been made on any considerable scale and have met with a measure of success. The Buddhist World Council, which met for two years in Rangoon and came to an end in 1956, occupied itself among other things with the extension of missionary propaganda in the West, and gave a new impulse to the work.

Germany, perhaps because of the unique experience of suffering through which it has passed in this century, seems to be one of the lands to which the Buddhist feels himself specially drawn. A Buddhist Association has existed in Germany since 1903, but numbers of adherents had remained very small. The scholar Edward Conze, who is himself a Buddhist, remarked some years ago that the weakness of Buddhism as a propagandist religion is its lack of organization; it knows only one form of organization, the monastic order, and so far that has been wholly lacking in the West: 'Monks and monasteries—these are the indispensable foundations for a Buddhist movement, if the purpose of the operation is the creation of a living social community'.[5]

But now this situation seems to be changing. The task of 'evangelizing' Germany was specially entrusted by the Buddhist Council to Ceylon. On 7 August 1956 the Prime Minister of Ceylon

[5] E. Conze: *Der Buddhismus* (1953), p. 203, quoted in G. F. Vicedom: *Die Mission der Weltreligionen* (1959), p. 131.

inaugurated the buildings of a missionary organization, in which a German and a Swiss Buddhist monk co-operate with others in the formation of the young missionaries who are to go out to the West. There is said to be a good library of German books. Missionary methods are studied on the most approved principles of Christian missionary academies. As a beginning three monks have been sent to Germany and have for the time being settled in Berlin; but the aim is that in time they should form their own monastery, and that this should be the centre for the training in Germany of Buddhist missionaries to the German people.[6]

Naturally the Buddhist in Germany presents his faith in rather modern form and in full agreement with what modern man can be expected to believe:

It is regarded as the special privilege of Buddhism that 'as the oldest world religion, some six hundred years older than Christianity, it stands, as no other religion does, in complete harmony with scientific thought, and fulfils all the demands with which reason and feeling can confront a man in his power of discernment and in his conscience'. It can thus never be in disagreement with the findings of science, the most recent achievements of our modern research-workers having been already known by the Buddha over two thousand five hundred years ago, even, for example, the parliamentarianism of modern democracy going back to the earliest days of Buddhism. In contrast to the cultural backwardness of Christianity, Buddhism commends itself as the promoter of progress, as the religion which, like no other, is based on reason.[7]

In Britain, the first practising Buddhist appears to have started his operations in 1906, and the first Buddhist Society of England was formed in that year. This gradually died away, and was replaced through various stages by the Buddhist Society of 1943, the creator and inspirer of which was the well-known lawyer Mr. Christmas Humphreys. In May 1954 a Buddhist *vihāra* or dwelling was opened in south-west London by visitors from Ceylon. At least one English Buddhist monk is in residence, and it is hoped that gradually the number will increase to ten, so that the body can become self-perpetuating without the necessity of recourse to the East for ordination.[8] Mr. Humphreys has written a popular account of Buddhism,

[6] Vicedom, op. cit. p. 132, quoting from *Einsicht*, 1957, pp. 27 and 154.

[7] Walter Holsten, 'Buddhism in Germany', in *International Review of Missions*, October 1959, p. 412.

[8] It is interesting to note that not all Buddhists are in agreement with this approach. *The Revolt in the Temple* (1953) speaks of the *failure* of this attempt to introduce

published in Pelican Books; it is said that more than 100,000 copies of this book have been sold, and this in itself is some indication of the extent of interest in Buddhism among English readers.[9]

More than a hundred Buddhist missionaries are believed to be at work among English speaking people in the United States, apart from those caring for the needs of the large number of American citizens of Japanese or Chinese origin; and Mr. Humphreys has asserted that there are more than a hundred Buddhist societies in America.[10] But it has proved difficult to obtain any detailed information as to the activities of these bodies, and the influence of Buddhism in America seems to be small, though the interest in the subject may be widespread.

What is the Gospel that Buddhism presents to its adherents to-day, and that it so confidently offers as the panacea for all the ills of the West?

Its starting-point is the fact and the reality of suffering. Everyone suffers, and everyone knows that he suffers. Following the example of some of the modern existentialists, we may refashion the old Cartesian saying in the form *Dolet mihi, ergo sum*—I suffer, therefore I am. How is the problem of suffering to be dealt with? Buddhism adopts the most radical of all solutions: abolish the entity, and therewith we shall abolish the sufferer; abolish the ego, which believes that it suffers, and there will no longer be anything that can suffer. This was the great enlightenment that came to the Buddha under the Bo tree.

The elimination of the self is the heart and the centre of all Buddhist philosophy. What we apprehend as human existence belongs to the realm of *anicca*, the impermanent and perpetually changing, in which there is no abiding reality. Such a realm is necessarily *anatta*, 'without soul'; there can be no place in it for a permanent centre of human consciousness. Man is not a unity; he is simply the coalescence of five *khandhas*[11] (the word is frequently

---

Buddhism in England: 'One of the main reasons for its failure was the establishment of a Buddhist *Vihāra* or place of worship in London. Buddhism is an intellectual doctrine, and its primary appeal is to people of intellect and deep culture. These are the very people to whom the idea of a *Vihāra*, or cathedral with statues and statue-worship, is irrelevant and indeed repellent.'

[9] Christmas Humphreys, *Buddhism* (reprint of 1958), pp. 225-7.

[10] Christmas Humphreys, op. cit. p. 229.

[11] This is the more correct form of the word; the spelling *skandha* is often found in more popular works on Buddhism.

translated 'aggregates') which happen to come together. These *khandhas*, the nature of which it is hard for the Western mind to conceive, are a little like centres of tension in a generally diffused ether, or in a field of energy. When the necessary five of them come together, they produce for the moment the illusion of consciousness and of an existing self.

The following is a brief account of the *khandhas*, as they seem to be generally understood in Buddhist thought. The first is *rūpa*, a familiar Sanskrit term meaning 'shape', or 'form', and this corresponds to all that presents itself to us as the physical properties of the existent. The other four are grouped together as *nāma*, the immaterial properties of the apparently existent. The first of this group is *vedana*, feeling or sensation. The second is *sanna*, perception or recognition. The third is *sankhara*, a word which even the experts in Buddhism find it extremely hard to define. Perhaps the nearest word to it is 'synthesis', the capacity for bringing together disparate elements of experience into a whole, 'the mental processes of discrimination and comparison between the ideas so brought into being.'[12] The fourth is *viññana*, consciousness, or perhaps rather better reflection, the capacity that man has to think about himself.

As a piece of psychological analysis this is remarkably apt and penetrating. Dr. de Kretser pertinently remarks:

In many respects, the Buddhist analysis of mental processes is supported by the findings of modern psychology. Man becomes a self-conscious . . . person (*viññānam*) when he is brought into contact with the external world, and becomes aware of it through his sense-organs. These sensations (*vedana*) organise themselves into percepts (*sanna*) which again through the process of ideation (*sankhara*) make self-conscious reasoning possible. This analysis may be found in the most elementary psychology books today, and yet it is remarkable that these mental processes should have been described so accurately by Buddhist psychologists more than two thousand years ago.[13]

Modern psychology in the West has had difficulty in determining what, if anything, it means by the term *psyche*; on the whole, however, it has held that there is some centre of ideation, some ego, by which all the shifting gleams of experience are held together in some kind of unity. Buddhism cuts the Gordian knot of the problem

[12] Humphreys op. cit. p. 94. The suggestion has been made that *sankhara*, a word of many meanings, should, when used of one of the *khandhas*, be translated 'will'. I do not think that this is correct.

[13] Bryan de Kretser, *Man in Buddhism and Christianity* (Calcutta, 1954), p. 38.

by radically denying the existence of any such unifying centre. Precisely this is the meaning of the term *anatta*, without soul.

It may be useful to make plain the radical character of this denial by a somewhat lengthy quotation from the *Questions of King Milinda*, a document of perhaps the first century B.C. which has been described by Dr. Rhys Davids as the masterpiece of Indian prose:[14]

Then the venerable Nagasena spoke to the king as follows—'Your majesty, you are a delicate prince, an exceedingly delicate prince, and if, your majesty, you walk in the middle of the day on hot, sandy ground . . . your feet become sore, your body tired, the mind oppressed, and the body-consciousness suffers. Pray, did you come afoot or riding?'

'Bhante, I do not go afoot. I came in a chariot.'

'Your majesty, if you came in a chariot, declare to me the chariot. Pray your majesty, is the pole the chariot?'

'Nay, verily, bhante.'

'Is the axle the chariot?'

'Nay, verily, bhante.'

' Is the chariot-wheel, the banner-staff the chariot?'

'Nay, verily, bhante.'

'Is it then something else besides pole, wheels . . . which is the chariot?'

'Nay, verily, bhante.'

'Your majesty, though I question you very closely, I fail to discover any chariot. Verily now, your majesty, the word chariot is an empty sound; what chariot is there here? Your majesty, you speak a falsehood, a lie. There is no chariot here. . . . Listen to me, my Lords. Milinda the King says thus, "I came in a chariot" and being requested, "Your majesty, if you came in a chariot, declare to me the chariot", he fails to produce the chariot. Is it possible, pray, for me to assent to what he says?'

'. . . Bhante Nagasena, I speak no lie; the word "chariot" is but a way of counting, term, appellation, convenient designation, and name for pole, axle, chariot-body, and banner-staff.'

'Thoroughly well, your majesty, do you understand a chariot. In exactly the same way, your majesty, in respect of me, Nagasena is but a way of counting . . . for the hair of my head, for , . . . sensation, . . . consciousness. But in the absolute sense there is no Ego (*atta*) to be found. And the priestess Vijira said as follows in the presence of the Blessed One:

> Even as the word of chariot means
> That members join to frame a whole;
> So when the *khandhas* appear to view,
> We use the phrase, a living being'.[15]

---

[14] Milinda is the Indian form of the name of the Greco-Bactrian King Menander.
[15] Quoted in Bryan de Kretser, op. cit. pp. 40–41.

The delicate logical problem of parts and wholes, and of the whole which is more than the sum of its parts, has occupied Western philosophy from the time of Plato onwards. With the details of the discussion we are not here concerned. But to the careful reader it must be obvious that the argument put to King Milinda by Nagasena is cogent, except for one single point: if any significance is attributed to *arrangement*, the lynch-pin has fallen out of the argument. In that case, 'chariot' is not simply a method of counting; it is a reference to a number of objects arranged in one particular way and in no other. But, leaving aside for the moment the question of the logical validity of the argument, the purpose for which it is put forward is perfectly clear; it is to destroy the concept that there is in apparent existents any permanent centre which could be called the self, or which could endure the experience of suffering.

Experts are divided on the question whether, with the abolition of the Self, the Buddha intended the abolition of God also. There is one much-quoted passage from the *Udāna-Sutta*, one of the sermons attributed to the Buddha, which imply that he did in some sense recognize the existence of God, or at least of something that remains amid the flux of that which never abides in one stay:

There is, monks, an unborn, not become, not made, uncompounded, and were it not, monks, for this unborn, not become, not made, uncompounded no escape could be shown here for what is born, has become, is made, is compounded. But because there is, monks, an unborn, not become, not made, uncompounded, therefore an escape can be shown for what is born, has become, is made, is compounded. (*Udāna* VIII. 3)

On the whole very little is said on such subjects in those traditions which stand nearest to the Buddha himself. It may be that he avoided the subject, because in the contemporary Hinduism against which he was reacting he found it cluttered up with endless and unprofitable disputation.[16] It may be that, propagating as he did a way of salvation that depends on man's own efforts and on nothing else, he felt that the introduction of the idea of God could only confuse the minds of his monks and distract them from concentration on the one thing needed. It may be that he felt the Supreme to be so august that nothing at all could be said about it,

[16] 'Hence, his dismissal of vain arguments. They belonged, he said, to "the jungle, the desert, the puppet show, the writhing, the entanglement of speculation". Brahmans who indulged in them were like wriggling eels.' R. H. L. Slater in *Modern Trends in World Religions* (1959), p. 244.

on the basis of the principle that 'the Tao that can be expressed is not the eternal Tao'. Whatever the explanation, classical Buddhism in its *Theravada* form is, and always has been, a form of belief which does not recognize the existence of God, and in this it seems to me to have remained true to the intentions of its original Founder.[17]

If the attitude of the ·Buddha towards God is in some ways ambiguous, the same must be said of the highest of Buddhist ideals, *Nirvāṇa*, the state of perfection to which the Buddhist monk most earnestly aspires. The word itself means simply 'nakedness' or 'emptiness'. It is not surprising that it has often been taken, both by Buddhists and by Christians, to mean sheer nothingness. The existence of the ego has been shown to be an illusion. The I has been resolved into its shifting and impermanent parts. Once a man has been set free from the illusion of personal existence, anguish comes to an end, and with anguish ends also the illusion of being. What can be left other than nothingness? So in a work of Northern Buddhism, when the Venerable Subhuti is asked, 'Even *Nirvāṇa*, holy Subhuti, you say is like an illusion, is like a dream?', he replies, 'Even if perchance there could be anything more distinguished, of that also I would say that it is like an illusion, like a dream. For not two different things are illusions and *Nirvāṇa*, are dreams and *Nirvāṇa*.'[18]

On the other hand, *Nirvāṇa* is not infrequently spoken of in terms of the highest bliss. This bliss is beyond anything that can be described in human words; therefore those who have experienced it almost always speak of their experience in negative terms, and it is this that gives the impression of pure negation. And yet this is perhaps a misunderstanding of that which they are trying to say. Buddhism is a religion of emancipation from illusion; beyond the illusion is there a reality so transcendent that it defies every human attempt to find expression for it? *Nirvāṇa* is fullness and not emptiness. The answer of some experts in Buddhist lore is that this is the correct interpretation:

[17] Dr. Bouquet, however, quotes a very interesting encounter of his own with a Burmese monk. 'Thus a Burmese monk once said to me that of course he and his colleagues did not believe in a Personal God, but when I quoted to him certain definitions in Christian theology: "God is Spirit", and "There is but One Living and True God, everlasting, without body, parts, or passions, etc.", he seemed surprised, and asked where they were to be found. I told him, in the Fourth Gospel and in the first of the Anglican Thirty-Nine Articles; and his rejoinder was: "If that is the official doctrine, we should feel no difficulty over it".' A. C. Bouquet, op. cit. p. 299.

[18] Quoted by E. Conze, in *Concise Encyclopaedia of Living Faiths*, p. 307.

The aspirant who has attained the highest Aryan wisdom and has thus come to the end of the way, knows the complete destruction of anguish. And that freedom of his, of which he is also possessed now, is founded on truth and is unshakeable. . . . These negative expressions are meant to indicate no more than that to name anything positively is at once to impose limits on it. The phenomenal may be described, analyzed and confined in lists. But not so the transphenomenal. . . . *Nirvana* is, and it will not fail the man who has so tamed himself and developed himself that he is prepared physically, morally and mentally, and in wisdom, for the vision of it, while he is deeply absorbed in meditation. Its unspeakable bliss cannot be described, it has to be experienced. It is for the here and now rather than a kind of heaven to be entered into by a virtuous man when he dies. Perhaps it has therefore become less difficult now to answer the question that many people find perplexing: Who is it that enjoys Nirvana if there is not much left of the man So-and-so after he has died? The question framed thus is inept and does not fit. Rather should it be asked: Who enjoys *Nirvana* here and now? The answer is the adept in meditation. For *Nirvana* may be seen in this very life.[19]

The two words which seem most constantly to recur in reference to the experience of those who have attained to *Nirvāṇa* are 'freedom' and 'peace'. A controversialist would gain nothing by attempting to score points off Buddhism on the ground of this apparent inconsistency, for a similar inconsistency lies at the heart of every form of mystical experience. The roots of Western mysticism are in the philosophy of Plotinus, and here the student is faced by exactly the same perplexity. Here too is the same demand for the stripping off of the accretions of a physical and material existence; here too the demand for an ascent of the soul through varying worlds of experience. But, if the aspirant asks 'Having stripped off everything, what do I then attain?', the answer may be 'Nothingness', or it may be 'The Vision of the All'. The experience may come as a sense of total denudation, even inanition; or it may come with the sense of a plenitude of existence almost too great for the experiencing subject to bear. How can such things be put into words? And how can the apparent inconsistency be resolved?

We must allow for possibilities of depth and subtlety in Buddhism such as are not easily attainable by the Western mind. Yet it has to be affirmed that, in what appear to be its purest and most classical forms, Buddhism does present itself as an extremely negative form

[19] I. B. Horner, in *Concise Encyclopaedia of Living Faiths*, pp. 292–3.

of human existence. Without doubt it denies all reality to the thinking self and seeks to eliminate it. For all practical purposes it is an atheistic system of belief; if it does not absolutely deny the existence of God, it removes him from the field of enquiry and aspiration. It leaves no room for any kind of worship, since there is no existent to which worship can be directed.[20] It holds out a goal which is described far more in negative than in positive terms.

What, then, is its attraction for modern Western man, and why do so many Western intellectuals affirm that they find the teachings of Buddhism more attractive than those of Christianity?

In part, we may attribute this simply to modern Western man's inability to live with himself. He has lost heart about himself and his own civilization; he has lost faith in its values and its potentialities for recovery from within. Ever since Europe discovered China in the eighteenth century and *Chinoiserie* became a fashion, there has been a tendency to look towards the East as the source of a wisdom more venerable and nearer to the truth than our own. Buddhism comes veiled in all the charm and mystery of the East, and this in part at least accounts for its appeal.

1. The figure of the founder of Buddhism, a little romanticized, but, as we have seen, not very far from the historical reality, is full of charm. It presents precisely that quality which modern man knows himself to lack—serenity. In every Buddhist country thousands of statues of the Buddha look down on city and village and field, and almost every one conveys the same impression—of tranquil calm, raised high above the strife and squalor of human life and that unease which men miscall delight. This, as we shall see, is a serenity that has been hardly won, but in a world so troubled as ours any price might seem worth the paying, if at the end such inner peace as this could be attained.

2. Part of the attraction of Buddhism is certainly to be found in its reaction against the intellectualism which has been the dominant characteristic of Western life since the Renaissance. This may account for the popularity of Buddhism in its Zen form, of which so far nothing has been said in this chapter.

---

[20] The Buddhist monastery has, of course, an intense and complex liturgical life: but this is not worship in the ordinary Western sense of the word, where the reality of worship is determined by the reality of the object to which it is directed. 'Wish takes the place of prayer in Buddhism. In the *Majjhima Nikaya* the Buddha says that the strong aspiration of a good man takes effect.... It is not the answer of God to a petition, but the response of Cosmic Law.' *The Revolt in the Temple* (1953), p. 204.

The word Zen, confusingly, arises from a double deformation. The Sanskrit word *Dhyāna* means meditation. In Chinese this took the form *Ch'an*. In Japanese *Ch'an* was transformed into *Zen*. The *Ch'an* sect is believed to have arisen in China in the sixth century. Zen Buddhism appeared in Japan in the ninth century, and began to exercise great influence from the thirteenth century onward. To put a complicated matter in a single phrase, the aim of Zen is *immediacy*.

At a first approach Zen utterances and dialogue present an appearance of total meaninglessness, bordering on lunacy. Everything is inconsequent, unrelated, fragmentary. Everyone knows the sound of two hands clapping together. What are we to make of it when we are asked to ponder the sound of a single hand clapping? Here is a typical, though more than ordinarily logical, specimen of Zen dialogue:

'Am I right when I have no idea?' asked an inquirer.

'Throw away that idea of yours', replied the teacher.

'What idea?' asked the pupil in perplexity.

'You are free, of course, to carry about that useless idea of no idea.'

But behind all the apparent absurdity there is a real and definite purpose. Whenever we think, we impose a pattern upon the flux of things. The structure which arises from our thinking is rational; we can wed thought to thought until we end with an imposing pattern of rational existence. We then imagine that our rationality corresponds to some rationality in the structure of being; we have the sense of having discovered that which we ourselves have imposed. It is a central tenet of Buddhism that there cannot be any rationality in what we imagine to be perceived by our senses, or in those senses themselves. All things are in flux; there is no order and no pattern. If we are to enter into contact with such reality as there is, this can only be achieved by thinking thought away, by cutting out ratiocination, and so entering into *immediacy* of apprehension. Almost from our earliest day we have been brought up to think, to infer, to construct. Therefore it is endlessly difficult for us to go to work the other way—to abandon thought as a prison and to go over the precipice of non-thinking. Some aspirants never achieve the goal; for even the most favoured years of discipline are likely to be required before they discover the undiscovered country.

It is not hard to see the affinity between this approach and much that exists in the West to-day. We shall come in a later chapter to another form of protest against the belief that the universe and all things in it are rational and that all problems can be solved by the patient application of the discursive reason. Here, by way of illustration, we may look at certain tendencies in modern art.

Traditionally the creation of a picture, or for that matter a novel, has been a highly intellectual process. The artist selects a frame, and carefully works out the manner in which he will give expression within those limits to his vision. From the untidiness and infinite fecundity of nature he will select only that which is germane to his purpose. He will simplify, and will represent an order, a tidiness, a completion such as are never to be found in nature itself. It used to be held that by doing so he would introduce the beholder into the mysteries of nature, and reveal to him things that he would never have seen for himself. Almost the whole of modern art seems to be a protest against this method and these ideas. Its aim is immediacy of impression and of expression, even if this involves, so to speak, drawing what is seen so close to the eyeball of the painter that normal perspectives cease to exist and vision in the ordinary sense of the term ceases to be possible. Is the result intelligible? Why should it be, if all that seeing can do is to make possible some kind of contact with an entity other than the self which is itself unintelligible? Is it beautiful? There we go again, imposing our own constructs on 'nature' and mistaking them for reality; no one has yet been able to explain what is meant by the word 'beautiful'. Why should we go on using meaningless terms?

The same sort of reasoning, or lack of it, seems to lie behind the writing of the so-called 'beat generation'. If I construct a story or an essay in advance, I am imposing by force my own simulation of reality on a world to which it does not belong. If I simply sit down in front of the typewriter and let my thoughts and my fingers stray at random, I am being loyal to the truth—we cannot say 'to reality', since 'reality' is precisely one of those constructs that we are trying to avoid.

It would be impertinent to deny all value to this approach. The West is over-intellectualized. It does tend to mistake its own formulations for the truth, to live in conventional patterns, and to be insensitive to anything that will not fall within those patterns. The rediscovery of immediacy, of complete honesty as to what we see and experience, and as to what we feel about our own experiences, would be a boon and a blessing to all of us. If Buddhism, in its Zen or any other form, can help us back to this primitive realism, it is to be welcomed.[21] We may wish at this point parenthetically to insert the reservation that it is not enough to find the way there; it is necessary also to find the way back. Zen Buddhism tends to treat mind and thought as always and in all things the enemy, the cause of darkness and distortion. We must not *a priori* rule out the possibility that the mind has a place in nature, and that it is there because it has a service to perform. Intellect without immediacy results in sterility. Immediacy without intellect results in chaos. There is, however, at least a possibility that the due marriage of one to the other might result in the production of healthy and interesting offspring.

3. The main attraction of Buddhism in the modern world, however, would seem to be that it offers a high and noble ethical ideal, and a reasonable discipline unencumbered with dogma and directed to the attainment of that ideal. Ethical excellence is, in Buddhism, only a stage on the way to deliverance, but it is a stage that must be passed through. And minute instructions, based on the experience of many centuries, are offered to the aspirant to guide him in thought and action at every point along the way.

This unquestionably chimes with the mood of many men in the present world. They are weary of uncertainty and are glad to be given rules, albeit very exacting rules, by which to live. They are weary of the clash of dogmas and sects and philosophies, and relieved to be told that all that can be forgotten in the accomplishment of a law that is itself the highest wisdom. This is the way to freedom, this is the way to peace. In the words of an old Buddhist classic, 'Immaterial things are more peaceful than material, cessation is more peaceful than material things.'

The general outline of Buddhist philosophy and of Buddhist method is so familiar that it can be very briefly sketched in.

The aspirant to wisdom is first taught the principle of seeking refuge: 'I take refuge in the Buddha; I take refuge in the Doctrine (*Dhamma*); I take refuge in the Order (*Sangha*).'

[21] As is well known, one of the symptoms or causes of mental sickness is unwillingness or inability to face the reality of one's own experiences and emotions. It is perhaps not fortuitous that a number of psychiatrists have become deeply involved in the study of Zen Buddhism as giving them the clue to that immediacy to which they wish to help their patients back.

These principles once accepted, the pupil will be introduced to the first principles of doctrine, and these have hardly changed at all since the four Aryan (noble) Truths, which the Buddha himself announced in the very first of all his discourses.

The first Aryan Truth is the Truth of Anguish. Birth, age and death are anguish, and so are all the states of mental suffering which men may experience. This is the truth of human experience.

The second Aryan truth is the Truth of the Arising of Anguish. This comes only from desire—the craving for the experience of the senses, for the process of becoming and of existing in the world of illusion. No one English word will exactly represent the Pali word *tanha*: 'It is the desire for what belongs to the unreal self that generates suffering, for it is impermanent, changeable, perishable, and that, in the object of desire, causes disappointment, disillusionment, and other forms of suffering to him who desires. Desire in itself is not evil. It is desire to affirm the lower self, to live in it, cling to it, identify onself with it, instead of with the Universal self, that is evil.'[22]

The third Aryan Truth is the Truth of the Stopping of Anguish; this involves the complete stopping, abandonment and rejection of this desire, this craving for existence.

The fourth Aryan Truth, which is the means to the attainment of the third, is the Aryan Eightfold Way or Path. This is defined in terms of right understanding, right aspiration, right speech, right action, right mode of livelihood, right endeavour, right mindfulness, and right concentration.

Each of these terms is carefully defined in the Buddhist Scriptures, and there can be no doubt as to what is intended by each.

Right understanding means the apprehension of the four noble Truths.

Right aspiration is the aim of renunciation of all desire. It includes also *ahiṃsā*, the purpose of not harming any living being.

Right speech is abstention from lying and slander, from unkind words and foolish talk.

Right action is abstention from stealing, and from wrongdoing in the world of the senses.

---

[22] Edmund Holmes, *The Creed of Buddha*, p. 68, quoted in Christmas Humphreys, *Buddhism*, pp. 91–2. Some Buddhist authorities distinguish three forms of *tanha*—*kāma-tanha*, desire for pleasures of the material world; *bhava-tanha*, clinging to existence; and *vibhava-tanha*, craving for immortality.

Right mode of livelihood forbids the earning of one's living by any trade that causes bloodshed, by the sale of intoxicating liquor, or by anything that causes harm to other beings.

Right endeavour aims at preventing the arising of evil mental states; the elimination of evil mental states that have arisen; the bringing into existence of good, or 'skilled', mental states; and the development of good mental states that already exist.

Right mindfulness means to be clearly aware of the body as body (and therefore of the dangers that necessarily attend our existence in the body), to be aware of feelings as feelings, of the mind as the mind, and of mental states as mental states.

Right concentration makes possible the entry on the four-fold way of meditation, which is open to the aspirant after perfection, when he has overcome the five 'hindrances' of sense-desires, of ill-will, of sloth, of restlessness, and of doubt or questioning.

Such is the way to *Nirvāṇa*. Together it comprises an impressive complex of psychological intuitions, of ethical and moral self-discipline, and of meditative aspiration. All these things are but the portal—beyond lies the goal of ultimate liberation.

4. For the modern man one of the most attractive things in this scheme is that in it he is entirely cast back upon himself. 'Therefore, O Ananda, take the self as a lamp; take the self as a refuge. Betake yourselves to no external refuges. Hold fast as a refuge to the truth. Look not for refuge to anyone besides yourselves. Work out your own salvation with diligence.' So the *Mahā-Parinibbāna-Sutta*, one of the most famous of Buddhist classics. The teacher may be a guide; but in the last resort the progress made by the aspirant will depend upon him and him alone. The Buddha attained to enlightenment by his own intense concentration; he called in no help from any god or saviour. So it must be with the disciple. God has been abolished, at least as far as any possibility of a practical relationship to him is concerned. There is no hope for a man outside himself; if he is to have hope, that hope must arise within himself—or rather in his inner apprehension of the meaning of the Buddha, the Law and the Order.

'Man for himself' That is the modern mood. The last thing that a modern man desires is to be told that he needs to be saved, or that he requires the help of a saviour. Such doctrine seems to smack of infantile dependence, and, as so many psychologists tell us to-day, our whole salvation depends precisely on growing away from that kind of infantile retardation. So naturally Buddhism has attractive power, when it is presented in the form summarized by a Christian writer in the following terms:

Buddhism is the faith and confession of courage. The message or *Dhamma* of Buddhism is a summons to courage: 'Come and see for yourself how our existence is really formed and ordered' ... Only the brave among us dare to respond to this summons, for it will require us to make a ruthless examination of our knowledge, to repudiate what we have imagined or wished our existence to be, and fearlessly to look at things as they really are. ...

In its two major traditions (*Theravada* and *Mahayana*) Buddhism either rejects outright any notion of a man getting "supernatural" help for his protest or it denies that such help can be expected until the individual has expended every energy in his possession for this purpose. In neither stream of Buddhism is there any place for the unrealistic who would dream their way into the lap of the gods, or at least out of the responsibilities of this cruel world; nor is there room for the lazy and slothful who are quick to find crutches or escapes while someone else does the work of redeeming our existence.[23]

5. We have not yet come to that claim which perhaps gives Buddhism its strongest appeal to the modern world. It claims to be the true gospel of peace.

The Buddha took over almost unaltered the old Hindu doctrine of *ahimsā*, harmlessness, abstaining from injury to any form of life. This has its roots in the doctrine of *karma*, the retribution in later lives for sins committed in the earlier, which itself is inextricably involved in the doctrine of transmigration. Souls can wander through every form of being; therefore life, even in its lowest form, is to be respected and preserved; no sin is greater than the taking of life, even though it be only the gnat or the worm that perishes.[24] If only all mankind would accept this simple gospel of gentleness and respect for life, no doubt strife, contention and war would cease for ever from the earth.

At this point the Buddhist, armed as he is to reaction against the West, can make a devastating attack on the supposedly Christian nations: 'You have controlled the greater part of the world for

---

[23] Edmund Perry, *The Gospel in Dispute* (1958), pp. 194–5.
[24] Of course, the use of the term 'soul' in this connexion is indefensible in terms of strict Buddhist usage. Where there is no soul, no soul can survive. All that remains when the body dies is 'a nameless complex of *karma*', of unpaid debts. When the right situation is once again produced for the coalescence of this residual *karma*, the illusion of human existence can again come about.

fifteen centuries. What have you done with it except to produce one devastating war after another? Christians have not even been able to keep the peace with one another. Not content with that, they have drawn millions of innocent Asians and Africans into their quarrels. Christianity has no effective Gospel of peace for the world to-day. Is it not time that the Christian stood aside and gave the Buddhist a chance?'

That this is the general belief of Buddhists is evident from a speech made a few years ago by U Chan Htoon, at that time Attorney-General of Burma:

Now we are threatened with another global war and total annihilation of mankind. The people of the world are greatly alarmed and very anxious to find some way out of this impending catastrophe. Buddhism alone can provide the way, and thus the World Buddhist Conference was held in Ceylon during May 1950 . . . one thing was notable at the Conference, and that was the unanimous belief of all those people present there that Buddhism is the only ideology which can give peace to the world and save it from war and destruction.

What was aimed at at the Buddhist conference was not to attempt to convert the followers of other religions of the world into Buddhists. But what we hoped for was this: people may profess any religion they like, but if their moral conduct is such as is in conformity with the principles of Buddha's teachings or in other words, they lead the Buddhist way of life, then there will be everlasting peace in the world.[25]

Clearly, in Buddhism the Eastern reaction against the West presents itself in its most formidable and challenging form. Few Christians have made a deep study of Buddhism as it is to-day—of what Buddhists are really thinking and feeling and of the faith by which they live. The true dialogue between the adherents of the two faiths has not yet developed. Yet it may be already possible to indicate a few of the lines along which the dialogue may be expected to proceed.

1. It is by no means clear that the Buddhist analysis of the self into the *khandhas* is as exhaustive as may appear at first sight, or that the elimination of the Self can be achieved so completely and so easily as some Buddhists seem to think. There is, first, the troublesome and elusive reality of memory, which can be neither evaded nor explained away. It is certainly the case that my body and

[25] Quoted in A. C. Bouquet, *Christian Faith and non-Christian Religions* (1958), p. 289.

my mind exist in a state of continual flux; but this is not the whole truth about them. No doubt the whole substance of my brain and every cell within it has changed a number of times in the last forty years; yet memory can leap back over those forty years, and reproduce with perfect precision events that took place and words that were spoken so long ago. There is something that persists. A line may be divided into an infinite number of points, but it does not for that reason cease to be a line. If Christians claim that some recognition must be accorded to the empirical ego, this must be attributed not to any vain craving after sentient existence but simply to a serious desire to do justice to all the evidence before us.

2. Buddhism affirms the existence of the *khandhas*. It cannot forever refuse to face the question of the ultimate origin of the *khandhas*. A contemporary Buddhist affirms that

according to Buddhism the universe evolved, but it did not evolve out of nothingness; it evolved out of the dispersed matter of a previous universe, and when this universe is dissolved, its dispersed matter—or, its residual energy which is continually renewing itself—will in time give rise to another universe in the same way. The process is therefore cyclical and continuous. The universe is composed of millions of world-systems like our solar system, each with its various planes of existence.[26]

But this is sheer assertion without the production of any evidence. The Christian is entitled to ask his Buddhist friend at least to consider the alternative possibility that all things have their origin in Spirit, the creative Spirit of God, and that all things are making their way back to God the Spirit who is their home.

3. Buddhism assumes that man can be his own saviour, and that by trying very hard to be good he can become good. But does the evidence support this view? The so-called Christian countries are not a strong commendation of Christianity. Are the countries which have been Buddhist for more than two thousand years a better commendation of Buddhism? For the moment the Buddhists of those countries can blame their low estate on the domination of the West and the corrupting influence of Christian missionaries; but this is an argument which will lose its force as the episode of Western rule in Buddhist countries sinks into the past as ancient history. And if there is any doubt as to the salvability of man by his own

[26] Maha Thera U Tittila, in *The Path of the Buddha*, ed. Kenneth W. Morgan (1956), pp. 77–8.

efforts, a very wide chink has been opened in the armour of the Buddhist's defence:

If one has to achieve moral living as a preliminary to attaining Nibbana, one may as well not begin. It is the moral problem that constitutes life's tragedy, and what is the use of telling us to solve it so that we may be able to attain to something else. . . . For it is useless to say that the availability of infinite time makes a problem solvable when it is the nature of the problem that defies solution. The moral problem is not that there is not sufficient time in which I and Society can become good, but that I and Society cannot become good.[27]

4. At two points, perhaps, the Christian, placing himself within the charmed circle of Buddhist belief may ask the Buddhist to question his own convictions, and to consider whether he does not find there arrows that point beyond the limits of the Buddhist solutions.

The first is the concept of *mettā*, a term which is generally translated 'goodwill' or 'benevolence'.[28] The classic passage on this subject is the *Mettā Sutra*, in which the Master himself is represented as saying:

As a mother, even at the risk of her own life, protects her son, her only son, so let him cultivate goodwill without measure among all beings. Let him cultivate goodwill without measure toward the whole world, above, below, around, unstinted, unmixed with any feeling of differing or opposing interests. Let a man remain steadfastly in this state of mind all the while he is awake, whether he be standing, sitting or lying down. This state of heart is the best in the world.

This is a fine and high ideal. We are not concerned at this point to discuss the similarities and differences between *mettā* and the Christian *agape*.[29] We are asking, on the basis of Buddhist conviction itself, how a place is to be found within the Buddhist system for any such feeling. Why should the aspirant after salvation be concerned about these other sentient beings? He knows that their existence is a mere illusion like his own. He has enough to do with the handling of his own anguish and deliverance from it. Why should he concern himself with others who, if they are to be saved at all, can be saved only by their own efforts?

[27] D. T. Niles, *The Preacher's Task and the Stone of Stumbling* (1958), p. 60.
[28] I note that Professor Perry, op. cit. p. 206, translates it 'love'; this seems to me misleading.
[29] On this see some wise words of Dr. A. C. Bouquet, op. cit. pp. 301–3.

5. The same question may be asked, with even more force, in relation to the remarkable concept, developed in the Mahayana form of Buddhism, of the Bodhisattva. The Bodhisattva is the man who has progressed so far on the way towards perfection that he could enter into *Nirvana*; but, for the sake of other struggling, imperfect souls, is willing to remain a little longer in the realm of *saṃsāra*, imperfection, or it may be accept yet another incarnation in this inferior world. 'He radiates great friendliness and compassion over all beings, and he resolves, "I shall become their saviour, I shall release them from all their sufferings".'

> 'The merit I achieved by all these pious actions, may that make me
> Quite able to appease the sufferings of all beings . . .
> Heedless of body, of goods, of the merit I gained and will gain still,
> I surrender my all to promote the welfare of others'.[30]

Once again, this is a high and noble ideal; but we are bound to ask how it fits in with our general picture of Buddhism. In Christianity the idea of self-giving for the sake of others (though this will not express itself in terms of merit) is of the very fabric of Christian thinking. In Buddhism it appears something like a foreign body. If this were to be taken as the starting-point for Buddhist re-thinking, might it not end by completely changing the Buddhist concept of life and of the world?

6. So far we have been dealing with arguable theses and counter-theses. But frequently argument proves futile, because the disputants are in reality starting from different existential decisions, which lie far below the level of consciousness or rational thought, and are therefore not amenable to the approach of reasoned argument. It seems to be so in even friendly discussion between the Buddhist and the Christian.

The Buddhist has made his existential decision on the subject of suffering. Suffering, anguish, is the worst of all things. Therefore suffering must at all costs be extirpated, even at the cost of destroying the sentient being that suffers. We must cut off the branch that we sit on, even though we should fall to destruction with it. We must root up the very tree of life itself. 'The door is open', so runs the Buddhist invitation, 'why suffer?'

Why suffer? That is the ultimate question. It comes to sharp and challenging expression in the contrast between the serene and

---

[30] E. Conze, *Buddhist Meditation* (1956), p. 59. This lines quoted are by Sāntideva, a poet of the seventh century A.D.

passionless Buddha and the tortured figure on the Cross. In Jesus we see One who looked at suffering with eyes as clear and calm as those of the Buddha. He saw no reason to reject it, to refuse it, to eliminate it. He took it into himself and felt the fullness of its bitterness and horror; by the grace of God he tasted death for every man. Others suffer; he will suffer with them and for them, and will go on suffering till the end of time. But he does not believe that suffering is wholly evil; by the power of God it can be transformed into a redemptive miracle. Suffering is not an obstacle to deliverance; it can become part of deliverance itself. And what he was he bids his children be—the world's sufferers, in order that through suffering the world may be brought back to God.

The Buddhist ideal is that of passionless benevolence. The Christian ideal is that of compassion. When argument has done its best, we must perhaps leave the two ideals face to face. We can only ask our Buddhist friend to look long and earnestly on the Cross of Christ, and to ask himself whether, beyond the peace of the Buddha, there may not be another dimension of peace to the attainment of which there is no way other than the Way of the Cross.

CHAPTER VI

THE PRIMITIVE WORLD

COMPARATIVELY few books on Christianity and other faiths include a study of the primitive world and primitive religions. Writers may be daunted by the difficulty of the subject. Yet clearly some such chapter must be included, if only because the proportion of the world's inhabitants with which it must attempt in some way to deal is so large. At least 40 per cent. of the world's population to-day still lives under primitive conditions; the outward conditions of their lives are reflected in their religious ideas and practices.

This reality tends to be concealed, since a great many of those who can correctly be classed as 'primitive' are usually included in the statistics for the greater religions. It is, for instance, taken for granted that everyone in India who is not a Muslim, a Christian, a Sikh, a Jain or a Parsi is a Hindu, and the figures are given accordingly. On the basis of such statistics, it may be held that the 'primitives' make up only a small part of the human race, and are to be found mainly in Africa and in the South Seas. But, in point of fact, as was pointed out in an earlier chapter, the religion of the inhabitants of most South Indian villages bears very little relation to classical Hinduism, as it has become familiar to students from the textbooks.

In a sense there is a justification for including many primitive people under the general umbrella of the great religions. All the great cultures have a deeply penetrative power; they create a climate, an atmosphere, which is different from that of the other great cultures. There is truth in the Buddhist claim that the *Dhamma*, the Law, is like a taste, and that the words of the Buddha are those which have a *taste* of peace, of emancipation, of *Nirvāṇa*.[1] Clearly, many elements of a more primitive way of looking at things survive in the life and the superstitions of a South Italian village, and parallels to those survivals can be drawn from many parts of the world.

---

[1] Cf. E. Conze in *Concise Encyclopaedia of Living Faiths*, p. 308: 'All Buddhist writings have a *flavour* of their own; and for thirty years I have not ceased marvelling at its presence in each one of them. . . . Those who refuse to taste the Scriptures for themselves are therefore at a serious disadvantage in their appreciation of the unity which underlies all forms of Buddhism.'

This does not alter the fact that it is Christianity which has given its taste, its flavour, to the life of the village, and that in a Hindu or a Buddhist village we shall find a different taste.

But, when all this has been allowed for, it still remains true that the world of the simple village-dweller is not the same as the world of one who has been brought up in the classical traditions of one of the great religions. The categories of his thought are not the same. The powers to which he believes himself to be related are not the same. He follows a different method in constructing for himself a world within which he can live. Of course it is not possible to reduce his concepts to so lucid and consistent a form as those of more highly developed religious systems. Yet his world is deserving of sympathetic study, and of deeply sympathetic study by those who believe that simple man also has been redeemed by Christ and has his own particular inheritance in the Gospel.

There is a further reason for directing attention to this primitive thought and understanding of the world. Nothing is more notable than the persistence of this kind of religious outlook in the midst of other forms of religion and civilization that are generally reckoned higher in the scale of human evolution. Sometimes the old carries on a surreptitious existence, banned by the law and carefully concealed from sight. In other circumstances, it maintains a parallel existence, hardly overlapping with the official cult.[2] Yet in others, it seems strangely to co-exist within the minds of generally sophisticated and 'modern' people.

Everyone has heard tell of the existence in Haiti and other Caribbean countries of the Voodoo cults. These are nominally Christian countries. Yet primitive Africa is very much alive in them; and this wholly different world lives just beyond the lights of the cities, and plays a great part in the life of almost the entire population. The better educated people do not care to speak very much about these things; they are almost certainly aware of them and know more than in most cases they are willing to reveal.

In Rio de Janeiro, one of the most sophisticated cities in the world, on New Year's Eve all along the beautiful beaches little fires are lighted and exotic African rituals are performed, with the burning of a black cock's feathers and other such strange survivals from the ancient African heritage. Those who come to look on are

---

[2] Nothing in the civilization of ancient Greece is more remarkable than the co-existence, almost without overlapping, of the Chthonian and the Olympic gods.

by no means only those of evidently African lineage. One of the most disturbing phenomena in Brazil in recent years has been the extremely rapid growth of the 'spiritist' movements, which are believed by now to have more than a million adherents. There may be Christian elements in a number of these movements; to a large extent they seem to represent the resurgence, and emergence into the daylight, of feelings and impulses that are very ancient and belong to a different world from that of Christianity.

Perhaps the strangest survival of all is to be found among the Indians in America. Some of the Indian peoples, such as the Navajos, live in considerable numbers on their reservations and have maintained a largely separate existence. Others, in smaller groups, appeared to have been almost wholly assimilated to the current patterns of American life. Many among them have, of course, become Christians. But during 1959 Mr. Edmund Wilson published in the *New Yorker* an extraordinarily interesting series of articles based on his contacts with the remains of the 'Six Nations', the Iroquois, in the north of New York State and over the Canadian border. It is quite clear from these studies that even among these people, who for more than a century have been overwhelmed by the surging tides of an alien civilization, something survives that belongs to a far more ancient pattern; it is this survival that keeps the Indian from ever feeling quite at home in the world in which he spends the greater part of his life, and in which he earns his living.

Admitting the extent and the reality of this world with which we have to deal, it still remains difficult to know how we are to approach it.

In the first place, though we speak casually of 'primitive man', we must remember that genuine primitives do not exist anywhere on the earth to-day. This point has been correctly noted by Professor H. H. Farmer:

There is the fact that we have no direct knowledge of the earliest beginnings of religion, of the true chronological primitive. The observation of present-day backward tribes plainly does not obviate this difficulty, for such tribes are after all our contemporaries, with as long a history behind them as we have ourselves, and the possibility of degeneration cannot be excluded; it is obviously illegitimate simply and uncritically to equate the backward with the chronologically primitive.[3]

[3] H. H. Farmer, *Revelation and Religion* (1954), p. 44.

It must further be remembered that by no means all of those whom we are pleased to class as primitives are mere barbarians; many of them are the bearers of considerable and elaborate cultures. For this reason it might be better to abandon altogether the use of the familiar word 'primitive', and to substitute for it 'pre-literate'. For it is the characteristic of all the forms of religion with which we shall be dealing in this chapter that they antedate the arrival of literacy, and that the details of them have had to be patiently gathered from non-literary sources. Yet this again must not be taken as evidence of boorishness or stupidity. Many other students would be able to echo the words of that acute observer E. E. Evans-Pritchard, who writes affectionately of his Nuer Friends:

The Nuer are undoubtedly a primitive people by the usual standards of reckoning, but their religious thought is remarkably sensitive, refined and intelligent. It is also highly complex.[4]

We are likely however to be perplexed by the enormous complexity of the material collected for us by missionaries, anthropologists and others. Is it possible to make any sense at all of what at first sight appears to be simply a meaningless jumble? Here the difficulty is not as great as might at first appear. It is important to recognize the wide differences that do exist between races and geographical areas. But certain patterns do emerge that seem to be real patterns in the material itself and not merely convenient classifications imposed by the mind of the scientific student. Man, at this simple level of living, seems to have certain methods of making himself at home in the world in which he has to live; and these recur in so many different parts of the world as to give us some confidence in thinking that they are part of the structure of the human mind as such, as it tries to take account of the reality that surrounds it.

There is the further question whether we can use the term 'religion' in speaking of the experiences of primitive man and of the rites and ceremonies in which he expresses them. Long ago, the founder of the scientific study of primitive man, E. B. Tylor, referred to the belief in spiritual beings as the minimum definition of religion.[5] But is such a belief necessarily religious? Professor Farmer, who starts from a rather high definition of religion as personal apprehension of one living God, naturally concludes that

---

[4] E. E. Evans-Pritchard, *Nuer Religion* (Oxford, 1956), p. 311.
[5] E. B. Tylor, *Primitive Culture* (1871), i. p. 424.

it is not—'To think that the world contains spirits or souls is no more religious than to think that it contains your next-door neighbour.'[6] It all depends on the definition of religion. We must recognize that primitive man has not separated out things neatly into spheres as we have done. The distinction between religious and secular is to him meaningless. The whole of life is to him made up of one single web, one single pattern. If we are prepared to understand religion in terms of a man's total reaction to the totality of life, we may be led to regard the primitive peoples as among the most religious people upon earth. If, on the other hand, we look for certain signs or ideas of higher religion, we may deny to them almost any religion at all. For practical purposes, we may find it best to adopt a compromise—to admit that among such people there is very widely diffused what, for want of a better phrase, we may call the religious spirit; that we shall find among them in germ some things that are almost invariably found playing their part in the higher religions; but also there will be many factors in their life and 'religious practices' that we shall disregard as having nothing to do with religion as that term is commonly employed.

One of the criteria that has commonly been employed for this purpose of discrimination is the distinction between magic and religion. From the time of Sir James Frazer and *The Golden Bough* (1st edn. 1890) it has been widely held that true religion is the expression of submission to the will of a deity and a readiness to be adapted to that will; whereas magic always involves the desire of the worshipper to get the deity under his own control and to use him for the fulfilment of his own purposes. 'Religion represents a submissive mind, magic an overbearing, self-asserting attitude.'[7] There is no doubt real value in this distinction. But, if we press the definition, how much of magic is contained in Christian prayer as practised by the ordinary Christian! A great deal in primitive practice is directed to maintaining good relations with the spirits and to getting them on your side; but this is not necessarily magical in the sense of being evil or depraved. The subject is far too complex to be summed up in one single phrase.[8] And probably the distinction that primitive man himself makes is one that falls outside the

[6] H. H. Farmer, op. cit. p. 89.
[7] See Nathan Söderblom, *The Living God* (1933), pp. 32 ff.
[8] A very full and interesting discussion of the problem is to be found in C. G. Diehl, *Instrument and Purpose: Studies on Rites and Rituals in South India* (Lund, 1956), pp. 1–20.

categories that we generally use. He is acutely aware of the difference between constructive and destructive activity, concepts that we shall endeavour to define more exactly later in the chapter. Though he certainly would not use the phrase, he would be inclined to include within the field of religion everything that falls under the heading of constructive activity; and this will include a good deal that the Western observer would be inclined to dismiss at once as magic.

No single clue will guide us through the labyrinth of primitive thought. Without waiting for everything to become clear, is it possible to begin to discern as already present in the mind of primitive man any of the factors that, as they develop more fully, give rise to the higher forms of human religion? It seems to me that four such factors are discernible.

The first is the part that primitive religion plays in enabling man to apprehend the world around him and his own experience as a unity. Man cannot live without some sense of outer and inner unity, though perhaps in this life the perfection of that unity is never to be attained: 'All these things make it difficult to suppose that even the most primitive and unreflective polytheistic religion could ever have been (so to speak) a pure and unqualified polytheism. Always there must have permeated it some sense that all the gods, despite their separateness, belonged together in the unity of one ultimate supernatural reality.'[9]

The second is the sense of personal confrontation—a sense that we shall recognize at a much higher level in the 'I—thou' with which Martin Buber has made us familiar. The concept of 'animism', the idea that primitive man attributes souls or spirits to things which in themselves are lifeless, is now rather out of date. It is now recognized that the reality is rather different. The whole world, as primitive man experiences it, is teeming and abounding with life. He himself is a part of it, and he has only imperfectly distinguished himself from all those other things which together make up his existence:

Any phenomenon may at any time face him, not as 'It' but as 'Thou'. In this confrontation, 'Thou' reveals its individuality, its qualities, its will.

---

[9] Farmer, op. cit. p. 104. A Chinese convert has referred to the wonderful *simplification* that comes with the acceptance of the revelation of God in Jesus Christ; the unity that previously had only been sought has now been found. Compare also J. Murphy, *Primitive Man, His Essential Quest* (1927), pp. 24–5, 29: 'An avenue of approach to the psychology of primitive man may be found in the Quest for Unity, which, it appears to me, is fundamental in human nature.'

'Thou' is not contemplated with intellectual detachment; it is experienced as life confronting life, involving every faculty of man in a reciprocal relationship. Thoughts, no less than acts and feelings, are subordinated to this experience.[10]

Thirdly, there is the fact of responsibility. The life of any primitive people or tribe is held together by an immensely complicated fabric of custom. Prosperity depends upon the due 'balance of powers', another phrase which we shall later have to elucidate. Each man is responsible for doing that which will maintain the life of the tribe and for avoiding that which will harm it. The ideas of 'good' and 'evil' are not abstractly apprehended and expressed in general terms as they are in Western manuals of ethics. But the ideas are not absent; in relation to highly concrete acts and situations primitive man is well aware of the distinction between 'approval' and 'disapproval', between 'a quiet mind' and 'a troubled mind', though he may not yet have any very clear idea of what at a later stage of development will come to be called 'good' and 'evil'.

Finally, there is the concept of the one High God, which seems to be present almost everywhere, even among the remotest and simplest of the peoples of the earth.

As to the existence of such a belief there can now be hardly any doubt. There are still a few unexplored corners of the earth, and no doubt there are still surprises awaiting the anthropologists and others who interest themselves in simple peoples. But the myth that affirmed the existence of tribes which have no religion at all has steadily been exploded by the progress of research; and some of the most striking evidences of a comparatively high level of religious understanding have been obtained among the peoples that live on the lowest level of subsistence and culture. Thus Fr. W. Schmidt (1868–1954), who has given more elaborate attention to this line of research than any other scholar, found that among the pygmies of Central Africa there is nothing that could be called animism, or ancestor worship, that almost universally recurring phenomenon among primitive peoples; but that there is a clear sense of the existence of one Supreme Being to whom all other existences, natural or supernatural, are subject.[11]

[10] Henri Frankfort and others, *Before Philosophy* (edn. of 1954), p. 14.
[11] Fr. Schmidt's ideas are set out in detail in a gigantic work in twelve volumes, *Der Ursprung der Gottesidee* (1926–55); briefly and conveniently for English readers in W. Schmidt, *The Origin and Growth of Religion: Facts and Theories* (London and New York, 1931).

As to the significance of this belief there is less agreement. Fr. Schmidt regards it as the evidence and survival of a primitive revelation of God to man, which through sin has become overlaid by magic, animism, polytheism, and other forms of error and delusion. Others would hold that this belief is not so much religion as elementary science or philosophy. Even the most primitive man is likely sooner or later to ask himself the question, 'Who made it?'; and the idea of a great 'All-Maker' would not seem to be beyond his comprehension. But on one point all students seem to be in agreement—the great High God plays very little part in the life or worship of those who in some sense believe in him. There are exceptions. Dr. Bouquet quotes a most interesting and unusual example from Northern Rhodesia of a hunter saying: 'I am tired of petitioning the *mizimu* (the departed spirits of ancestors). Let us pray to Leza (the local name for the High God).' The prayer is recorded in the following terms:

O God, our father, do not turn thy back upon us. We know that all the animals are thy children; we too are thy children, and thou gavest them to us for food. Other people come to this place and kill game. Why should we go home empty-handed? We pray thee give us success in our hunting.[12]

But this seems to be the exception. 'In many primitive peoples the High God appears to be regarded as a somewhat otiose and functionless being, who, after creating the world wandered away into a far region, and so is now no longer very relevant to the practical affairs of life; he is not the object of a cult, nor is sacrifice offered to him.'[13]

The folk-tales of many peoples explain that in olden times the sky was quite near the earth; then the High God became offended with men, for some transgression which may or may not be specified, and withdrew himself to a distance at which he is no longer approachable by man. Our further studies may gradually make plain the relation of this set of ideas to other concepts in the religious world of primitive man.

Primitive custom and practice, when first studied, presents itself as a patternless and inconsequent chaos, so much so that some

---

[12] A. C. Bouquet, op. cit. p. 257, quoting from C. R. Hopgood, in *African Ideas of God*, ed. E. W. Smith (1950). Christian and missionary influences are very widely diffused in even remote areas of Africa; and it is necessary to reckon with the possibility that this African may have been stimulated by some memory of Christian prayer to God the Father of all.   [13] H. H. Farmer, op. cit. p. 107.

Western observers have been led to the idea that primitive man is incapable of logical thinking. But to the one who lives enmeshed in such a system things present themselves in a very different way. Everything is related, reasonable, and necessary. His thought is logical, but the logic is not that of the white man. Is it possible to find the key, and to think the thoughts of primitive man with him?

One of the most notable attempts at 'thinking black' has been made by the Franciscan Fr. Placide Tempels in his book *La Philosophie Bantoue*.[14] Fr. Tempels goes to the very heart of the question, and asks what is the fundamental concept in the thought of the Bantu people amongst whom he was living. He finds the answer in the term 'force' or 'power'. The European thinks in terms of 'being' or 'existence'. The African thinks in terms of 'vital force' or 'energy'. Anything which exists is a 'force'. This vital force can be increased, or it can be threatened or diminished. When a man's vital force is on the increase, he is well. If an African is tired, he says 'I am dying', a phrase which sounds ridiculously exaggerated in European ears, but which to the African is perfectly sensible, as implying the sense of a diminution of vital powers which unless repaired or checked will lead in the long run to his decease. Much that the European observer might be inclined to class as 'magic' is, in African eyes, simply 'setting in motion certain natural forces placed by God at the disposal of men for the reinforcement of their natural energy'[15]. An African Roman Catholic priest, who naturally has an exceptionally clear understanding of the point of view of his own people notes that 'the duty of the increase of the vital forces, which can only be accomplished in community, is the primal duty of our Muntu [= "man", singular of Bantu], and the point on which all his efforts converge'.[16]

It is important to emphasize the all-embracing character of this concept:

Since all being is energy (*force*), and is being only in so far as it is energy, it follows that in this category 'energy' are subsumed all 'existents'—God, men living and departed, animals, plants and minerals. Since all being is energy, all these existents are apprehended by the Bantu as forces,

[14] Elisabethville, 1945. The English translation, *Bantu Philosophy*, published in Paris by 'Presence Africaine' (1959) was not known to me when I wrote the above.
[15] P. Tempels, op. cit. p. 28. Our translation.
[16] Fr. Vincent Mulago, in *Des prêtres noirs s'interrogent* (Paris, 1956), quoted in *Mission et cultures non-chrétiennes* (Bruges, 1959), p. 52.

sources of energy. This general concept is hardly used by the Bantu, who are by no means incapable of philosophic abstraction but in general express themselves only in concrete terms. They give everything a name; but the specific quality of these things presents itself to their minds as this or that specific form of energy, and not as a static reality.[17]

The happiness and prosperity of a tribe depends on the conservation and strengthening of its vital force. The various forces exercised by different individuals must be kept in proper balance; and the necessary steps must be taken to guard against deleterious forces, against anything that might cause a diminution of the existing vital force.

In the understanding of primitive man the tribe consists not only of its living members, but also of the ancestors, those great ones who are no longer visible, but who watch over the tribe and care for its interests, and with whom good relations must be maintained by the tribe. It must not be supposed, however, that all the dead are 'ancestors'. Some were so feeble in life that no serious account need be taken of them after their death. Some left no descendants to keep alive their memory. Some may even be classed as harmful or dangerous spirits. In that case, certain rituals are performed in order to prevent such a dead man from ever having any relations with the living, from ever becoming 'incarnate' again in the tribe, and this is the extreme diminution of vital force. In some cases the tribe will go so far as to disinter the corpse of the bad man, burn it, and scatter the ashes. In this case, the man is believed to have gone to 'the accursed place' from which no one has ever yet returned; he is now totally dead, and can exercise no 'force' of any kind on anyone at all.

The 'great ones', on the other hand, are the beneficent spirits, who have laid down the ordinances of the tribe and whose behests must be obeyed. Only if these ordinances are most carefully observed will the true balance of forces be maintained and the tribe continue in prosperity. But, if the tribe is dependent on the ancestors, the ancestors may be dependent on the tribe; their vital force needs also to be kept at its proper level, and may fail unless the tribe does its duty in the matter of gifts and offerings and libations. This sense of the dependence of the dead upon the living, of the need of each to have someone who will perform for him the rites of the dead and will keep his memory alive, is one of the deepest strains in human

[17] P. Tempels, op. cit. p. 33.

nature. It accounts for the practice of adoption, so common at Rome even in the height of its classical civilization—the man who has no son by nature must take to himself a son who can perform the needed rites for him. An extension of this idea is that even the gods are dependent on men for their well-being. This is one of the primitive traits that comes out in ancient Indian religion, and notably in the Brahmanas. With increasing emphasis on the sacrifice and on the due performance of the ritual with exact regard to every movement and every phrase, the gods themselves are depicted as dependent on the sacrifice—how can they continue to exist, if their due share of the sacrifice does not come to them? And so the Brahman on earth who carries out the sacrifice is really greater even than the gods; is it any wonder that he passes as a god among men?

'Man' is a central concept for the primitive. But man must not be thought of just as the individual. He is himself, and his ancestors, and his clan, and his descendants, and his possessions; his vital force can be diminished by anything that happens to any of them; if injury occurs he will be sick until the right reparation has been made and his vital force has been restored. An interesting example of this principle is recorded by Fr. Tempels. In 1945 one African had entrusted to another the care of a lamb. Not long after, the guardian's dog was found feasting on the unfortunate lamb. It was hardly likely that the faithful dog had itself killed the lamb; no one could deny that it had been seen eating it. The guardian started by sending a lamb to the injured man; he then sent a second, and a third; and finally a gift of fcs. 100, a considerable sum for an African at that time. No trial had been held, and the guardian had not been condemned to pay a fine. He had simply recognized that his friend had been caused pain, had suffered a diminution of his vital force; only when all these payments had been made was the friend able to say, 'Now I am happy; now I am *a living man* again.'[18]

Here we encounter the central principle of the repair or the renewal of the vital forces. If the balance has been destroyed or impaired, action must be taken. The ancestors have revealed the way in which propitiation is to be made, or a new store of vital force is to be released. It is this principle of reparation that will explain much that to us seems grotesque or horrible in the primitive way of life.

It is well-known that head-hunting is a custom that has prevailed among primitive peoples in most widely separated regions of

[18] P. Tempels, op. cit. pp. 117–18.

the earth. Naturally the Western powers have regarded this as a purely barbarous habit, and have done their best to suppress it wherever they have been in control. Very different is the attitude of primitive man. In certain cases head-hunting is the expression only of the desire for personal glory or for vengeance. In most cases it appears to have far deeper roots. It is connected with profound beliefs as to the nature of fertility and of the power of the human spirit residing in the head. Natural forces controlling the fertility of the fields must be increased; a head is required. The balance of forces in the world has been disturbed; a head, naturally the head of a man of another tribe, is required to restore the threatened balance. Head-hunting is not an enterprise lightly or wantonly taken in hand; among certain peoples it is carried out only as the climax of cere-monies that have lasted for several years. In some areas it played so central a part in the social life of the people that the prohibition of it by a Western government has been noted as one of the most serious factors resulting in the decay of a people and the decrease of population. The vital forces have been touched and diminished at a literally vital point. So to primitive man head-hunting is not murder; it is a solemn ritual, unfortunate of course in its consequences for the man whose head happens to be taken, but in principle productive of the greatest good to the greatest number.

Some such idea seems to have dominated the Aztec civilization of Mexico, at the time when stout Cortes and his men first made contact with it. The gods demanded a steady tribute in living human hearts. It was the task of the Aztecs to supply the tribute, and, if they failed to do so, ruin would fall upon them and upon all the world. Montezuma and his lords seem to have been kindly and reasonable people; but, when strife began, the Spaniards knew very well what would be the fate of those who were taken prisoner. They would be kept for a time in prison, well fed and cared for. But, when the appointed time had come, on the top of the high pyramid the sharp stone knife would tear open the victim's belly, the living heart would be plucked from the still living body, and offered to satiate for the moment the appetite of the insatiable gods.

Primitive man has thus made for himself a world which is complete, by his standards rational and well ordered. He knows where he is. Every individual knows his station and his duties. Every member of the clan and tribe lives supported by all the other members seen and unseen. The anthropologists have gone to great trouble to explain all this to us, and to make clear the coherence of the world of primitive man from his own point of view. There is one factor in the situation to which they seem to have paid less than the necessary attention. That factor is fear.

Shortly before writing this chapter, I had the privilege of a long conversation with the distinguished German missionary Christian Keysser, who had penetrated perhaps further than any other European into the recesses of the minds of the peoples of New Guinea. This was the point on which he laid greater stress than any other. Primitive man is never free from fear. His life is hedged round at every point by rules and taboos. If any rule is infringed, retribution will be terrible. While a mother is out, a child has sat in the hut in a place in which it is not entitled to sit. The child must be killed. Why? Because the ancestors have said so; if the due retribution is not exacted, the ancestors will be angry and may withdraw their support from the tribe; then the pattern is broken and everything falls in ruins.

The ancestors are within the structure of society, and are so to speak recognizable sources both of help and of fear. But primitive man is well aware also of those other uncanny forces that fall outside the tidy world that he has created for himself. He knows quite well the distinction between what the West has learned to call sympathetic magic and sorcery, between good and placable spirits and the evil power that goes about seeking what it may destroy, and into contact with which certain men may enter for their own evil purposes. No one can understand the real situation of primitive man without taking serious account of the three motive powers of shame, guilt and fear. His life is not so full of care-free happiness as the tales of some travellers have given us to understand. 'The native aboriginal is above all fear-ridden. Devils haunt to seize the unwary; their malevolent magic shadows his waking moments, he believes that medicine men know how to make themselves invisible so that they may cut out his kidney fat, then sew him up and rub his tongue with a magic stone to induce forgetfulness, and thereafter he is a living corpse devoted to death.'[19]

Nevertheless, when we have allowed for this darker side, it has had to be admitted that primitive man has had considerable success in creating a world in which he can live, in finding that unity the quest for which seems to be one of the basic factors in the human

[19] S. D. Porteus, quoted in *Reader in Comparative Religion* (1958), p. 273.

approach to life. He has brought together in what is to him an intelligible scheme man and his environment, the living and the dead, human and animal neighbours. His world may be a very small one, bounded, as in many cases in New Guinea, by a tribe of not more than a thousand members, and all beyond may be a world of the unknown and of perpetual hostility. But here at least a man is at home; he knows just where he belongs, and there is a real simple piety in the performance of those duties which his position in society has laid upon him.

It is this situation which is threatened throughout the whole of the primitive world to-day. The safe, small world of primitive man is collapsing about his ears.

In much contemporary writing the blame for this situation is thrown on the missionaries. They burst in on simple tribes which did not want them, condemned what they did not understand, and so tore in shreds the fine-spun web of tribal existence. We need not pause at this point to consider how much truth there is in this one-sided picture. For, if it is true that in a number of areas the missionaries were the first in the field, it is also true that the trader, the adventurer and the government servant were not far behind. Europe and America have washed up as a resistless tide over the primitive lands; wherever they have come the result has been the casting down of landmarks and the destruction of the ancient ways of life. We may well wish that it had not been so. It is futile to imagine that the tide can be turned back. This is impossible. Almost everywhere primitive man has entered on the crisis of his existence.

We may note three directions in which this crisis has affected the being both of the individual and of the people.

1. The whole of primitive life is organized in terms of the clan or the tribe. The most terrible punishment that can be inflicted on anyone is to be cut off from the tribe, and so to be indeed a lonely man, cut off from the vital support of his fellows at all the points at which he most needs it. But, with freedom of movement, immense numbers of tribesmen have left their tribes to live and work for long periods in the cities of the white man. 'Detribalization' is perhaps the most acute problem of Africa to-day.

Almost the first consequence of this separation of man from his tribe is the emergence of the individual as individual. In the old life at home within the tribe everything fell into a pattern; the occasions for personal decision were few and far between. This must not be exaggerated, as though in the tribe there was never anything but a communal decision. Even in the most closely integrated tribe there are differences of gifts and personality. One hunter is more skilled than another. The hunter has to decide in which direction he will go to look for game, though even in this matter he will seek the co-operation of the *bakisi ba luvala*, the tutelary spirits of the chase.[20] Very different, however, is the situation of the young man who is living far from his home. Here there are no clues and no traditions. The familiar checks and impulses no longer seem to hold. Everything has to be a matter of individual decision, without precedent and without assurance. There the law is that of common sharing; here it seems to be that of individual possession. There is hardly a point of reconciliation between the two opposing worlds.

A great many young men work for part of the year in the city, and then return home for a rather shorter period. On their return they find it almost impossible to enter again into the life of the tribe. They are, in fact, unassimilable. Even where there is no lack of goodwill, where there is a real desire to become as they were before, this proves almost impossible—they have become new men with a wholly different outlook. They have become accustomed to freedom. The possession of money gives them a sense of personal independence. The elders and the chiefs find themselves bewildered and affronted by a spirit of self-assertion to which they are wholly unaccustomed. The ancient reverence seems to have gone; the foundations of existence have been shaken.

2. In the second place, the ancient hierarchical structure of tribal existence is being fiercely called in question, and in many cases by political leaders who themselves have only recently emerged from it. All the younger African political leaders—Dr. Milton Obote, Léopold Senghor, Dr. Julius Nyerere, to name only three—came up through Western, usually Christian schools, and there imbibed Western ideas of democracy. Such men wish to introduce in their countries with the least possible delay a fully democratic system based on the principle of 'one man, one vote'. Such a planning of life is irreconcilable with the ancient and traditional ordering of the tribal system. There nothing is ever decided by a vote. The elders (or sometimes all the men of the tribe) meet and discuss, not infrequently with great democratic liberty of

[20] See P. Tempels, op. cit. p. 128.

discussion. But in the end the decision is given by the chief, or by the small group of elders who have in their keeping the ancient traditions of the tribe.

Over large parts of Africa the real contest is not, as is generally supposed, between the black man and the white; it is between the old Africa and the new. This is already apparent, for instance, in Ghana. The inland kingdom of Ashanti, which was independent of Britain until 1900, has by no means forgotten its proud status of only a few years ago. The Asantehene of Kumasi is one of the strongest and most influential chiefs in the whole of Africa. It is no accident that the policy of Dr. Nkrumah, upon his accession to power, was marked by a strong tendency to diminish, if not to destroy, the authority of the chiefs in favour of a more individual pattern of democracy. Conversely, the Smith regime in Rhodesia is eager to shore itself up by restoring the waning power of the chiefs over their people.

3. Thirdly, the inner being of primitive man is marked to-day by a painful schism. He feels the irresistible attraction of the new; he knows also something of the terrible price that he will have to pay if he accepts it.

If an African, still living within the tribe, is asked to say honestly what he inwardly most strongly desires, his answer will be that he wants to be like the white man. The interpretation of this saying is obvious, if we recall Fr. Tempels's affirmation that primitive man thinks in terms of forces and not of existents. The first thing that is evident about the white man is that he is strong. He has uncanny control over mysterious forces. If the black man can discover the white man's secret, he will himself learn to control these powers, and this will lead to a great increase of his own life-force.

For primitive man the crisis of history is not marked by the distinction between B.C. and A.D. It is marked by the coming of the white man. In many parts of Africa the new age burst upon the tribesmen less than fifty years ago, within the memory of men still living. In the interior of New Guinea it is still taking place to-day. The white man is not liked. He may even be hated. But he must be imitated because he is strong. A great part of the white man's magic is believed, not without truth, to reside in his book. The passion for education which is manifest in so many of the simpler parts of Africa is not in every case the expression of a pure and disinterested desire for knowledge; it has in it something of the medieval alchemist's search for the philosopher's stone. A certain desire to be acquainted with the white man's God may not have much to do with true religion; it, too, may be part of the search for the secret of the white man's power.

Such an action in one direction could not but produce reaction. At one end is the sheer conservatism of the older chiefs who will not countenance any change in the ancient ways of life. At the other is the sophisticated attempt to prove that all things African are good, and that the old ways are better than the new. Not long ago in Canada a young African who had passed through a mission school and been baptized, rather startled a group of his Canadian fellow-students by saying, 'On the whole I am more a pagan than a Christian, and is that such a bad thing to be? In the tribe I learned discipline and the laws of the tribe. The old women told me that I was always being watched, in the day-time by the big light the sun, and in the night by the small lights, the moon and the stars; whatever I did would be known, and if I broke the law of the tribe, what I had done would certainly come to light. Was that a bad way of educating the conscience of a boy? And what have I gained in Christianity that is better than what I had in the tribal system?'

It must be taken as certain that there are many things of great value and beauty in the ancient ways of life, and every encouragement must be given to those who are seeking to discover these values and to conserve them in the modern world. In a very real sense, Europe has created Africa. What was a congeries of mutually unknown or hostile tribes is now a self-conscious unity, trying to discover its own soul and to establish its contribution to the world. The modern educated African speaks of his 'Africanism', though he might be hard put to it to explain exactly what content he puts into the word. The *évolué* of French-speaking Africa has perhaps been even more completely integrated into Western culture than his English-speaking brother. He now speaks of his *négritude*, and this too is still a somewhat vague concept as yet lacking clear and defined content. But, whatever be the process of discovery, one thing is already quite certain. There is no way back. Elements from the past may be conserved and used; but, for those who have entered into contact with a wider world, the way back to primitive existence is barred. It is the expression only of a certain sentimental nostalgia. There is in reality only one way, and that leads forward into an as yet largely undiscovered world.

Four forces are at the moment competing for the soul of Africa, and, with modifications, the same can be said of other parts of the world that are in a similar stage of transition. The first is sheer secularism—the glittering civilization that comes in mainly from America, with neon lights, powerful cars and electrical appliances. The second is communism. No one knows how deeply communism has penetrated into the African mind. Where nationalism and political independence are the burning concerns of the day, it is probable that communism finds for the moment a somewhat barren soil. But it is not without significance that Russia has recently created a great and well-endowed Institute of African Studies in Moscow, and that Chinese communists are surveying and building the great railway that will link the copper-mines in Zambia with Tanzania and the sea. A temporary set-back is apparently again being followed by communist advance. The third force is Islam. The advance of Islam is certainly less rapid than it was fifty years ago. But in certain areas it is still successful in presenting itself as the natural religion for Africa, and as the African's ladder from a lower to a higher level of civilization. Whether it can finally satisfy his spiritual needs is another question. And finally there is Christianity. A century ago there was hardly a Christian in tropical Africa. To-day at least one-sixth of the total population is Christian. In the Congo the proportion rises to a quarter, in Uganda as high as one half.

Which of these rival forces is going to prove most successful in the conflict for the soul of Africa between 1960 and the end of the twentieth century?

We are open to admit that in the past the Gospel has sometimes proved itself a disruptive force. Missionaries have come in with no understanding of the way in which the primitive mind works. They have confused the Gospel with Western ways of living. They have learned very imperfectly the languages of those among whom they worked. They have tried too quickly to change ancient and long-established custom. But by now a great many lessons have been learned. The younger Churches have come to self-consciousness. The vast majority of those who preach the Gospel in Africa are Africans and not Europeans. Has the time, perhaps, come to ask what role the Gospel can play constructively in the Africa that is to be?

*   *   *

What shall they preach?

We may at once answer that they must preach, as always, the message of the Father, and of the Son, and of the Holy Ghost. The Gospel does not change from generation to generation. This is the correct and fundamental answer. Yet at the same time it is true that new and exciting perspectives of the preaching of the unchanging Gospel do present themselves, when we ask questions not merely concerning the message as preached but also concerning the message as heard.

One of the most valuable sections in Canon Taylor's study of the growth of the Church in Buganda is that in which he makes clear the difference between what the missionaries preached and what the Baganda heard. The missionaries, devout Anglican Evangelicals, preached in a rather conventional way salvation through the blood of Christ. Yet what was really heard by the Baganda was something that perhaps the missionaries had taken for granted and had not specially emphasized:

The message which was received and implanted and upon which the church in Buganda was founded, was primarily news about the transcendent God. 'Katonda', the unknown and scarcely heeded Creator, was proclaimed as the focus of all life, who yet lay beyond and above the closed unity of all existence. This was in itself so catastrophic a concept that, for the majority of hearers, it appeared to be the sum of the new teaching. . . . The revelation of a transcendent, personal and righteous God was not relevant, but revolutionary to the Baganda, yet that was the Word which they heard. The fact that they did hear it, and did not at this stage, for the most part, hear the message of the Saviourhood of Christ or the power of the Spirit, though these were the themes that were being preached, suggests that this was the Word of God to them, and it was independent of the word of the preacher.[21]

There can hardly be any doubt that the intelligent Baganda, like other African peoples, already possessed some faint knowledge of the High God. Dr. Bouquet suggests that 'there is strong evidence of the belief in a High God having come down with Hamitic immigrants from the north, perhaps from Ethiopia. In this case it may have a Judaeo-Christian origin.'[22] It is also true that the Baganda

[21] J. V. Taylor, *The Growth of the Church in Buganda* (London, 1958), pp. 252-3.
[22] op. cit. p. 264.

has been in contact with Muslims. Nevertheless there seems to me to be no reason to doubt that the Baganda belief in a High God was of purely African origin. But, as in other areas, the High God was a remote and faint existent, in whom the Baganda were not very much interested, and whom they did not suppose to be very much interested in them. Now through the preaching of the missionaries he had suddenly become a very important figure indeed. It is hard to overestimate the significance of the revolution that has thus been brought about.

Of the Baganda Christian to-day, Canon Taylor writes:

They are certain of one thing—that they believe in God. What is often lost sight of by missionaries, and by all the more spiritually and intellectually advanced Christians, is the enormous significance of this faith in God. It has to be seen against the background of the old world-view, in which the whole of existence was 'consubstantial', with no fundamental differentiation drawn between inanimate, human and super-nature. To say 'I believe in One God' is suddenly to see a gulf appearing between the here and now, and the beyond; further, it is to see the known network of inter-relation, which constitutes my life, terrifyingly related in some way to him who is independent of those relationships.[23]

The apprehension of the reality of the one God who stands outside the unity of all things that man has created for himself is bound to be revolutionary in its effects. We can summarize this revolution under three headings:

1. In the first place, the preaching came to the Baganda from outside the limits of their familiar and fairly comfortable world. Their security of living in their own ways had already been threatened by the arrival of Arabs from the coast and by contact with the monotheistic ideas of Islam. Perplexity was greatly increased by the appearance of the Christians, especially since these came in sharply contrasted Anglican and Roman Catholic groups. The initial assumption would naturally be that the white man has his own religion which is no concern of the black man. But it was this that the white man denied. He claimed that he had been sent by the High God, whom the African dimly discerned, precisely because that High God was deeply concerned about his African children, and had now through the preaching come to seek his own. These were thoughts that could not be fitted into any existing categories.

[23] J. V. Taylor, op. cit. p. 227.

Yet this was the message that the Baganda heard, because there was in their minds something already prepared to respond to these notes in the preaching.[24]

2. No sooner is the High God recognized as a living reality than a people such as the Baganda must begin to reconsider their relationship to all other peoples. It has been made plain to them that the High God is interested in them only because he is equally interested in all other peoples as well. Hereby another shattering blow is dealt to the idea of the self-sufficiency of the tribe within its own world of men and ancestors and gods. God can be known as Father only if he is understood to be the universal Father; it is precisely this that many African converts identified as the new thing that came to them through the preaching. How well the Baganda had grasped this new truth is seen in the zeal that they displayed for the preaching of the Gospel beyond their own limits to the neighbouring peoples. The most famous example is that of Apolo Kivebulaya, who penetrated the pygmy forest and translated the Gospel of Mark into the pygmy language; but he was only one of a great many pioneers who carried the new teaching to regions which the white man had never penetrated.

3. Thirdly, the teaching introduced the Baganda to the distinction between nature and grace. They would not, of course, use these classical terms to describe their new experience, and a few words are necessary to explain the phrase in this connexion. It seems plain that relationship between man and his ancestors and his gods, as the primitive understands it, is not contractual. With the particular spirit whom the hunter chooses to help him in his hunting the relation may be contractual; if the spirit fails to give the expected and desired success, the hunter may repudiate that spirit, cease to make offerings to it, and cast down the little shrine that he has made for it in the forest. But with ancestors and gods it is not so. They and the tribe belong together, and they cannot get rid of one another. Relations may be strained; disorder in the scheme of things may have to be repaired. But, in the most literal sense of the term, a nation cannot change its gods. In other words, all these different existents are seen as holding together within an order of nature that cannot be changed.

[24] The great Swiss missionary H. A. Junod notes how readily Africans respond to the idea of God. It is as though they were hearing again an old tale almost but not quite forgotten. There is an element of the familiar as well as of the unknown.

Once the High God has been apprehended as a living and near reality, the believer passes from one order of being to another. Almost the first thing that the inquirer is taught is that he can never get this God under his control. This is a God afar off, who will always maintain his sovereign freedom in all his relationships with man. In seeking him, man can do nothing to propitiate or to reconcile him, for he is not like the uncertain and capricious deities whose anger comes and goes and can be averted. In the world of nature man can restore the threatened or disrupted order by head-hunting or whatever the prescribed medicine may be. In confrontation with the living God, man encounters a world order, which has indeed been broken by sin, but which man himself can do nothing to restore. Movement, if any, must be in the other direction. There is a covenant; but it depends solely on the will and mercy of God and not on any natural relationship on which man can rely. The first outlines of the doctrines of election and of grace are beginning to emerge.

The reader familiar with the Old Testament will recognize at once how similar this pilgrimage of the African is to the pilgrimage of Israel. Probably at first the African finds himself more at home in the Old Testament than the New, and more especially in the sublime stories of the early chapters of Genesis. This is as it should be. Unless the doctrine of creation has been well and truly understood, it will not be easy to build on it a genuinely Christian doctrine of redemption.

The danger is that the new convert may hear the message of the Old Testament and may genuinely accept it. But this of itself will never make him a Christian. He must pass on from the doctrine of the Father to the doctrine of the Son. But here once again we may note a rather sharp separation between the message as it was proclaimed and the message as it was heard.

The missionaries plunged immediately into the New Testament, and proclaimed salvation through Jesus Christ as they themselves had experienced it. To them it meant primarily salvation from sin through conscious repentance and faith. The African heard the message, but to him it probably conveyed something else. The salvation which Jesus offers translated itself for him primarily into the message of salvation from fear. Jesus is the conqueror of the demons.

If the African understands the New Testament in such terms, he is actually coming nearer to its first readers than is easy for modern secularized man. The world of the New Testament was also a world full of spirits and of fear. The hundreds of magical papyri which have been dug up in Egypt and made available in printed form bring that world very near to us. The altar to the Unknown God in Athens was not, in reality, evidence of the questing of man's spirit after the as yet unrevealed Supreme; it reveals that haunting fear that, when all known spirits have been propitiated, there may still be one that has been forgotten. As in the Old Testament, there is the eager desire to know the spirit's name, since knowledge of the name conveys a certain power over it and the possibility that harmful influences may be averted.

To the one who lives in this haunting world of fear, Jesus draws near as the victor over the powers of evil. He speaks to them with power and they are powerless to resist his will. The resounding 'Fear not' of the New Testament fell on early Christian ears, not only as the guarantee of the divine presence in times of hardship and persecution, but also as an assurance of protection against that dark world of the real existence of which the Christians believed themselves to have so many clear evidences.

The primitive tribe which accepts the Gospel usually manifests its adherence by some outward sign, such as the destruction of the idols, the burning of sacred symbols, or some other ritual act in which the turning away from the old gods is made visible and tangible.

But ancient fears are not so easily dispersed as this. All missionary history shows the extent to which a duality can persist even within an apparently flourishing Christian Church. The members are sincerely Christian in that their intention is to follow the new way. At the same time a deep feeling persists that it may be as well to keep on good terms with the old gods. This may come out in convulsive forms, like the regression to primitive paganism which was one of the accompaniments of the Mau Mau terror in Kenya. It may break out in such forms as the curious 'Cargo' cults of the South Pacific, an evident attempt to capture the white man's magic by using some of the white man's methods. Much more often it persists in a quiet way, in the use of charms and incantations, in recourse to witchcraft and divination by respectable Christian people; and this goes on to an extent unsuspected by the white missionaries and even by the indigenous clergy.

This became plain in, for instance, the so-called Alice movement in Northern Rhodesia.[25] Those who came under the influence of the remarkable woman who headed this movement were required to give up all charms, fetishes and other objects which belonged to the dark realm of non-Christian observance. The quantity of objects delivered up was enormous. Even more startling was the standing in the Church of some of those who were led to make this revelation of themselves. The consternation cannot have been greater at Ephesus when those who had been practising curious arts came forward and confessed their deeds, and brought their secret books.[26]

Now all this is to be interpreted in terms not so much of sin as of fear. Unless the first deliverance from fear has been fully accomplished, unless Jesus has really been enthroned as conqueror of the demons, the believer is still living half in the old naturalistic world in which the spirits have power; and the time has not yet come in which his ears will really be opened to hear teaching concerning sin, righteousness, repentance and forgiveness.

It is easy to see why this first deliverance has in so many cases remained imperfect. Sheer numbers have made it difficult to give adequate teaching to the converts. Missionaries have had a tendency to condemn things that they did not fully understand. Inevitably their flocks have become secretive, and have failed to tell their pastors things that they have revealed without hesitation to the anthropologist. The first converts tend to be puritanical, and even more severe than the missionaries in their condemnation of all that belongs to the dark world. Only free and patient discussion of *everything* in the light of the Word of God can set men and Churches free from this impasse. Christ is the Saviour of all that can be saved from the old way of life, and from the traditions of tribe and people. But he can be Saviour only if he has first been destroyer. Reconstruction can begin only if the sovereignty of the old life has been totally extinguished, and the people have really made their Exodus from the dominion of the ancient spirit world.

We have seen that the gravest crisis of primitive man to-day arises from the disruption of society and the state of inner schism which that produces. Missionaries have been blamed for many things for which they have not really been responsible. Yet, by their

[25] Fergus Macpherson and W. V. Stone, *The Alice Movement in Northern Rhodesia* (International Missionary Council: Department of Studies, Occasional Paper, no. 1, 1959).   [26] Acts 19. 18, 19.

insistence on individual conversion, they have tended to exacerbate what was in any case bound to become in time a galloping evil, and to hasten unduly the detachment of the Christian from the traditional community to which he has belonged.

It was by reaction against this danger that the German missionaries in New Guinea were led to adopt a very different approach to the problem of conversion. They were dealing with small isolated tribes, often of not more than six or seven hundred members. Their method was to go on with patient instruction, until the whole tribe was prepared to declare itself ready to break with the past and with the old evil ways. Until this declaration had been made, no one in the tribe would be baptized. Thus the solidarity of the tribe was maintained, and the convert was saved from the dangers of isolation from that corporate life, on the support of which the individual is so deeply dependent.[27]

Rather similar has been the experience of those engaged in the so-called 'mass movements' in India. There the unit has been not the tribe but the village. It has usually been found wise to wait until a whole village is prepared to decide; then, once again, the social continuity is maintained without the divisions and disruption that individual conversion may involve. In quite a number of cases the old Hindu temple has been baptized to become a Christian church.

The merits of this method are self-evident. The dangers must not be overlooked. All too easily the new social unit, the Church, can take the place of the old, the tribe or village, without due understanding of the radical nature of the transformation that has taken place. This is at once evident if more than one Church or mission is at work in the area. In parts of the Telugu country in South India large numbers of the Mala community had become Anglicans; large numbers of the Madiga community had been won by the Baptists. In many villages it was possible to find both a Mala (Anglican) and a Madiga (Baptist) church. Conversion had doubtless solved a number of problems *within* the existing community; it had not led the Christians to face in the radical way that the New Testament demands the central problem of *all* community. The new man in Christ is not the old man patched up; the new Society can use all that is good in the old—it cannot simply be the old refurbished.

---

[27] Very little material is available in English on this method and its success. G. F. Vicedom, *Church and People in New Guinea* (1961), gives a good and clear account of the method pioneered by Christian Keysser.

We have seen the significance of the preaching of the Father and the Son. The logic of the situation drives us on to see the necessary place in missionary work of the doctrine of the Holy Spirit.

For we cannot spare primitive man the agony of becoming an individual, if he is ever to find his place in the elect community of free men. If we desired to leave primitive man in the anonymity of the tribe, circumstances would not allow us to do so—the old tribal system is breaking up. But, even if it were possible, the true preaching of the Gospel leads a man into a new responsibility for decision, which cannot be evaded if he is ever to become truly Christian. But once he has come to the point of such decision he has broken through the trammels of primitive and purely tribal existence.

Once again, we must not exaggerate the uniformity of life even within the most fully integrated tribe. Some individuals develop qualities of leadership, others of subservience. Human individuality is far too rugged and persistent a thing ever to be permanently suppressed. But the limits within which individual decision is permitted are narrowly drawn, and are mostly on the safe ground of the familiar and well-worn. When a man comes to the point of saying 'Yes' or 'No' to Jesus Christ, no one can help him. At that point he must stand alone, and take a decision for which he and he alone is responsible. And this decision, by definition, involves going forward into a future which is uncharted and unknown. In confrontation with the living God he has emerged from the limbo of half-personality into the reality of personal existence.

I do not think that anyone who has worked among very simple people can doubt the reality of this change. Those who live within the limits of the natural society seem to be all so very much the same, their reactions conditioned, their decisions predictable. The moment the Holy Spirit, the Lord and Giver of life, enters in, man is set free from his environment to be himself. The pressure of society, almost as acutely felt in industrialized mass society as on the simple level of the tribe, tends to make us all very much the same as one another; when God gets to work, he seems to make us all as different from one another as could be, and to be glorified by the infinitely diverse development of personality.

As we have seen, the breakdown of the tribal order is producing the individual, and the emergence of the individual is hastening the breakdown of the tribal order. In many areas this is happening in the worst possible way. Yet perhaps the process itself is not altogether to be condemned as evil. Tribal existence has much beauty. But it involves also hampering limitations on the expansion of human powers, the restriction of the individual to traditional paths, the loss of much that could be contributed by the creative inventiveness of the individual. We admire the cohesion of the tribe. Would we ourselves wish to go back and live within its limits? Are we surprised that the emancipated young man from Johannesburg finds himself unassimilable when he returns to the tribe?

The problem is as old as the age-long problem of the transition from status to contract. The Christian question is this—is it possible that the transition from a society based only on order to one based on freedom should be carried through without the wastage and destruction of human substance that is generally evident when primitive man is brought suddenly into contact with a material civilization? The Christian answer should be found in the doctrine of the Holy Spirit. The Gospel came to set men free—free from their own past in darkness, free from the dark world that is the other side of this world, free from all that is cramping and hampering in tradition. But it does not proclaim the barren freedom of sheer individualism which is no better than death. Freedom is given in order that men may enter into the community of grace.

The tribe is the natural community. The Church is the willed community. It is brought into being by the will of the Father, whose gracious purpose it is that all should have a home upon earth. It is kept in being by the will of men, who commit themselves to it in order that fellowship in freedom may become the great human reality. The Church, the community of the Holy Spirit, ought to be there to help men of all tribes and peoples through the painful process of rebirth, in order that they may find again on a new and higher level all that was of value in the closely corporate life of the family and the clan.

To what extent is the Church proclaiming this Gospel, and making it a living reality in the lands where rapid social change is the order of the day? To this question it is extraordinarily hard to give one single answer. But two grave weaknesses in the Christian witness, as it exists to-day, may be pointed out.

In the first place, in most Christian communities the quality of fellowship is very poor. Where all have come recently from the same background, something of the old corporate quality of life seems to survive. But precisely where this quality of fellowship is most needed, namely in the cities where detribalized man feels his loneliness in all its bitterness, there are few churches in which the stranger can be quite certain that he will be made welcome, and which provide such a quality of life as will draw him in with the feeling of belonging and being at home. Even in church the Christian tends to be an individual and not a member who finds himself enriched by the corporate life of the whole body.

Few Protestant Churches or Christians have a clear sense of their membership in the world-wide Body of Christ. Here the Roman Catholic fares better. From the very first day he is taught that he is a member of *the* Church. This Church has a visible centre in Rome. It has a visible head, the Pope. For the Protestant the idea of the Church is all too often hidden behind the structure of the local church and of the missionary society. But this, as we have seen, is one of the vital points in the dialogue between the Gospel and primitive man. The figure of the High God cannot really come alive and carry meaning, unless it is clear that the Father on high cares for all men equally, and that those who enter into covenant with him are thereby equally entering into covenant with all their brethren on earth.

Here we touch the ecumenical dimension of the preaching of the Gospel. Perhaps at no other point is it more clear that the ecumenical movement needs to become more missionary, and the missionary movement needs to become more ecumenical.

CHAPTER VII

FAITH AND NO FAITH

THE title of this book makes an assumption which until recently most people would have been prepared to grant but which in our own time has come under fire from a variety of directions. We have seemed to take it for granted that, if human beings are not Christians, they will be adherents of some other known religion—Hinduism or Islam or some other—or that at least they will manifest some form of faith which, even if it cannot be classed as specifically religious, bears some relationship to what we commonly understand by religion. Is that assumption any longer valid? Do we not live today in a world in which a great many people have not merely abandoned religion in any recognizable form, but are settling down quite happily to live without anything that could be described as faith?

Our understanding of the problem will depend a little on the meaning we attach to the word 'faith', a term which is clearly flexible, and has in fact been understood by different people in a variety of ways. Paul makes the contrast between walking by faith and walking by sight (2 Corinthians 6.7). Faith is related to that which is invisible but need not for that reason be any the less real; sight means here, not the act of seeing or the capacity of vision, but the thing seen, which can be observed and intellectually handled. Today the contrast would probably be rather differently expressed. Modern man is prepared to accept affirmations based on observations and experiments which can be repeated and are equally open to all, the conclusions from which are based directly on the evidence or on inferences from that evidence. Assent to such affirmations seems to him the only assent worthy of a reasonable man. Faith, in his eyes, has to deal with that which is accepted on authority, because someone said it a long time ago and other people have since repeated it a great many times; or on faulty deductions from inadequate evidence; or on a 'leap of faith' made in defiance of such evidence as there is; or on sheer fantasy, which lives in a world entirely different from that with which the reasonable man has to do.

We may later question the adequacy of such a definition or interpretation of faith. There can be no doubt that something like

F'

this is what a great many people imagine Christians to mean when they use the word 'faith', and that Christians have made themselves vulnerable either by failing to make clear what it was that they were talking about, or by using the word 'faith' in what is really an indefensible sense. It is not surprising that the reasonable man, which sometimes means no more than the man who has acquired at school an elementary knowledge of natural science, feels himself to be standing on firm ground, which he contrasts to his own advantage with the quicksands and quagmires of faith.

It is this attitude which can be summed up in the single word 'secularism'. But before we come to consider this particular point of view, it may be well to spend a little time on three other attitudes to which the term 'secular' can rightly be applied, but which, as we shall see, do not exclude the possibility of faith quite so radically as the current secularism which claims for itself the honourable title 'scientific'.

I

Ask a Christian from where he thinks that the greatest danger to religion threatens, and he is likely, especially if he is an American, to answer 'from Marxism'.

This is by no means an unplausible answer. It is claimed that religious liberty exists in Russia, but this is understood to mean that there must be the fullest possible freedom for anti-religious propaganda, as well as for the practice of religion. Anti-God campaigns are launched with the full approval of 'the party'. No secret is made of the fact that the Marxist regards religion as a mere survival from the capitalist past, that he is perplexed by the toughness with which religion refuses to accept its dissolution before the advancing power of science, and that he looks forward with hope and expectation to the day when religion will finally disappear. It is not only Christianity which is threatened; Judaism and Islam are equally under the ban. But Christianity is perhaps more suspect than the others because of its international character and its close connection with the hated world of capitalistic power. Religions can continue to exist only if they limit their concerns rigidly to what happens within their places of worship, and make no attempt whatever to intervene in the social, political and international affairs which the State has claimed as belonging exclusively to itself.

All this is true. But Karl Marx himself must not be held responsible for everything that passes as Marxism today. In the work of the prophet himself the Christian will find much to interest him, and much which he can appreciate.

In the first place, Marx has brought us back firmly to the terrestrial realities, which religious people have been inclined to overlook or to treat with less than the seriousness which they deserve. There is no authority in the Gospels for this kind of 'religious' attitude; Jesus is much concerned with loaves and fishes and other very material entities. He tells us that we are not to take anxious thought about such things. But, though he reminds us that man shall not live by bread alone, he never for a moment doubts that man shall live by bread. 'Give ye them to eat' still stands as his command to his Church. If at any time the Church has been inclined to spiritualize this command, to think that it has fulfilled its duty by providing man with spiritual food and so preparing him for life in heaven as a compensation for poverty and hardship on earth, the word of Christ is there to rebuke it. As William Temple once remarked, Christianity is the most materialistic of all the great religions of the world. It does take the terrestrial realities seriously. If we had ever been inclined to forget the words of Christ, Marx is there to make sure that in the modern world we cannot do so. It matters immensely that man should have enough to eat and to wear, and a reasonable home to live in, and such social and economic conditions as favour genuinely human life. When these things are lacking, man becomes alienated from himself, he loses the truly human quality of life. It is the aim of Marx to restore to him the integrity of his own being. With this aim the Christian cannot quarrel, though he may take exception to some of the means chosen by the Marxist for the accomplishment of his aim.

Secondly, Marx has been responsible for a new understanding of history which is almost universally accepted. We are all Marxists to a far greater degree than we are consciously aware. The *Communist Manifesto* was first published in 1848. It took about a generation for its significance to dawn on historians. But, if we contrast history as written before 1878 with history written since that date, we cannot but become aware of the change. Earlier history was written in terms of dynasties and wars and political changes. Now the economic factor plays an important, sometimes a decisive, part in the development of the art of history-writing. For instance

Professor E. J. Hobsbawm of the University of London published in 1968 a book with the title *Industry and Empire: An Economic History of Britain since 1750*. His argument is not at every point convincing; he himself points out that on many matters the fundamental research has not yet been done. But his basic contention is sound. Kings, queens and politicians play their part. But, if we wish to understand human history, we must recognize that changes in methods of production, distribution and communication affect the lives of men more than all but the most revolutionary changes of political organization. In the life of India the extension of the railways was more significant than the Act through which responsibility for India was transferred from the East India Company to the British government, and than the notable proclamation of Queen Victoria in which the change was made known to the world.

Thirdly, Marx claimed, not without reason, to have made Hegel's dialectic stand on its head, and to have established the principle that the business of the philosopher is not to understand the world but to change it. Marx held that history advances according to irreversible and immanent laws; but he also believed that, through scientific understanding of these laws and a willing 'acceptance of necessity', it is possible to serve the inevitable revolution and to advance its cause, just as the refusal of necessity may slow down the progress of the revolution, and this is the unpardonable crime.

It is sometimes said that, at a time at which the Churches were deaf to the cry of misery that arose from the new industrial proletariat, Marx heard the cry and was moved by compassion to champion the cause of the so-called working class. Two arguments can be brought to bear against the accuracy of such a statement. Recent research has shown that the Church was very far from being deaf, at least in England, to the needs of the poor, and that in some of the worst affected areas an overwhelming majority of the clergy were behind the great Lord Shaftesbury in his campaign for the better conditions provided by the Factory Acts. And compassion is hardly a virtue which one would associate with the real Karl Marx. He was an angry, contentious, authoritarian man, who managed to quarrel with almost all of those who had at one time or another been his associates. He himself affirmed that his interest in social conditions was purely scientific. He reviled the industrialists not so much because they oppressed the poor, as because they had become anachronistic, having failed to recognize the proletarian revolution that was already on its way and to foresee the consequent demise of capitalism.

But on the duty of the man of vision to see to it that society changes and is changed the Christian can heartily concur with Marx. There has been a strain of pessimism in Christian theology, a concentration on the eschatological hope and the second coming of Christ, which is easily compatible with a *laissez-faire* attitude towards politics and economics, and the supposition that in these regions nothing can really be changed for the better.[1] It is not surprising that much attention has been attracted by the book of Professor Jürgen Moltmann: *The Theology of Hope*.[2] Moltmann is one of the younger German scholars who has made a deep and sympathetic study of Marxism, and is much concerned about the possibility of Marxist-Christian dialogue. He has come to his views on Christian responsibility by way of Karl Marx rather than by way of the New Testament; but the challenge he has thrown out can only be welcomed by those who have long believed, with Frederick Denison Maurice and all his disciples, that society can in a measure be transformed and that it is the business of Christians to transform it.

So far Christians can go with Karl Marx himself. But even in Marxism as it has further developed they can discern something that it is hard to describe by any other word than 'faith'.

Marx was a Jew who had been baptized. He was well acquainted with Christianity and seems to have found it hard to get away from it. His system sounds at times almost like a parody of New Testament teaching. Here too is an innocent victim, the proletariat, through whose sufferings the world is to be redeemed. Here is the eschatological hope, the coming kingdom—only here it is the kingdom of man, and not the kingdom of God. But the eager expectation with which the convinced Marxist looks forward to the coming of that kingdom, his absolute certainty that he has the clue to the future and that that future is in his hands, is something that the Christian

[1] The attempt of the World Council of Churches to put out a clear and challenging statement on the Christian Hope in preparation for the Assembly to be held at Evanston in 1954 was frustrated by the refusal of the continental theologians to recognize the possibility of any hope this side of the second coming of Christ.

[2] Original German edition *Theologie der Hoffnung*; English translation London 1967. The original German quickly ran through five printings. In view of the strongly this-worldly character of Moltmann's thought, it is ironical that in the catalogue of the London Library which I gratefully use, his book appears under the heading 'Religion: Future State'!

can understand, since it is no more than a transcription into another key of the certainty which he entertains himself.

Moreover, the Marxist conviction, no less than the Christian, has shown its capacity to breed martyrs. We in the West are more aware of the massacres for which the Marxist has been responsible, of the martyrs whose blood he has had upon his sword. It is important not to forget the other side—the communists who remained true to their convictions during the German occupation of France and gave a lead to the resistance, and the many in other countries who have endured oppression, imprisonment, and sometimes death for the sake of what they believed to be the truth.

These are the aspects of Marxism which have made possible the development of a Marxist-Christian dialogue of a type and on a scale that would hardly have been thought possible at the date (1960) at which these lectures were originally given. Originating in France, the impulse has spread to Germany, to Czechoslovakia and to other countries on the continent of Europe. Faith can always speak to faith. It may be that the way of agreement is long and hard. But here as so often it is the first step that costs the most; the great thing is that the first step has been taken, and that there is no thought of turning back from the beginning that has been made.[3]

II

A second form of no-faith, or of qualified faith, is that which calls itself scientific humanism, or simply humanism for short. This is associated especially with the name of Sir Julian Huxley, the learned biologist, who has also been President of the United Nations Educational Scientific and Cultural Organization, and whose aim is neatly summed up in the title of his book *Religion without Revelation*.[4]

It is the idea of revelation to which Sir Julian specially takes objection. In the world of science man is left on his own. He has to observe, to classify, to form theories, reject or modify them, and thus laboriously to understand and to master his world. No outside

[3] I have before me as I write an account of the first international meeting of Christians and Marxists (June 1967), published in the German periodical *Stimmen der Zeit* for July 1967, pp. 48–54. One of the speakers was Professor Moltmann.

[4] London 1927; new edition 1959. The same ideas are set out by a large variety of writers in the work, *The Humanist Frame* (London 1961) of which Sir Julian Huxley was the editor.

power will come to his aid and supply him with information which would otherwise be inaccessible to him. The idea of special divine aid to man belongs to the childhood of the race and should now be discarded. To believe that such aid is possible, still more to regard ourselves as in any way dependent on it, would be to condemn ourselves to perpetual infancy. We must stand upon the dignity of our manhood, and accept the responsibility and the risks without either timidity or rashness.

The responsibility, as Sir Julian sees it, has become specially heavy in our time. Up till now the progress of evolution has been haphazard and uncontrollable by man. Now science has put into our hands the means by which we can discern the direction in which evolution is going or ought to go, and we ourselves can take a hand in determining, to some extent at least, the direction. A somewhat similar view had been reached, though not along exactly the same route, by the Jesuit palaeontologist Pierre Teilhard de Chardin. It was this that led Sir Julian to interest himself in Teilhard de Chardin's views; in consequence the world was presented with the edifying spectacle of the sceptical English biologist writing the preface to the most celebrated work of the pious and basically orthodox French Jesuit, *The Phenomenon of Man.*[5]

Certainly there have been times at which Christians have understood revelation in the sense to which Sir Julian takes exception—as the communication of information to which men would not otherwise have access. It is doubtful whether any intelligent Christian holds that view today. Once this little misunderstanding has been cleared up, it is clear that there is much in the attitude of the humanists which Christians can only welcome and approve. There has been a great tradition of Christian humanists, who have delighted in all the manifestations of man's creativity, and have made their own contributions to his investigation of his world.[6]

Moreover, it is to be noted that many humanists desire to find a place for many things to which Christians attach particular value. They appreciate art. They recognize that, if human life is to be safe and orderly, there must be a place for morals and ethical principles.

[5] *Le Phénomène Humain* (Paris 1955): English translation *The Phenomenon of Man* (London 1959).
[6] Here it may be well to note a distinction between German and English usage. *Humanismus* in German could imply concentration on the human to the exclusion of the divine; ordinarily in English usage the word humanism does not have this connotation, and the expression 'Christian humanist' involves no logical contradiction.

Some would even find a place for religion, provided that this is purely immanent—it must be no more than man's reverence for the highest ideals that he himself has been able to discover. What, asks the humanist, has morality to do with the idea of God? Why drag in religion as a support for something that can perfectly well stand on its own feet? We have plenty to occupy us in a world that we know; why direct our attention away to a transcendent world, which, as Christians themselves admit, is unknown and to a large extent unknowable?

We shall postpone to a later stage of our argument our discussion with the humanists on fundamental issues. We will simply note in passing that they seem a little unduly optimistic in their attitude to the evils in the world and in human nature. It is not self-evident that reason alone can deal with the unruly and aggressive elements in human nature. We can admire and approve their exemplary diligence in their vocations, the integrity of their thought and of their lives. We share their sense of the greatness of what it means to be a human being and of the responsibility laid on the men of the atomic age to conserve and not to destroy. We can applaud their faith as far as it goes, and hope that they may discover in time that they must go further, if they are to be consistent in following the argument which has led them to their present position.

III

There is a third approach to the secular, which must detain us a little longer, though it claims to fall within the field of Christian faith, while making use of language which is unfamiliar and uncongenial to many Christians.

When, in 1928, Christians from all over the world (but not from the Roman Catholic section of the Christian Church) met at Jerusalem for the second World Missionary Conference, the attention of the members was drawn to the great increase of secularism, a negative outlook which must be regarded as the antithesis of the Christian faith and the greatest danger to it. Some were prepared to go so far as to suggest that the adherents of all the theistic religions should form an alliance to defend the religious outlook on the world against the secular menace. When the World Council of Churches was formed, many lay people supposed this to be an alliance of *religions*, in which Hindus and Muslims no less than Christians would find their place. This was, of course, a misunderstanding; there are inter-faith movements, but this has not been the direction which the contemporary ecumenical movement has taken.

A quite different approach was adopted by a number of Christian theologians, who posed the question whether the secularization of thought must necessarily be regarded as such an evil thing; should not Christians perhaps regard it as part of God's providential ordering of the world, as something that they ought to welcome rather than to reject? The principal champion of this view was Professor Friedrich Gogarten, who in 1953 published a book with the title *Peril and Hope of the New Age: Secularization as a Theological Problem.*[7] Gogarten distinguishes between two views of nature—the mythical, in which nature is understood as possessing mysterious powers, before which man must bow in insignificance; and the rational or secular, in which man sees nature objectively as something which it is his right to investigate and to master. This is what is meant by the secularization of the world. It is in ancient Israel that the protest is first raised against the 'sacralizing' of all being, against the supremacy of fate, against the divinizing of kings and kingdoms.[8]

These ideas have become familiar to English readers, not directly from Gogarten, few of whose works have been translated into English, but through Dr. A. van Leeuwen's book, *Christianity in World History*, the popularity of which is vouched for by the fact that a second printing was called for only a year after the first appearance of the book. Van Leeuwen develops the ideas of Gogarten extensively and persuasively. This secular view of the world derives from Christian ideas, and in particular from the idea of God as creator. It is this secular approach that has made possible the development of science in the modern world. Hence, although science has often detached itself from its Christian roots, this is a development of which Christians ought not to be afraid, and which they ought rather to welcome. In any case, this tendency is now irreversible. Western culture is an offspring of the Christianization of the West. Wherever Western culture has spread, it carries with it the destruction of the mythical view of the world, which is still

[7] *Verhängnis und Hoffnung der Neuzeit: Die Säkularisierung als theologisches Problem* (Stuttgart 1953).

[8] A. van Leeuwen: *Christianity in World History* (London 1965), p. 331.

that of all the non-Christian religions. It may seem that the Western world is growing less religious than it was; but this does not seriously matter, since 'Christianity is now operating in the shape of a technological culture, which may be said to be its secularized form'.[9]

Van Leeuwen's book is based on wide, though uneven learning. But it is confusing, and often the exact direction of the argument is difficult to grasp. This is partly due to a fundamental defect of terminology. At one point in the quotation given above, reference is made to the 'sacralization' of everything. The correct term for the opposite process is 'desacralization', and to this word van Leeuwen, and his translator, should have confined themselves. Instead, he tries to make a distinction between 'secularization', in the sense indicated above, which he regards as a good thing, and 'secularism', which he regards as a bad thing. But the distinction will not be clear to the ordinary reader, and endless confusion will be the result.

In English the contrast between the 'secular' view of the world and the 'religious' is that between a world from which God has been once and for all excluded, and which therefore is to be understood only in three-dimensional terms, and a world in regard to which the possibility will be at least entertained that there is another aspect which can never be reduced to the three-dimensional, and which therefore holds out as arguable the hypothesis that God exists and that he matters. The danger is that, under the influence of Western science and technology, the heirs of ancient cultures in India and elsewhere may not merely carry out the necessary task of desacralization, but may move onwards to the point of secularism, that is, to the total abandonment of anything that goes beyond what men can touch and see and handle.

Experience shows that this is no mere theoretical danger. When the British government, from 1855 onwards, undertook the task of introducing Western education into India, out of consideration for the feelings of the non-Christian peoples of that country a guarantee was given that there should be no religious or moral teaching in the schools controlled by the government, though there would be freedom for such instruction in schools set up by religious bodies. Even a century ago the daily and periodical press in India was flooded with bitter protests from writers of all classes against the

[9] J. Macquarrie: *God and Secularity* (London 1968), p. 58.

'godless' education that was being provided—old traditions and ways of looking at things were being destroyed, respect for the past was being uprooted, a vacuum created which evil spirits of every kind were rushing in to fill. Dr. van Leeuwen is aware of this danger, and does mention it; but he attaches far less weight to it than it deserves. If these results really follow on the preaching of the Gospel, the non-Christian peoples of the world might well find in this an additional argument for the total exclusion of Christian missionary work from their countries.

Moreover, it is not the case that the entry of the scientific and technological understanding of the world will immediately be followed by the disappearance of the mythical or magical view. The human mind is not swayed only by logic. One of the problems of all missionary work, and of all educational work in countries where the Western tradition is a newcomer, is the apparently unlimited capacity of the human spirit to hold together two ways of looking at things which are logically irreconcilable with one another. Oil and water can co-exist without commingling; so can the scientific and the magical understanding of the world. Advertisements in the Indian papers reveal the regularity with which students about to take an honours examination in physics will purchase an amulet 'guaranteed to supply the wearer with the ability to pass every examination' to help them in the examination room. The African schoolboy knows perfectly well that cholera and typhoid are water-borne diseases. But, if there has been in his village an outbreak of disease in which six people have died, he may well be convinced that witchcraft has been at work. If his missionary mentor takes him to task and points to the evidence supplied him by scientific knowledge, the boy is perfectly ready with his answer: 'How do you account for the fact that only twenty people in the village fell ill, and that of those fourteen recovered and only six died?' To him it is self-evident that the infected water could not have brought about the death of the victims, unless it had been rein-forced by magical powers used to the detriment of just those six people.

We shall do well to exercise some caution in our approach to this idea of 'secularization', especially when on the basis of it large generalizations are made as to the kind of witness that 'religious' people ought to be attempting to bear in the modern world. Two other points in van Leeuwen's important book serve to warn us of the need for accuracy in speech, and for knowing just what it is that we are talking about.

We have just put the word 'religious' in inverted commas, and not without reason. It has never yet proved possible to arrive at a definition of the word 'religion'; but the nature and the range of religion, and therefore of what it means to be 'religious', is precisely the subject that we are discussing in this chapter. A quotation from Dr. van Leeuwen will illuminate the point. Speaking of the meeting between Christianity and the non-Western civilizations and religions, he writes

Whether they will or no, these are entering upon an epoch in which 'religion'—in the traditional sense of a dominating social pattern—can no longer sustain itself, or at least can do so only at the cost of existing in a perpetual state of tension.[10]

Now it is clear that every writer must be free to use every word in a sense of his own choosing. If Dr. van Leeuwen wishes to use the word 'religion' as equivalent to 'a dominating social pattern', he has every right to do so, and it is kind of him to point out to us that this is what he does mean. But attention must be drawn to the fact that, though this may be the meaning of the Dutch word *religie*, in English 'religion' has never been used in this sense. It is true, as was pointed out long ago by Christopher Dawson,[11] that every great religion has clothed itself in a culture and a social system, and that every great culture and social system looks back to a religion as its foundation. But to identify the two is to abandon the distinctiveness of religion, and to give in to those cultural anthropologists, who regard religion as simply relative to a variety of cultures, and appear to have abandoned the quest for truth. 'Religion' in English raises precisely the question whether there is anything outside the three-dimensional world to which man has access and which he ought to take seriously; what matters in religion is precisely that which distinguishes it from culture.

With what is religion concerned, and what is the range of its interests? The failure of a great many Christians has been in their tame willingness to limit religion to the 'religious sphere'—to what people do in church, or in one particular area of their life which has little to do with everyday affairs. Hence the protest of Dietrich

[10] op. cit. p. 422.   [11] See pp. 214 ff. of this book.

Bonhoeffer in favour of 'religionless Christianity', a phrase which has given rise to endless confusion.[12] But, if we take religion seriously, it has to do with everything. There is no area of man's life with which it is not concerned; the old distinction between 'sacred' and 'secular', or between 'sacred' and 'profane', convenient as it is in practice, cannot be systematically maintained.

At one point Dr. van Leeuwen seems to recognize this aspect of religion. When speaking of Christian missionary work, he applauds the comprehensive approach, as set forth in for instance the writings of J. Merle Davis:

Under this approach, evangelization is cure of sick bodies, of broken-down, inefficient, and eroded farms, of illiteracy, of insufficient and unbalanced diet, insanitary homes, impure drinking water, of a subsistence level of existence, of filthy villages, of the moral, mental and spiritual stagnation of corrupt practices and conditions. Every effort upon this wide and comprehensive front of Christian service is a part of the Evangel and is required to enable the individual to reach the fulness of the stature which is in Christ.[13]

Davis is here putting forward a view which was almost universally accepted by missionaries, Protestant and Roman Catholic, at the time at which he was writing. If they did less towards the implementation of these noble ideals than they could have wished, this was due rather to the niggardly support from the older Churches by which their efforts were cramped and hampered at every turn than to failure to recognize the breadth of the missionary obligation.

Having accepted this, van Leeuwen goes on to find fault with Davis for what he takes to be the 'limited dimensions' within which he has developed his ideas. Davis had written:

In view of the rapidly growing secularization of all modern life which is defeating the religious interpretations of non-Christian as well as Christian culture, the comprehensive programme of the Church takes on enormous significance. . . . To abandon these areas to the domination of irreligious forces and to fail to make them vehicles of the Christian

---

[12] The difficulty is that Bonhoeffer was using 'Religion' in the German and not in the English sense of the term. It would be quite correct to translate his expression in English as 'religious Christianity', a Christianity which concerns itself with everything, as religion ought to do!

[13] op. cit. p. 427. The quotation is from J. Merle Davis: *Old Buildings on New Foundations* (New York/London 1947), p. 233.

witness amounts to a betrayal of God as Creator of all and In-dweller in all of life.[14]

On this van Leeuwen comments:

Why do we suddenly launch our criticism when the modern welfare state and all sorts of private agencies make use of exactly the same means? What mysterious religious powers does the Church possess that alone beneath her aegis can a penicillin injection and the alphabet become the instrument of God the Creator, while in other hands they would appear to be deadly poison?[15]

It is immediately clear that van Leeuwen has not taken the trouble to understand the writer whom he has been quoting. Merle Davis, writing in 1947, cannot be found fault with for not knowing a use of the word 'secularization' which was invented by Gogarten in 1953. It is quite clear that he means by it what van Leeuwen would describe as secularism, the arrogant claim by man to exclude God from his own world, and to suppose that salvation can come to that world through technology alone without any recognition of the spiritual dimension. Merle Davis is right, and van Leeuwen is wrong. If there is any truth in Christian faith at all, the Church must go on endlessly proclaiming to the world the dangers that lurk in man's Promethean arrogance, in his conviction that he can do it all himself, in that reductionism through which man is imprisoned within space, time and matter, and forbidden to look beyond them. The Churches in South India had had such experience of the consequences of this Promethean vanity of man in the field of medical training that, for the sake of human beings and of the values that the Christian believes to be inherent in human life, they felt themselves compelled to set up, at enormous expense their own centre for the training of Christian doctors and nurses.

But the point has come at which we must turn from these modified forms of secularism, humanism, or secularization, and look at the secularism, self-confident and unashamed, which confronts us in many areas of the world today.

IV

Isaac Newton, with his *Principia Mathematica* (1687), and John Locke with his *Essay on the Human Understanding* (1690), were the harbingers of the modern world. For almost three centuries there

[14] op. cit. p. 425 quoting Davis, op. cit. pp. 232 f.   [15] op. cit. p. 429.

has been uninterrupted and unparalleled progress in human knowledge in every sphere. Theoretical knowledge usually comes first; the practical applications follow after. Faraday (1791–1867), through his tremendous achievement of developing means by which the power of electricity can be brought under the control of man, was perhaps, more than any other man, the Titan of the modern world. We can trace an unbroken line of advance from his discoveries to the explosion of the hydrogen bomb and the landing of the first men on the moon. The universe is far richer than we had ever imagined; its resources are at our disposal today, in a measure never dreamed of by our ancestors.

A race of men is growing up which is content to inhabit this new world of knowledge and desires no other. An army of research workers all over the world is engaged in pushing back the frontiers of knowledge in all directions. The acceleration of progress is so rapid that most of the books and papers written ten years ago are out of date today. The time-lag between the discovery of new forces and the application of those forces to production, to the increase of riches and the enhancement of human life, is growing less and less. There seems to be no limit to the dominion that man can exercise over his world.

Men of this type are characterized by a generous and serious optimism. They have little use for the pessimistic prophecies uttered by those who have not grown used to the climate of this new world, or who see peril where the scientist is much more likely to discern promise. For instance, we have been told countless times that, if the population explosion continues at its present rate, the earth will not be able to support the population that will weigh upon it in the year A.D. 2000. It may well be questioned whether so rapid an increase in numbers will really contribute to the well-being of the human race; but there can hardly be any doubt that the riches of the earth will be equal to any forseeable increase in population. The agricultural scientist can point to the fact that, though the application of scientific method to the fields of India has hardly been begun, India was able in a year or two to double its production of wheat, so much so that, methods of better distribution having been neglected, a glut had been brought about in the producing areas.

If the attention of the new man is drawn to areas of human conflict, and it is suggested that man's material advance has far outstripped his ethical and spiritual progress, he is likely to reply that this is largely a matter of education and social conditions. Education has remained far too much in the hands of priests and pedants, who are still inculcating the ethics of the dark ages. What is needed on every level is the liberating influence of science. When scientific method has eliminated poverty, we shall see everywhere the emergence of the new race of men, qualified to enjoy the liberty that has been won for them by the toil of centuries.

If it is suggested to him that science has as yet shown no sign of eliminating death, or postponing the inevitable date of the extinction of all life on this planet, he is not long at a loss for an answer. In the first place he may well say that he can face his own death with equanimity. He has tried to live honourably and to leave the world a little better than he found it; why then should he be afraid to fall asleep when his time comes? And, as for the race, if life becomes impossible on this small planet, why should we think it impossible that man may find means to project himself to some other inhabitable world and begin the process all over again? The climate of the moon appears to be unfavourable to any kind of life that we know; but why should we assume that this will be the situation in all the various worlds that remain to be explored?

We are not going to catch our secularist out too easily; we shall certainly not do it with slick questions and easy traps.

There have been secularists in all ages. The modern type of secularism may perhaps be thought to begin with the famous answer of the French astronomer Laplace to the Emperor Napoleon. Napoleon had said: 'Monsieur Laplace, they tell me that you have written this big book on the System of the Universe, and that you have not once mentioned God in it.' 'Sire,' replied Laplace, 'I had no need of that hypothesis.' In that context, Laplace was perfectly right. At the beginning of the eighteenth century Newton did bring God into his physical and mathematical speculations as to the nature of the universe; by the end of the century the scientists had opted for the total autonomy of their realm, and believed that it would be to the advantage of both science and religion if each went its separate way.

Science had had a rather difficult time freeing itself from the tutelage of philosophy and religion. Galileo's troubles had come mainly from the philosophers, who held with Aristotle and with his commentators that all motion above the lunar realm must be perfect, and therefore perfectly circular—they were not prepared to admit that the planets might have elliptical orbits. Others found themselves hindered by traditional interpretations of the Scriptures, which were regarded as infallible, and with which therefore the findings of science must not be allowed to conflict. Only gradually was the scientist able successfully to vindicate his right to make his own observations, to form his own hypotheses, and to state his own conclusions, without regard to anything except the integrity of his own conscience. The honest Christian can only applaud his liberation, though he may deplore the confusion into which at times scientists have fallen between unproved theories and really established conclusions.

Theology no longer attempts to dictate conclusions. We live in an age of the contrary tendency—for science to dictate the conclusions to theology. What can the modern secular man, schooled in the rudiments of science, believe? This is taken to be the standard of credibility. Some theologians have taken this as the yardstick by which to measure their own theology, and not surprisingly have come up with some very negative conclusions. Best known among these are the writers of the 'Death of God' theology; but it seems that this was no more than a passing phase of Christian exploration, which has already reached its point of maximum influence. There are, however, in the field of theology more serious voices than these.

We may take as, perhaps, the most important of these voices that of Paul M. Van Buren, in his book *The Secular Meaning of the Gospel* (1963). This is an exceedingly able work, though it has to be confessed that it is not altogether easy going for the reader who is an amateur. Part of the interest of the book lies in the fact that it is autobiographical, and, without obtruding the fact, is a record of the author's own passionate search for truth. He had been for years a convinced and orthodox Barthian, believing that the answer to every kind of question would be found in the correct exposition of the Word of God. It was clear at that period of his development that, if he began to slip, he would slip a very long way. The British logical positivists and linguistic analysts threw at him a number of puzzles to which he could find no solution in the categories in which he was then thinking. His dilemma can be paraphrased very simply: 'I am a modern secular man, and I think in the categories of the modern secular world. What, then, can I, without doing violence to my own conscience, accept of traditional Christianity?' The answer would seem to be 'Remarkably little'. Modern secular man has no use for the transcendent. Therefore any faith that he can accept must be purely three-dimensional; it must move only in the realms of the historical and the practically ethical. So it becomes very doubtful whether we can use the word 'God' at all; if we do use it, it is likely to be in a sense very different from any other sense in which it ever has been used before.

Yet Van Buren is, in fact, much less negative than might be supposed on a first reading of his book. Like others of his kind, he cannot get away from Jesus of Nazareth. What specially impresses him in the life of Jesus is that he is the man who is truly free. Now this is excellent New Testament theology. Freedom is one of the great New Testament words. 'If the Son shall make you free, you shall be free indeed' (John 8.36). 'For freedom Christ has set us free; stand fast therefore' (Galatians 5.1). I would myself be prepared to construct a complete Christian theology with freedom as its basis.

Why then does Van Buren break off, just where we might expect him to begin? The reason may be that he is making certain assumptions without realizing that he is making them, and that, if he worked backward to these assumptions, he might find his conclusions profoundly modified. Apart from the assumption that this is a universe in which freedom exists, an assumption which many thinkers would passionately refuse to accept, he seems to me to assume that it is in some way better to be free than to be a slave. But how does he know?

Aristotle, whom the Middle Ages regarded as 'the philosopher', and whose word for them carried almost incontrovertible authority, had laid it down in his *Politics* that there are men who are fitted by their nature to be slaves, and for whom therefore it is the best possible destiny to be the slaves of those whose nature is noble. That this was very much more than a theoretical proposition will not be doubted by those familiar with the story of the great debate in Valladolid in 1550, between Bartolomé de Las Casas, the friend of the Indians in Latin America, and Juan Ginés de Sepulveda, the upholder of the ancient ways, on the question whether Indians of the western world have full human rights or not. We may think that Van Buren is right in regarding freedom as 'better', but we must not allow him to get away with an assumption that his view is self-evidently correct.

It is the word 'better' that constantly perplexes the thoroughgoing secularist, in whose world there should be no place for transcendence of any kind. What does the word mean? In some contexts this is self-evident. 'This is a better knife than that.' The word 'better' here would seem to mean simply 'more effective'; a knife is an instrument made for the purpose of cutting, and if, in any particular situation, one knife cuts more effectively than another, the term 'better' seems both clear and appropriate. But the meaning is not always so evident. 'This house is better than that.' Here 'better' could mean 'less likely to fall down', or 'aesthetically more pleasing to the eye', or 'better adapted to my particular purposes', these purposes being unspecified; or simply 'more comfortable to live in'. In each case there is a reference to standards, which are not self-evident either from the word 'house' or from the word 'better'.

And what are we to make of the remark 'Mussolini was a much better man than Hitler', which I once heard fall from the lips of a German diplomat who had known both men well? The speaker seemed to imply that he knew the purpose for which man exists on the earth, and therefore the way in which men ought to live, and that he was judging the two men by their greater or less conformity to what he regarded as an established and acceptable ideal. But how did he know, and by what standards was he judging? Do such standards exist? Who invented them? Is there universal, or even general, agreement about them? Or do we mean simply that a larger number of people would be likely to approve of Mussolini than would approve of Hitler, regardless of any possible objectivity in their judgement?

Such questioning is not mere playing with words. It may make clear to us that more is implied than we are always aware of in the apparently simple words we use, and that awareness of our own unspoken presuppositions is one of the necessary steps towards lucidity of understanding and consistency in thought. And the careful analysis of a single word may take us far in the direction of asking fundamental questions.

In almost every situation there are seven questions that can legitimately be asked. Of these four—Who or What? When? Where? How?—are proximate questions. There are three ultimate questions, 'Whence?' 'Whither?' and 'Why?' Where did it all come from? Where is it all going to? Why are things the way they are?

The physical scientist is perfectly entitled to say that he is content with the first four questions, and for the purposes of his discipline never finds it necessary to ask any others. Once again, it is M. Laplace with his 'I had no need of that hypothesis'. The chemist knows perfectly well that, if he pours hydrochloric acid on manganese dioxide, chlorine will be released. He has some idea of the strange process of reconstruction which takes place in the two substances he has mixed. But he has no idea at all *why* these particular changes take place. And for the immediate practical purposes of his demonstration, he has no need to ask 'Why?'

This does not mean, however, that these questions cannot or should not be asked. The scientist may well say that he never himself wishes to ask these questions, and is of the opinion that, if asked, they cannot possibly be answered. This does not, however, give him any right to say that other people should not ask these questions, if they wish to do so, or to maintain that the questions are in themselves meaningless.

In point of fact, it is extraordinarily difficult to remain firmly within a three-dimensional universe, and not to ask, or imply, any questions that go beyond these limits. The moment we begin to think seriously about this universe, the less easy does it become to maintain that all the explanations that we need are given within the visible and measurable aspects of things.

For example, the chemist will tell us that, if tomorrow we pour hydrochloric acid on manganese dioxide, chlorine will be released. How does he know? He can say that it happened yesterday, and that it happened today. But the assertion that it will happen tomorrow belongs to the realm of faith and not to that of knowledge; the scientist has called in a dimension of which he himself may hardly be aware. He may have established a strong probability; about the future he can establish no certainty, and it is faith in the stability of the universe, a stability that is not demonstrable, which takes the place of the certainty which we can never have.

The great mathematician J. E. Littlewood, in a charming little book with the title, *A Mathematician's Miscellany*, stated that everyone knows that, if you put a kettle on the gas, it is probable, but not certain, that it will boil. If everyone really knew this, the world would be a far better place than it is. Few things do more harm than the confusion between high probability and certainty. Littlewood, the mathematician, knew well the difference between the certainty with which a mathematical conclusion can be derived from mathematical premisses, and the uncertainty that comes in the moment we adapt mathematical or logical categories to the consideration of a world of space, time and matter to which they can never be wholly appropriate. To make his point perfectly clear, Littlewood works out mathematically the probability of a celluloid mouse surviving for a week in hell; and, to balance this, the contrary probability of a live mouse freezing in a similar situation. It must be admitted that the probability is low—except that possibly Littlewood had not read his Dante, and did not know that Dante's hell in its lowest reaches is cold, not hot, and that his Lucifer stands for ever at the centre of the earth in everlasting frost.

We are led on to see that it is not irrational to ask, What kind of a universe is it that gives us such confidence in its uniformity that we live in it as we could not possibly live in a universe that was purely chaotic? For, if there is one thing that is absolutely certain about this universe it is that it is a universe in which purposes can be formed and carried out. I planned this chapter; when it comes to the point of writing, my brain, and my hand, and the paper, and the ink converge, and what had been merely a purpose becomes an accomplished fact. The chapter is written. President Kennedy announces that a man will be landed on the moon. For ten years thousands of men work together with this one single purpose in view. Countless millions of dollars are expended. Endless experiments are made and rejected. But still the work goes on. And in the end the dream comes down from heaven to earth; what Jules Verne foresaw in 1865 as a splendid possibility has now become something that has actually happened.

It is time to come back to our three ultimate questions—Whence? Whither? Why?

How did it all start? The Christian submits a hypothesis which appears to cover the phenomena more effectually and completely than any other. Spirit is prior to 'matter'. 'Matter', as we have learned from our physicists in recent years, is only a manifestation of energy. If asked to define the word 'spirit', the Christian might answer, 'pure energy, and the source of energy in all other things that are'. On this view, the emergence of spirit as self-consciousness, ability to ask the kind of questions that we are now asking, the capacity to know God as we are known by him, is an inevitable consequence of the nature of the initial impulse. But we become aware of a paradox. The emergence of spirit, as apparently the climax of a long development, takes place at a time at which the disintegration of the universe through the dissipation of energy is already far advanced. What then is the nature of that Spirit from whom the initial impulse was derived?[16]

Where is it going? As far as this planet is concerned, we can say with almost certainty that in the course of time life on it will become impossible. One of the wandering bodies of the heavens coming a little too near us might cause a shock that would blast us all out of existence in a moment. Or the natural process of cooling might make this earth uninhabitable by any kind of life that we know. And it must be taken to be rather doubtful whether this kind of life could really propagate itself again upon some distant planet. Is that the end? The Marxist and the secularist must answer, whether cheerfully or regretfully, Yes. The Christian, viewing all space and all time, asks to be allowed to draw attention to another possibility. If the origin of all things is spirit, it cannot be thought impossible that the innate tendency of all things is to return to that Spirit from which they came forth. In man this tendency becomes conscious and deliberate. Man seeks a unity with God, because he knows that that unity, once established, can never be destroyed. This, or something like it, is what Paul meant by his mysterious affirmation that the creation itself 'will be set free from its bondage to decay and obtain the glorious liberty of the children of God' (Romans 8.21).

Why? We have affirmed that the universe, as we experience it, is so far reliable that within it it is possible to make and carry out purposes. But does the universe as a whole make sense? Even the most tentative answer can be given only in terms of purpose. Is it possible to conceive of one single purpose so vast that all the myriad phenomena of the world as we know it can be related to it? If God exists at all, and really is Lord of all this vast universe, as well as of thousands of other universes as to the existence of which we have no clue, it seems likely that he has literally countless purposes, as to which we cannot even hazard a guess. But, as far as this one world is concerned, the Christian is prepared to hazard the guess that

---

[16] It is not possible to disprove the alternative view of the eternity of the universe, As is well known, Professor F. Hoyle and others hold the view that creation is continuous, and that as energy is lost in one form, it comes into being in another. This is a technical problem that must be left to the experts. The question is whether the universe, as it is now, can be regarded as ultimate, and not derived from anything else.

Spirit, in letting loose that energy through which our world came into being, had in mind one single central purpose—the aim of enjoying for ever the fellowship of intelligent and free spirits which had freely chosen to live in fellowship with him. If this really was the aim, it would explain many things. If the purpose had been to make all men as comfortable as possible all the time, the world would have had to be very different from what it is. But, if freedom is a condition for the fulfilment of the purpose, the element of risk, of suffering, of disaster, of apparent failure, cannot be excluded. In such a world the Cross of Jesus is not out of place.

In at least one passage, the Bible does seem to contemplate the sudden dissolution of all terrestrial and material things, when 'the heavens will be kindled and dissolved, and the elements will melt with fire'.[17] But such a climax the Christian can face with equanimity since it is clear that spirit cannot be touched by material disaster. The end would be the beginning. Spirit at present is called to use the material as its instrument and to recognize it as its temporary home. But, if all these things were destroyed, spirit would simply enter on a new freedom, a new creativity to which the inborn recalcitrance of matter would offer no further obstacle.

This argument has been presented, as far as possible, in terms which avoid traditional Christian platitudes. We have simply tried to indicate the questions which we would like our secularist friend to ask, pointing out to him that these questions really arise out of the discipline which he is pursuing, if he will pursue it to the very end, and that, though the answer can no more be guaranteed for these than for the thousand other questions which he asks in his professional capacity, it is not necessary to despair at the outset of at least a tentative, and therefore provisionally satisfying, answer. He is deeply concerned about his own rationality, and will not be fed on dreams and vague desires. We can assure him that our concern also is with the right use of reason, but that it is also our concern not to exclude any of the questions that can be asked, and not to exclude the possibility that the answer might come by way of dialogue with an unseen power and not through the exercise of our own powers of ratiocination alone.

It may be well to conclude this section with a rather more positive statement of what it is that we have been after, in words that can leave no doubt in the mind of our secularist friend as to the challenge

[17] 2 Peter 3.12.

which is being presented to him, and the direction in which we hope that his mind may be led to move:

From some of the books being put out nowadays, one might conclude that atheism had proved its case and is the only possible belief for any educated and up to date person. . . . This is an utterly ridiculous and arrogant claim. I should say myself that theism is a much more *reasonable* belief than atheism and always has been. . . . The very fact that there is a world rather than just nothing, that this is an ordered and structured world rather than just chaos, and that this world has brought forth spiritual and personal beings, makes atheism a most improbable thesis.[18]

V

We are left with the most difficult problem of all: how are we going to persuade the secularist to ask the questions which, for his own good, we are convinced that he should be asking? If there is one thing that is quite certain, it is that, if you never ask a religious question, you will never get a religious answer.

This problem, however, cannot be dealt with simply as a problem of religious or Christian apologetic. Here we are face to face with the appalling impoverishment of the human spirit that can be seen going on all around us. The spirit of man is enriched proportionately to the variety of responses that it can make to the multiplicity of the environment, physical, natural, living and human, by which it is surrounded. We in the West live in an affluent society; we have been delivered from many of the fears under which our ancestors laboured. But apparently a terrible price has had to be paid for our deliverance. As evidence we need look no further than our speech. Compared with the fresh, racy, imaginative utterance of village dwellers, even though they be illiterate, our speech is flat, worn-out, prosaic, abstract, tedious. Something has gone wrong with our response to the world. Together with our material wealth we seem to be bent on imposing our spiritual poverty on all the world.

The point can be illustrated from the spectrum, into which clear light is refracted by the prism. Most of us can see clearly the seven colours, made up of the primary colours and their combinations. We are well aware that what our eyes can see is not the entire spectrum, but only a part. There are other rays, of which we can observe the effects, but which we shall never see. At one end are

[18] John Macquarrie: *God and Secularity* (London 1968), p. 108.

the ultra-violet rays, the power of which will not be doubted by anyone who has stayed out too long unprotected under bright sunlight, and at the other end the infra-red rays, the use of which in photography and other ways is steadily being extended. But those who are partially colour-blind can see fewer colours than those who are more fortunate; and those who are completely colour-blind see everything as a monochrome in which there is no distinction of colours at all.

The pressure of Western civilization, and of the kind of education which is increasingly fashionable today, seems to produce on a massive scale emotional and spiritual colour-blindness. The spirit of man is being impoverished by the limitation of his responses to life and its challenges; we are becoming starved in the midst of overwhelming plenty.

If there are seven colours of the rainbow, there are at least seven aspects of the wonderful world by which we are surrounded to which we ought to be able to respond. There is the aspect of the existent (natural science); of the event (history); of the beautiful (aesthetics); of mental process (psychology); of the better and the worse (ethics); of the transitory and the permanent (metaphysics); of ultimate obligation (religion). To how many of these aspects have we been qualified, by the education we have received, adequately to respond? And will our children be better educated than we, or worse?

The most distressing characteristic of our civilization is its capacity for the destruction of beauty and the creation of ugliness. The peoples whom we class as primitive have a limited awareness of beauty; yet they seem to possess an instinctive understanding of proportion and hardly ever produce anything displeasing to the eye. The aspect of our great cities reveals at once all that we have lost, and the failure of our educational systems to produce in young people the furious spirit of protest against the shoddy, the merely mechanical, the second-rate, the simply hideous, which would make sure that in a generation the abominations produced by a prosaically technical civilization would be swept away.[19]

Natural science, well and wisely taught, can be an introduction into the good life. But, clearly, as it is taught in many of our schools, it makes contact with reality under only one of our seven aspects— the existent, which we desire to understand and to control. The end

---

[19] I am not saying that our civilization cannot produce beauty. Some types of aeroplane are really beautiful; and so are some modern cities, but all too few.

of such education is not the good life, but technical expertise; the effects of this can already be seen in the incipient boredom of the welfare state.[20]

Christian faith is not to be identified with 'religion' as the seventh of our aspects. The most admirable thing about the secularist is his unconditional devotion to the truth, and this may be said to be his religion, just as for the Marxist the cause of Marxism, for which he is prepared to die, has many of the characteristics of a religion. Christian faith is concerned with the universe as a whole, and with every aspect of it, including the life of man as a spiritual being and the life of man in society. It is for this reason that the Christian must protest against such emphasis on one aspect as would exclude consideration of the others, or would paralyse the potential response of the developing individual to them.

In the old days, when the Bible was the recognized basis of good learning, education, for all its mechanical character and technical imperfection, corresponded far better than our contemporary education to the realities of the world, and to the variety of responses that are required of men. That kind of education, like every other, could be and often was mishandled; but even when only moderately well conducted, it was in the best possible sense of the term both human and humane. It is impossible that the clock should be put back; the way out of a dilemma is always forwards and not backwards. It is the business, however, of every Christian to be deeply concerned about the kind of education that is being given to the younger generation. At what is this education aimed? Is the aim merely technical excellence in one of the so-called scientific areas of knowledge? If so, the Christian must proclaim his dissatisfaction; he cannot be content with anything less than an education that sets each generation of young people in the way to the full level of response to reality of which human beings are capable. This does not mean that he is primarily concerned about religion in the narrow sense of the term; as a follower of the man Christ Jesus, he is concerned about the human substance, which is so gravely imperilled by many of the tendencies of the present time.

It may well be that, until our educational systems are reformed,

[20] In Britain the latest figures show a remarkable swing away from science and back to the humanities. The cause of this is not yet adequately known; it seems to have something to do with the feeling that a scientific education does not offer the prospect of congenial and satisfying employment.

dialogue between the Christian and the secularist will be difficult. It is no use talking to a colour-blind man about the use of colour in the French post-impressionists, nor to a tone-deaf man about the beauties of polyphonic music. In so far as a secular education has conditioned the minds of our young people, they are incapable of seeing and hearing when the subject of discussion is the Christian faith. For a period, perhaps a long period, this may make the task of the Christian apologist extremely difficult. It may be almost impossible to find any wave-length on which communication is possible.

It is fortunate that human beings are rarely logical. The Christian may find the situation far more favourable to him than he has any right logically to expect. Young people refuse, as they always have done, to become just what their elders wish them to be. They will pay far more than they can afford to hear a first-rate rendering of Bach's *Mass in B Minor* or Handel's *Messiah*, perhaps with only the dimmest idea of the spiritual dimension of what they are going to hear. The secularist himself can sometimes be heard indulging in a perfectly reckless use of the words 'good' and 'bad', which ought not to be in his vocabulary, and be found engaging at great personal cost in causes participation in which can far more logically be defended by a Christian than by a secularist. It may be the business of the Christian simply to sit still and to listen. 'The still, sad music of humanity' continues to sound. It may be that we still have far more common concerns than we imagine, and that dialogue may be possible on a far deeper level than is immediately apparent.

CHAPTER VIII

THE EXISTENTIAL PILGRIMAGE

EXISTENTIALISM is a word that has only recently come into currency. It stands not for one single coherent doctrine, but for a certain attitude to life which is recognizable in a number of thinkers of very varying backgrounds and tendencies. It is possible that Existentialism has already had its greatest vogue; it seemed to answer to a special need of men, particularly of the younger generation, in the period of disarray and confusion after the Second World War. Of this period and its attitudes Paul Tillich has written:

It is not an exaggeration to say that today man experiences his present situation in terms of disruption, conflict, self-destruction, meaninglessness and despair in all realms of life. This experience is expressed in the arts and in literature, conceptualized in existential philosophy, actualized in political cleavages of all kinds, and analysed in the psychology of the unconscious. The question arising out of this experience . . . is the question of a reality in which the self-estrangement of our existence is overcome, a reality of reconciliation and reunion, of creativity, meaning and hope.[1]

When Tillich wrote these words, they were certainly true of a great many men. It is not certain that they are quite so true to-day, especially of the younger people of this age, to whom the memories of war and disruption are growing faint, and who seem to be discovering another kind of reconciliation to life.

Nevertheless, Existentialism deserves attention as being perhaps the most characteristic product of Western thought in the twentieth century. And, as always happens, what began by being the possession of an élite, initiated into the mysteries of a not always very intelligible jargon, has managed to filter through into the consciousness of the ordinary man, and existentialist phrases have become part of the current coin of everyday speech.

What, then, is Existentialism?

Any serious study of the subject must go back to Søren Kierkegaard who, long years after his death, has come to be recognized as one of the most creative thinkers of the nineteenth century.[2]

---

[1] Paul Tillich, *Systematic Theology*, i (1951), 49.

[2] Others would go back further still. Professor David E. Roberts opens his excellent study of *Existentialism and Religious Belief* (1959) with a chapter on Pascal. A place will

The best starting-point for the understanding of Kierkegaard is, perhaps, his hostility to the philosophy of Hegel, on which like most of his contemporaries he had been brought up. Hegel's thought was the last great attempt in the West to create a world-system of thought in which everything will find its place and nothing will be left unaccounted for. It was this concept of the function of philosophy that aroused Kierkegaard's wrath; his fiercest diatribes are directed against 'the System', for he is convinced that there are many things that cannot be reduced to system, and the chief of these is man in the richness and reality of his personal, every-day existence. So he starts by laying down the principles that '(A) a logical system is possible; (B) an existential system is impossible'.

An existential system cannot be formulated. Does this mean that no such system exists? By no means; nor is this implied in our assertion. Reality itself is a system—for God; but it cannot be a system for any existing spirit. . . . It may be seen, from a purely abstract point of view, that system and existence are incapable of being thought together; because in order to think existence at all, systematic thought must think it as abrogated, and hence as not existing. Existence separates, and holds the various moments of existence discretely apart; the systematic thought consists of the finality which brings them together.[3]

Kierkegaard is often hard to understand and has in consequence often been misunderstood. He loved to express himself in oracular and paradoxical form, a habit which he had learned, not to his own advantage, from Hamann, 'the Magus of the North'. His message was so strange and contrary to all the thinking of his time that he hardly expected to be heard, and seems to have felt that he could draw attention to what he wished to say only by dressing it up in the most startling and provocative form possible. It is, further, true that Kierkegaard's thought is always in movement; if what he says is not clear, this in some cases at least is probably because he does not himself know exactly what he wants to say.

certainly have to be found also for Johann Georg Hamann (1730–88), to whom Kierkegaard constantly admits his indebtedness. Hamann is almost completely unknown in Britain; but there has been a great revival of Hamann studies in Germany, the fruits of which will eventually become known in the English-speaking world. See a brief note in the *Oxford Dictionary of the Christian Church*, p. 605. The first full-scale study of Hamann in English, Professor R. Gregor Smith's *J. G. Hamann: A Study in Christian Existence* (1960), was published shortly after this chapter was written.

[3] *Concluding Unscientific Postscript* (Eng. trans. 1941), p. 107.

It is necessary at the outset to clear away certain misunderstandings. Kierkegaard is often regarded as the source and fountainhead of 'the flight from reason' which has been a sorry feature of our times, and he is often quoted in their defence by those whose flight from reason is grounded in nothing more admirable than the laziness which is unwilling to wrestle with the real problems of thought. It is clear through all his writings that Kierkegaard was prepared to pay the utmost deference to reason, if it is kept in its proper place. What he was implacably opposed to was that kind of systematizing reason, which works out a simple solution for a problem and presents an answer—only by dint of disregarding all those factors in the situation which, in point of fact, make any such simple answer impossible.

Again, Kierkegaard's constant use of the term 'absurd' seems to me unfortunate. 'Christianity is the absurd, held fast in the passion of the infinite.'[4] In English this can so easily be taken to mean 'the ridiculous, the totally irrational'. I do not believe that this is in the least what Kierkegaard meant by the word. In mathematics a surd is 'that which cannot be fitted into the pattern', the remainder that is left over when we have done our best to find a neat and tidy solution. In some such sense as this, 'the absurd' for Kierkegaard is that which never can be reduced to any kind of rule. It is the exception, the individual, the irreducible, that which can never be proved though it can be apprehended. If we have come to know anything, we have in a real sense made ourselves masters of it; we can set it to do our bidding, as the scientist makes use of the principles that he has discovered. In this sense Christianity cannot possibly be known, since in relation to it man is always the servant and not the master. It remains 'the absurd', since it can be neither proved nor reduced to rule. What relationship can a man, then, take up to 'the absurd'? No other relationship is open to him but that of faith—and faith to Kierkegaard always means adventure without the certainty of finding or reward.

We are now ready to consider the three great principles of Existentialism as Kierkegaard understands it.

1. In the first place, the ethical is the realm of generalization, of common rule and order. Ethical rules will serve as a useful general guide for conduct; but no ethical rule will ever be exactly applicable to the particular situation of an individual man. It cannot be more than an approximation. Any man is likely to find himself in a

---

[4] *Concluding Unscientific Postscript*, p. 192.

situation where the ordinary rules of ethics simply do not apply. Convention and human formulations no longer help, and he finds himself driven to act in a way for which the only appropriate term is paradox.

For Kierkegaard the classic example of this is the story of Abraham, when he was bidden by God to offer up his only son Isaac. In the Prelude to *Fear and Trembling* Kierkegaard gives four remarkable interpretations of this story, and then goes on to discuss its implications. The central problem is the question, 'Is there such a thing as a teleological suspension of the ethical?'[5] To this Kierkegaard would answer 'Yes'. The individual cannot truly rise to the point of being an individual, unless he is prepared, at whatever cost, to raise himself above the level of the universal, the general rules of the ethical, and to act as he, that particular man, is called upon to act at that particular point of time. Kierkegaard is no doubt trying to understand, even to rationalize, his own strange action in breaking off his engagement to Regin Olsen with whom he was deeply in love; but, whatever the origin of his thought, it has led him to a discovery of fundamental importance.

2. Secondly, we are led to the question as to where the fullness of man's personal reality can be experienced. Kierkegaard's answer is that this can come about only in the direct confrontation of man with God. This is an experience unlike anything else in the world. It can neither be taught nor learned. The increase of knowledge and the lengthening down of Christian history do not make it any easier to believe than it was in the beginning. No man can live another man's Christian experience. Each is in the nature of the case unique and different from any other, and no direct communication of such experience from one to another is possible. One may guide another some distance on the way; but each in the end must make for himself the leap of faith.

But faith must not be misunderstood in terms of assent to a particular kind of doctrine. It means total self-commitment, witness to what is believed, and in the modern world necessarily suffering. Kierkegaard satirizes the kind of Christianity which was understood in terms of intellectual apprehension:

If one would call medieval Christianity the monastic-ascetic type, one might call the Christianity of our age the professor-scientific type. Not all, it is true, could become professors; but nevertheless all acquired a certain

[5] *Fear and Trembling* (Eng. trans. 1941), p. 79.

professional and scientific cast of mind. And just as in the first period not all could become martyrs, but all stood in relationship with the martyrs ... so in our time all stand in relationship with the professor, the professor is the genuine Christian. . . . To the professor corresponds Christianity as objective teaching, as mere doctrine.[6]

In sharpest contrast with this is the reality of a faith which acts on that which it has apprehended:

To *suffer* for the doctrine. It is this which changes everything endlessly with respect to becoming a Christian, this which imposes endless weight. . . . To *suffer* for the doctrine. But there can be no question of that in these times when Christianity has fully triumphed and all are Christians! I could be tempted to say, 'Woe, woe unto thee, thou hypocrite!' But that I will not do. . . . No, the requirement of suffering for the doctrine is at this instant just as much in force and just as applicable as it was at the beginning.[7]

3. It is at this point that the thought of Kierkegaard approaches that of Karl Marx. Many philosophers, and many ordinary men as well, have held that, when we have understood something, we have done our duty by it. Kierkegaard and Marx take the view that understanding is true understanding only when it is conceived as a preparation for action; he who has understood is thereby committed to presenting a challenge to that which is. The business of the philosopher is not simply to understand the world but to change it.

The Existential thinker is the interested or passionate thinker ... Feuerbach and Kierkegaard prefer the term 'passion' for the attitude of the Existential thinker. In his beautifully written *Grundsätze der Philosophie der Zukunft*, Feuerbach says, 'Do not wish to be a philosopher in contrast to being a man ... do not think as a thinker ... think as a living, real being ... think in Existence'. 'Love is passion, and only passion is the mark of Existence.' In order to unite this attitude with the demand for objectivity, he says: 'Only what is an object of passion—really is.' The passionately living man knows the true nature of man and life.[8]

The thought of Kierkegaard slept for fifty years after his death; and then awoke to a new and vital creativeness in our own century.[9]

[6] S. Kierkegaard, *Judge for Yourselves* (Eng. trans. 1941), pp. 203–4.
[7] Ibid. pp. 211, 213.
[8] Paul Tillich, *Theology of Culture* (1959), pp. 89–90.
[9] When I first became interested in Kierkegaard in 1928, I could find nothing in English to read about him except the article by Dr. Alexander Grieve in Hastings's *Encyclopaedia of Religion and Ethics*; and at that date not a single one of his works had been translated into English.

Kierkegaard himself might have considerable difficulty in recognizing all the brood which he has hatched. Yet in all the thinkers who would call themselves Existentialists we shall recognize something of his spirit, and some of the principles for which he stood.

In no other thinker of our time is this so clear as in the work of Martin Heidegger (b. 1889). I am not competent to give a full account of Heidegger's philosophy; nor would our space permit it, if I could. But he has exercised so deep an influence on many of the younger men, and so much of his rather obscure terminology is in process of passing into common usage, that we must make the effort to grasp at least something of what he is talking about.

1. Heidegger calls his philosophy the philosophy of being. It has generally been assumed by thinkers that we know fairly well what we mean when we say 'I am'. But is this really the case? If we are to think at all, must we not start with a careful analysis of the nature of man's existence? If we attempt to do so, we may find that the problem is far more complex than we had supposed at the outset.

The first point to note is that for Heidegger existence is always existence in this world. He has made a radical break with the rationalist tradition of Western thought, and with the idea, familiar to all who have made any study of scholastic thought, that Essence precedes Existence, and that Existence can in some way be derived from Essence. We must never think of man in terms of substance or nature—generalized concepts that have no relatedness to this particular man in his situation of to-day. Nor must we suppose that we can think of man as a pure 'ego', a detached individual, as though he could be separated from the history that has made him what he is, and from the world, which includes the world of other selves, that surrounds him and in which he has to move.

This is how I exist, and only starting from here can we understand the nature of that existence and its problems for me.

2. Secondly, Heidegger insists passionately that existence is always individual and cannot be reduced to any form of classification.[10] This runs counter to the methods and approach of a good deal of modern science. The tendency there is to treat man like any

---

[10] Here we note a close parallel with Kierkegaard, though it is not possible to say whether Heidegger learned this principle from Kierkegaard or elsewhere. The same note rings out in the pages of another distinguished existentialist thinker, Karl Jaspers: 'We are completely irreplaceable. We are not merely cases of universal Being.' *Vernunft und Existenz* (1935), p. 19, quoted by Tillich in *Theology of Culture*, p. 103. This is one of the points at which Christian and Existentialist thought most readily meet.

other object of observation. The so-called social sciences spend their time in working out new formulae for the classification of man. It is not to be denied that such studies have a value for purely pragmatic ends; but, if we imagine that they can bring us any nearer to understanding the reality of man as man, we shall be sorely deceived.

3. For, to take up the third capital point in Heidegger's argument, there are two possible forms of being in the world. *Things* exist in one way. *Man* exists, or can exist, in another. For the existence of things Heidegger uses the term *Vorhandenheit*, which really means 'just being there'—they have significance for man only in so far as he can make use of them, in so far as they can serve as instruments for his purpose. *Existenz* is the being of man as a conscious subject, with awareness—awareness of himself, of the world and of other existences.

But herein lies the heart of man's problem. 'Nature', existence, is not given to him on a plate, ready and complete. He is a creature of potentialities, strangely compounded of Being and Not-Being. He is confronted all the time with two possibilities of existence, and all the time he is condemned to freedom of choice.

The two possibilities are characterized by Heidegger as authentic and unauthentic existence. Unauthentic existence is that of the crowd, where everything is ruled by conventions as to what one does and does not do, where a man hardly needs to make any deliberate personal choice but can drift along in the almost perfect anonymity of the crowd. The more perfectly he adapts himself to what is expected of him, the less effort he will have to make to exist in this unauthentic fashion. But by accepting this kind of life man rejects his own true existence, and falls down almost to the level of an object, a thing. 'Man-in-being' can lose himself to the being that meets him in the world, and be taken over by it.[11]

The reality of existence is to be found only in choice, in decision, in the deliberate acceptance of the authentic and rejection of the unauthentic existence. A man must become independent of others, of their judgement of him, of what they expect of him, and take his stand just upon what he authentically is, in the expectation of what he can become. There are no outward norms, no rules by which he can be guided (Heidegger has excluded God from his scheme of things). If we call the inner voice 'conscience', we must not interpret the word in the traditional sense of the voice of God; it is rather man's

[11] M. Heidegger, *Sein und Zeit* (8th edn. 1957), p. 36.

communing with the deepest levels of his own being, which we noted earlier as one of the possible forms of mystical experience.

This is freedom. Yet freedom is always accompanied by anxiety. Heidegger makes a distinction between fear and anxiety. Fear is always related to something which is in the world, which is conceived as terrible—or rather the empirical world itself is regarded as a sphere out of which something terrible might emerge. But this belongs to the realm of unauthentic existence. It is an unauthentic mood, and from this the man who has chosen authentic being is by definition free. And yet he is a prey to 'anxiety', that most characteristic of all the moods of modern man.

To what is anxiety related? Heidegger's answer is 'to Nothingness'. At this point Heidegger's own thought is so obscure that any exposition of it is bound to be obscure. Yet it is this concept almost more than any other which seems to have been found fascinating by generations of eager readers. An attempt must be made to understand the part that it plays in his system.

The mood of 'nothingness', of total meaninglessness, is not unfamiliar—it is closely related to that 'accidie' of the medieval monks, which might be a fleeting anguish, but could become a serious and dangerous mental illness. Boredom is one of its contemporary signs. 'Not boredom with a particular book or play or form of work, but finding oneself drifting in the abyss of existence as in a mute fog which draws everything into a queer kind of indifference. The sense of wholeness here comes out in the fact that *everything* is meaningless, pointless, tasteless, colourless.'[12] When this mood is on us, it is impossible to say 'Yes' to life, since life itself has become unbearable. What we do to the totality of being in this mood cannot be termed 'annihilation' (*Vernichtung*), since after all it goes on existing. Heidegger invents for this attitude the new word *Nichtung*, nihilation, the total personal rejection of that which is.[13]

But, if man feels like this on occasion, that can only be because there is something in the very nature of being to which the mood corresponds. Man's life is constantly threatened by non-existence; it is that which makes most men shy away from the decision in favour of authentic existence. Yet, even when this decision has been

---

[12] David E. Roberts, *Existentialism and Religious Belief*, p. 176.

[13] It is this word and concept that Sartre represents by the extraordinarily clumsy and unnatural word *néantisation*, reducing that which is to the state of the *néant*, nothingness.

made, the free man may be assailed by anxiety. He finds that there is a strangeness in the real world; he is not at home in it, and as long as he is in it his existence is continually threatened. It is only a courageous man who can look straight in the face of nothingness and accept it, accept his own existence as 'thrown forward to its own end'.

Outward help there is none. There is nothing in Being that could stretch out a hand to man in his perplexity, since Heidegger has rejected as puerility every idea of a personal God. Man has nothing to rely on except his own inner resources. Yet it is just at this point that, in the opinion of Dr. Macquarrie,[14] the Existentialist system is open to the approach of the reality of God. Heidegger has rightly seen that the truth of man's life lies in relatedness. The man who has chosen authentic existence is related to his own self in a new way, he has a new understanding of his own being. He can find relationships with other authentic selves at a level far deeper than the superficial encounter which passes as such in the unauthentic world. But, if man has not entered into relationship with God, the source and ground of all Being, is he not bound to be pursued by such an anxiety as Heidegger has so penetratingly analysed?

For in this fundamental malaise, which springs from man's very being, there is disclosed not only the self and the world, but also God. The disclosure does not indeed yield the explicit knowledge of God, but directs man to God as the ground of his being. . . . For what is this anxiety or dread, this basic malaise, this uneasy restlessness, this feeling of not being at home in the world, this disclosure which shatters the illusory contentment and security of everyday existence, but the *cor inquietum* of Christian experience? . . . Confronted with the disclosure of that anxiety which relates to nothing in the world but arises from his own being, man has an alternative to that flight into an inauthentic existence of surrender to the world—namely, recourse to God, Who is the ground of being, Creator of both man and the world.[15]

The thought that we now commonly call Existentialist was slowly maturing in Germany between the wars. After the end of the war, it burst upon the world almost with the force of a revelation through the genius of a group of French writers and thinkers. We shall briefly consider three of these writers as examples of the very various directions in which Existentialism can develop.

[14] John Macquarrie, *An Existentialist Theology* (1955). Though this book deals mainly with Bultmann, it contains the best short account of the thought of Heidegger known to me in English.   [15] J. Macquarrie, op. cit. p. 71.

All of them were marked by the scars of the tragedies through which France had lived—the surrender of 1940, the German occupation, the glories and squalor of the resistance, the deep disillusionment that resulted from the futilities that followed upon the liberation. The mood is perfectly expressed by a character in one of Gabriel Marcel's plays:

Do you not sometimes get the impression that we are living—if it can be called living—in a broken world? Yes, I mean broken, just in the sense in which a watch can be broken. The spring is no longer working. As far as outward appearances go, nothing is changed. Everything is in its right place. But, if you put the watch to your ear, there is nothing to he heard. You understand; this world—what we call this world, the world of men— at one time or another it must have had a heart—but now you get the impression that this heart is no longer beating.[16]

As a consequence of this mood of brokenness, and since existential thought by its very nature does not lend itself easily to systematization, a great deal of French Existentialism has found expression in novels and plays rather than in the form of systematic exposition. Yet there have been a number of more or less systematic attempts to communicate the nature of this strange new world in which these writers feel themselves to be living.

One of the most significant of these is Jean Paul Sartre's *L'Être et le Néant*,[17] with its sub-title 'An Essay in Phenomenological Ontology'. It is hard to imagine a greater contrast than that between Sartre's brilliant, witty and pungent handling of contemporary French in his plays, and the inflated, pretentious style of this monster volume—complex, repetitive, and in many places almost unreadable. It is hardly possible in a few pages to give a clear idea of what it is all about.

In Sartre (b.1905), as in so many of his contemporaries, we find evidences of a violent reaction against the narrowness and smugness of the well-to-do French *bourgeoisie*, a group that seems between the wars to have come as near as is possible to Marx's imaginary picture of the bourgeois world. In this atmosphere of getting and spending, imagination is at a discount; everything is ruled by convention, and all the moves in the game can be foreseen and calculated in advance. This is the picture given, for instance, by Simone de Beauvoir of her own youth, when there seemed to be only three possibilities for a

---

[16] *Le Monde Cassé* (1935).
[17] Paris, 1943 (Eng. trans. *Being and Nothingness*, 1957).

well-brought-up young woman—to make the customary *mariage de convenance*, to enter a convent, or to choose her own way in the world and to pay the price in total separation from her family.

With such a background it is not surprising that for Sartre the central problem is that of freedom. But this is not seen as a great and joyful privilege. Man is thrown into the world free, and his freedom is laid upon him as a dreadful burden from which he cannot escape: 'I am condemned to be free.'[18] Once again, there is nothing to help him. If Heidegger is uninterested in the idea of God, Sartre has positively and almost vindictively rejected it. The norms and standards accepted by the majority of men, merely because they come from the past, are irrelevant and can give no guidance. Man is alone, and it is his business to create himself:

Freedom coincides at its roots with the non-being which is at the heart of man. For a human being to *be* is to choose himself; nothing comes to him either from without or within himself that he can receive or accept. He is wholly and helplessly at the mercy of the unendurable necessity to make himself, even in the smallest details of his existence. Thus freedom is not *a* being, it is *the* being of man, that is to say his non-being. . . . Man cannot be at times free and at other times a slave; either he is always and entirely free, or he is not free at all.[19]

In Sartre 'the absurd', which as we saw for Kierkegaard meant 'that which cannot be reduced to rule', has come to mean that which is totally meaningless and irrational. There are no meanings in life except those which man himself projects upon it. His business is not to relate himself to some existing values, but to create his own values as he goes along. The nature of an act cannot be foreseen until it has actually taken place. So, if we refer to any act as moral, this must be taken as a judgement not on the act in itself, but on the man who acted—did he act in the full exercise of the freedom which is the prerogative and the burden of man?

Sartre is keenly aware of the difference between the existence of objects and the existence of persons. One of his besetting fears is that of being reduced to the level of an object. Therefore 'the other' is to him always a threat, a menace, and not a means of liberation into fellowship. How is this to be understood? Another looks at me. As he fixes me with his eye, I become the *object* of his thought—he thinks of me as this or that—Frenchman, writer, merchant, or whatever it may be. By doing so he reduces me from the level of a personal

[18] *L'Être et le Néant*, p. 515.   [19] ibid. p. 516.

subject to that of an object, a thing. So he menaces my freedom, he appropriates me and enslaves me to himself. 'It is clear that the whole of this dialectic . . . rests upon the complete denial of *me* as subject, that is to say upon the denial of communion. For Sartre this word has no meaning at any possible level, not to speak of its religious or mystical sense.'[20]

Now, here as so often, Sartre has stumbled upon something that is of great importance. It is the fact that we constantly think of one another in less than personal fashion, that in our minds we do reduce others to the level of objects or things. But Sartre's reaction to this is one that is very familiar as a symptom in those who are suffering from one form or another of mental ill-health—the identification of oneself with the thought of another: 'If someone has thought of me as inferior, then I am inferior, and that is painful.' The reality of the situation is entirely different. If someone has thought of me in an unworthy way, or as something different from what I really am, or merely as a specimen of a class, he reveals his own imperfection and may have done himself grave harm. But he has done nothing whatever to me, *unless I identify him with myself.* The truly free man is the one who can go on his own way without being unduly elated or depressed by what others may think of him.

Sartre seems never to have conceived the possibility of a genuinely 'I—Thou' relationship.[21] He is familiar with the cool appraising stare of the destructive other. He seems never to have encountered that other and unmistakable look in the eye of, it may be, someone we have never seen before, which sends out an immediately apprehensible message as from an 'I' to a 'Thou', and asks for an answering message in return. Once this personal relation has been established, there can be no question of the one self destroying the other or desiring the destruction of the other. Each enjoys the other in freedom, and maintains the freedom of the other. Each is to the other a cause of the enrichment of life. All this Sartre seems unable to understand. According to him, I can seek to possess the other—in that case I reduce the other to the status of an object, of a thing; or I can allow myself to be possessed, and in that case I permit myself

[20] Gabriel Marcel, *The Philosophy of Existence* (Eng. trans. 1948), pp. 54–55.

[21] The phrase has become familiar through the thought of another thinker, who probably would not call himself an Existentialist, though he is often classed with them (as by Will Herberg in his book *Four Existentialist Theologians*)—Martin Buber (1878–1965). The whole basis of Buber's thought is precisely that distinction between persons and things with which we are so much concerned in this chapter.

to be reduced to the level of an object, a thing. In neither case is love or community possible.

The point to which Sartre is prepared to carry this perverse understanding of human relationships comes out well in the astonishing passage in which he deals with generosity[22]:

Giving is a primitive form of destruction. . . . So generosity is above all else a destructive function. The passion to give, which at certain moments seizes certain people, is above all else a passion for destruction. . . . But this passion for destruction, which underlies generosity, is nothing else than a passion to possess. Everything that I abandon, everything that I give, I enjoy in a superior manner by means of the gift that I make of it. . . . But at the same time the gift casts a spell on the one to whom I give it. . . . To give is to impose servitude on another. . . . Generosity is thus a feeling structured by the existence of the other, and which manifests a preference for appropriation by way of destruction.[23]

This is cleverly written but perverse. And here perhaps we touch the root of the perversity of much in Sartre's writing. He has never understood the true nature of human relatedness. Man is lonely. But his loneliness is not such as Sartre has imagined it to be; there are other selves that can reach out to us in sympathy and helpfulness, but they cannot do so, unless we in our turn are open to receive what they are able to give.

It is not surprising that the final word in Sartre's philosophy is one of rather acid pessimism and frustration. On man is laid the heavy burden of perpetually creating man. Yet this is an aim that can never be achieved; and if it could be achieved, what would be the value of the achievement?

All human reality is a passion, in that it forms the plan of losing itself in order to lay a foundation for being, and at the same time to constitute that Consciousness (*En-soi*) which escapes contingency by being its own foundation, the *Ens causa sui*, which the religious call God. So the passion of man is the opposite of the passion of Christ; for man loses himself, in so far as he is man, in order that God may be born. But the idea of God is self-contradictory, and we lose ourselves in vain. Man is a futile passion.[24]

Albert Camus (1913–59), whose tragic death was a very grave loss to European literature, had many points of contact with Sartre,

---

[22] I note that Gabriel Marcel also deals with this passage in *The Philosophy of Existence*, p. 60, calling it 'his astonishingly distorted analysis of generosity'.
[23] *L'Être et le Néant*, pp. 684–5.   [24] *L'Être et le Néant*, p. 708.

and for a time worked closely with him in Paris.[25] But whereas Sartre represents a gospel of meaninglessness of which the logical conclusion would seem to be despair, Camus seems to represent Existentialism feeling its way towards the belief that there may after all be meanings and values, and that out of despair a new hope may be born.

If it were necessary to select one book as representative of Existentialist thinking and striving, I would be inclined to choose Camus's *L'Homme Révolté* (The Rebel).[26] In this extraordinarily able book Camus traces the principles and the imperfections of the European revolution. He is himself committed to the principles of revolution. Yet he is deeply disturbed by the evident fact that revolution leads to killing, and to the justification of much that is evidently unjustifiable. 'We have arrived at the period of premeditation and of the perfect crime . . . it is philosophy which can serve for every purpose, even for that of transforming murderers into judges.'[27] How has this come about?

The text of the book may be said to be the famous phrase of Nietzsche, 'God is dead'. To understand this, it is necessary to look back to the context in which Nietzsche (1844–1900) used the phrase. He does not regard himself as the violent iconoclast, dethroning a God who is still sitting in authority on his throne; he is the cool observer, remarking the fact, which others do not yet seem to have noticed, that Dagon has fallen from his throne, and asking what is to be done about it.

Nietzsche set out his idea in the form of a parable. A madman ran into the market-place calling out 'I seek God'. The bystanders, who did not really believe in God, were amused and said, 'Why? Is he lost? Has he taken a sea-voyage? Has he emigrated?' But the madman cried out again, 'Where is God gone? I mean to tell you. *We have killed him*, you and I! We are all his murderers! . . . Is not the magnitude of this deed too great for us? Shall we not ourselves have to become God merely to seem worthy of it? There never was a greater event—and on account of it, all who are born after us belong to a higher history than any . . . hitherto.' But the madman was before his time. The meaning of his message could not reach his hearers. And so he went into one church after another, and intoned

---

[25] The period of co-operation and the rupture between the two men has been pitilessly displayed by Simone de Beauvoir in her Goncourt Prize novel *Les Mandarins* (Paris, 1954).   [26] Paris, 1951. Eng. trans. 1953.   [27] op. cit. p. 13.

his *Requiem aeternam deo*. When asked what he was doing, he replied, 'What are these churches now, if they are not the tombs and monuments of God?'[28]

Nietzsche, with the penetration of genius, had fixed upon the great new phenomenon of his time, the gradual fading out of the consciousness of God from the mind of Western man. What had begun in the second half of the nineteenth century has gone very much further in the twentieth. What are we to do about it? One answer obviously would be that we must put God back upon his throne—if he is dead we must bring him back to life, because we cannot do without him. But that, says Nietzsche, is exactly what cannot be done. God, being dead, is dead for good. We have to recognize that the old ideas of transcendence, the old static values of goodness, truth and beauty are gone for good. There can never be a replacement of the old transcendence. There can only be an endless striving forward in response to the dynamism and upward striving of life. This is the meaning of the will to power.

Man in the past has been dependent upon God. In order that man might enter into the fullness of his inheritance it was necessary that God should die. Once man has recognized the reality of the situation, he can move forward into the stage in which man is transformed into Superman; no longer dependent on a Creator, he is himself the creator of his future.[29]

We recognize the familiar Existentialist pattern of 'man for himself'. But is it really the case that man can exist without any form of transcendence? Is it possible that the nihilism, the despair, the self-destruction, the mutual destruction, by which the progress of the revolution has been marked, are due just to the disappearance of the transcendent dimension? Is the affirmation that 'God is dead' quite such good news as it appeared to be to those who first affirmed it?

Camus does not come to the point of openly accepting this conclusion. Yet towards the end of his book there is a rather striking change of mood.

This comes out first in what Camus has to say about art. The strict revolutionary, if he is an orthodox Marxist, should not be able

---

[28] F. Nietzsche, *Die fröhliche Wissenschaft* (1882).

[29] The distorted application of Nietzsche's ideas by the totalitarians has shed discredit on his name. Naturally, no Christian can accept his ideas; but it is important to recognize that he was a serious thinker, trying to do justice to the realities of life as he had apprehended them.

to admit the possibility of art at all. There is no room in his world for imagination or creativity. Science excludes both. Nothing new can ever really happen, because history is merely the explication of that which in principle was there from the beginning. Equally, the fully consistent Existentialist should not be able to admit the existence of art. For all things exist in the fugitiveness of a perpetual becoming in which there can be no meaning or order. A good deal of modern art seems intended precisely to express this meaninglessness, the brokenness of man's inner life. But traditionally the artist is the man who fixes reality in a moment, who expresses that unity of the universal and the particular after which Hegel aspired. 'The great creators are those who, like Piero della Francesca, give the impression that the fixation has just taken place, that at that precise moment the projector stopped dead.'[30]

Is the artist merely imposing on things an order and a beauty that are not there at all? Or is he right when he says that his creativity is of the nature of response, a discovery of a deeper reality than that which lies merely on the surface of things?

Nietzsche could refuse to admit the existence of any transcendence, moral or divine, maintaining that to admit any such transcendence would lead men to take a low view of this world and this life. But it may be that there is a living transcendence, of which beauty is the promise, which could lead us to prefer this mortal and limited world to any other possible world.[31]

The revolution is based on the conviction that this world can be made better than it is. The artist lives in the same tension between 'that which is' and 'the better world'. Is he entirely wrong? It is not enough simply to exist. Every man craves for some principle of unity within his existence, some hint at least of meaning. The artist is expressing for us that which is within us all:

It is not enough to live. Man needs a destiny, and that without waiting for the arrival of death. It is therefore correct to say that man has the idea of a better world than that which now exists. But 'better' in this sense does not mean *different;* it does mean *unified.*[32]

The second point is the recognition that the grim revolutionaries have banished the idea of joy from the world: 'For this reason they have wished to wipe out joy from the picture of the world, and to postpone it to a later date.' But when the revolution has reached this

---

[30] *L'Homme Révolté*, p. 317.   [31] op. cit. p. 319.   [32] op. cit. p. 324.

limit of destructive malice, the true revolutionary must call into existence another revolution against it:

> We are already at this extremity. At the end of this darkness, it is inevitable that a light should appear. Already we divine its existence, all that is needed is that we should struggle in order that it may come into existence. Beyond nihilism, amid the ruins, we are all preparing for a rebirth. But few are yet aware of this. . . . We shall choose Ithaca, the faithful earth, bold and yet sober thinking, lucid action, and the generosity of the man who knows. In the light, the world continues to be our first and our final love.[33]

Camus himself would never admit that he was moving in the direction of what a Christian would call faith. He affirmed that his famous novel *La Peste* (1947) (*The Plague*, 1948) was in fact one of the most anti-Christian of all his works. This strange book is the story of the city of Oran under an imaginary visitation of the plague, and of the actions and reactions of the men who have to live with this terror. Once again, man cannot turn to any transcendent reality, to any God, to help him out of his misery; his only resources are in himself. Yet out of the terror emerges beauty, and a picture of what can only be called a kind of secularized and non-religious saintliness. At the end the doctor Rieux, who has endured the suffering of the whole period of tragedy, leaves on record his judgement that 'in times of disaster one learns that there is more in men to admire than to despise'. He is the type of all those men who, for all the torments of their own inner self-contradictions, knowing that they cannot be saints, do not admit that disaster should tyrannize over mankind, and take upon themselves the responsibility of being doctors.[34]

But is this very far from Christian faith? Camus avoids asking the obvious but ultimate questions. What kind of a world is this that can produce in the men who dwell in it compassion for their kind? And why in the world should any man take the trouble both to feel and to exercise that compassion? In his more recent works Camus seemed to have shied away from this kind of question, as though he were afraid of the final point to which his thought might lead him. But there were those among his admirers who felt that sooner or later he would be compelled by his own honesty to recognize all that was implied in the admissions that he had made. Death came too soon, and interrupted the pilgrimage. But perhaps it is not unfair to

---

[33] *L'Homme Révolté*, pp. 376–7.
[34] *La Peste*, p. 331.

describe the thought of Camus as 'Existentialism in search of a faith'.[35]

In the third of our trio of thinkers, Gabriel Marcel, Existentialism has found a faith.

Born in 1889, Marcel is rather older than the other French Existentialists. And throughout his career he has followed a highly individual way. Interested from a very early age in philosophy, Marcel found himself increasingly dissatisfied with what he read. The only true starting-point for a philosopher must be the incredible richness of the actual data of everyday life; this being so, the more we reduce things to a system, the further we shall move from reality. Science can build up assured results; it is not so with philosophy:

The stage always remains to be set; in a sense everything always starts from zero, and a philosopher is not worthy of the name unless he not only accepts but wills this harsh necessity. . . . This perpetual beginning again, which may seem scandalous to the scientist or the technician, is an inevitable part of all genuinely philosophical work; and perhaps it reflects in its own order the fresh start of every new awakening and of every birth. . . . The conviction that reality cannot be 'summed up' . . . came to me very early. . . . It seemed to me from then on that there was a danger of making an illicit use of the idea of integration, and that the more one relied on the richest and most concrete data of experience, the less this idea appeared to be applicable to reality.[36]

It is interesting to note that in those early days Marcel had not heard of Heidegger or Jaspers. He was working on his own, and we may suppose that similar causes produced rather similar effects. Clearly the attitude to which Marcel had been led was a profoundly religious one; it is not altogether surprising that in 1928 he felt himself led to ask for baptism in the Roman Catholic Church.

How, then, as a Christian does Marcel remain in the ranks of the Existentialists, and can he point the way for us towards a Christian understanding of Existentialism? It may be convenient to sum up what we have to say on this subject under the three heads of Incarnation, Mystery and Sensitiveness.

[35] In the *Journal de Genève* for 26 February 1960 I found quoted this very striking word of Camus: 'The certainty of a God who would lend significance to life is far more attractive than that of the power to do evil with impunity.' I do not know the source of the quotation.

[36] G. Marcel, *The Philosophy of Existence* (1949), pp. 93-4.

1. The plain fact is that man is not simply a thinking instrument. We must take account of him in the totality of his existence; and that means, to start with, that we must recognize the elementary fact that man is a body, and that it is in the first place through the body alone that all experience comes to him. This is the basic affirmation of Existentialism, as against the rationalism which would tend to identify the reality of man with his thought, and which since the time of Descartes has dominated the greater part of Western philosophical thinking.

This amounts to saying that it is impossible to make any real distinction between

Existence
Consciousness of oneself as existent
Consciousness of oneself as linked to a body, as incarnate. . . .
In the first place, an existential view of reality cannot be other, as it seems, than that of an incarnate personality.[37]

A little further on Marcel speaks of incarnation as 'the central datum of metaphysics . . . the situation of a being who is revealed to himself as linked to a body'.[38] Marcel is, of course, not using the term 'incarnation' in any technical or theological sense. He is merely recognizing the unity of human personality as the basis for the unity of human experience and human thought. But it can hardly be doubted that this apprehension is related to Marcel's Christian faith. When his concepts were enlarged to include the idea of revelation, it seemed to him natural and appropriate that revelation should come by way of incarnation, through the actual entry of the divine into the conditions of earthly life as we experience it.

2. For Marcel the difference between a problem and a mystery is fundamental, and it is related to the difference between contemplation, a purely rational activity, and engagement, in which the total man wrestles with the complexities of an existential situation:

A problem is something which I encounter, which I find set out before me in its totality, and which through that very fact I can apprehend and set to work to solve—whereas a mystery is something in which I am myself engaged, and of which it is therefore impossible to think except as of a sphere in which the distinction between 'in front of me' and 'within me' loses its significance and its initial value. . . . Certainly it is always possible (both logically and psychologically) to degrade a mystery by turning it into a problem. But that is always a harmful method of operating; its

[37] G. Marcel, *Être et Avoir* (1938), pp. 9-10.   [38] ibid. p. 11.

sources must be looked for in a certain corruption of the intelligence. What the philosophers call 'the problem of evil' is a specially instructive example of this degradation.[39]

Once again, it is to be noted that Marcel is not using the term 'mystery' in a technically Christian sense; indeed his use of the term is not that which is to be found in the New Testament. But it is part of his standing protest against the shallowness of the clear rationalist picture of the world in which nothing is left to the imagination; and in this way it draws near to the Christian apprehension of the universe in depth.

3. As a Christian Marcel has entered into the world of faith. What place does he now accord to philosophy? Does he attribute to it any particular usefulness? Like other Existentialists Marcel has given expression to a great many of his ideas through drama and autobiography. Even in his Gifford Lectures he can hardly be said to have reduced his thinking to systematic order—he would perhaps say that, if he had done so, he would have killed it. Yet it is clear that he does regard philosophic thinking as a genuinely human activity, and one which can have a special value of its own:

The immense service which philosophy could perform for us . . . would be to awaken us increasingly, even before our death, to that reality which unquestionably surrounds us on every side, but to which, as a result of our situation as free beings, we have the terrible power of presenting a systematic refusal. Everything shows more and more clearly that it is possible for us, in some fashion, to seal hermetically the prison in which we choose to live. . . . On the other hand, in proportion as we learn to pay attention to the invitations, often faint but innumerable, which stream out from the invisible world, all perspectives are transformed. I mean that they are transformed *here* in this lower world; for in the same breath life itself is transformed and clothed with a dignity to which it could not possibly aspire, if regarded as no more than an excrescence produced in some strange fashion in a universe which of its own nature is alien to spirit and to all the demands of spirit.[40]

In Gabriel Marcel the Christian dialogue with the Existentialists has begun from within the ranks of the Existentialists themselves. A further illustration of this is to be found in the theology of Rudolf Bultmann. Bultmann has become widely known through his plea for the 'Demythologisation' of the New Testament—the

[39] G. Marcel, *Le Mystère de l' Être* (Gifford Lectures), i. 227.
[40] G. Marcel, *Le Mystère de l' Être*, ii. 187.

removal of the mythological elements from the New Testament in order that the proclamation of it may become intelligible to the men of to-day—and the somewhat confused controversy that has raged on this subject since the publication of Bultmann's Essay in 1941.[41] But it seems likely that in retrospect this controversy will not seem after all very important. The real significance of Bultmann's thought lies in his attempt to take hold of Existentialist thinking as the right philosophy for the understanding of the New Testament and for the exposition of it in the modern world.

Bultmann's debt to Heidegger is self-evident. He starts from the same problem. What is being? But in a very real sense Bultmann begins where Heidegger stops. What he is concerned about is man's being before God. Heidegger has rejected the idea of God on Existentialist grounds; Bultmann would agree in rejecting any idea of God which is no more than a rationally constructed hypothesis, just as he rejects any theology of the 'natures' of Christ. God in himself must remain for ever unknown to me. But there is another possibility, the possibility of 'God-for-me', of a God who turns himself to me in order that I may turn to him.

This opens out the familiar contrast between authentic and unauthentic existence. To a large extent Bultmann accepts Heidegger's analysis of the latter. It is the world of use and wont, of conventional judgements, of the loss of liberty in the adaptation of the self to norms; here man feels 'the other' as a threat, becomes wary of him, closes himself against his brother. Man can escape from this lower and unauthentic world when he turns to God; and this can only be accomplished through an act of self-commitment, of decision for God. The word *Entscheidung*, decision, is one of the most characteristic of all Bultmann's words.

The change from the unauthentic to the authentic is set forth by Bultmann under three main headings:

1. There is, first, the concept of a new understanding of the self, of man's situation in the world and before God. Even Paul's conversion is understood in terms of this new understanding. But of course, 'understanding' in Bultmann's sense of the words means far more than any mere intellectual process:

If by understanding Bultmann meant primarily a theoretical activity, then to speak of a new understanding of the self would seem to be a very

[41] On all this, see in considerable detail G. Miegge, *Gospel and Myth in the Thought of Rudolf Bultmann* (Eng. trans. by S. C. Neill, 1960), with a very full bibliography.

inadequate account alike of the teaching of Jesus, the conversion of the apostle and the Christian life. But in the sense of understanding which has been explained, and which seems close to the New Testament meaning of the term, a new understanding of the self means nothing less than a complete reorientation of the entire personality. It is equivalent to a new life.[42]

2. This new life is to be understood in terms of liberation from the past. Here at last we meet a word which we have not yet encountered in our study of the Existentialists—forgiveness. Unauthentic existence is passed in the vicious circle of cause and consequence, from which there seems no way to break free. Man is what his history has made him; he is weighed down and imprisoned by the past. But authentic existence means precisely liberation from the past. What has happened can, of course, never be undone; but the man who has decided for God is the free man; the past can no longer tyrannize over him and determine his future. The forgiveness of God, declared in the Cross of Jesus Christ, stands between past and future, to rob the past of its power and to declare the future open with its illimitable possibilities.

3. This means that the future is a reality. It is the character of authentic existence that it is open to the future. It is here that Bultmann the Christian radically parts company with Heidegger. He recognizes the reality of the various threats to human existence. But the last word is not with nothingness; God has revealed to man the reality and the assurance of eternal life.

If asked how he knows all this, Bultmann has his reply ready— and here again we shall note how far he goes beyond the Existentialists. The God of whom he speaks is not a lay figure; he is a God who acts. In the death and resurrection of Jesus Christ God has come towards us, has decisively manifested the nature of authentic existence and challenged us to accept it. It is only through 'decision', acceptance, that we can know of the doctrine whether it be true or not.[43]

It is clear that there are already lively, and not altogether hostile, contacts between Existentialism and Christian faith. Before summing

---

[42] J. Macquarrie, *An Existentialist Theology* (1955), p. 66.

[43] The weakness of Bultmann's position is that he ascribes so little importance to the actual historical Jesus, and that he takes up a very negative attitude to the resurrection of Jesus as a historical event. But this falls outside the scope of this chapter, in which we are concerned only to consider the Existential aspects of Bultmann's thought.

up this chapter by indicating briefly the way in which we may hope that the dialogue will advance, we may turn aside to consider a point which may be of interest to British readers.

All the Existentialists so far mentioned in this chapter have been continental writers—French, German and Danish. Is there, then, no English Existentialism? This point has been touched on by Professor Paul Tillich, and a negative answer returned:

England is the only European country in which the Existential problem of finding a new meaning for life had no significance, because there positivism and the religious tradition lived on side by side, united by a social conformism which prevented radical questions about the meaning of human 'Existence'. It is important to note that the one country without an Existentialist philosophy is that in which during the period from 1830 to 1930 the religious tradition remained strongest. This illustrates once more the dependence of the Existentialist philosophy on the problems created by the breakdown of the religious tradition on the European continent.[44]

There is a point which, I think, Tillich has missed—the change which came over British philosophy just at the time when the great religious impulses of the nineteenth century were beginning to die down. Hegelianism had a very long life in England. Introduced to Oxford by Benjamin Jowett about the middle of the century, it was adapted to the English mind by T. H. Green (1836–82), and maintained in slightly different forms by F. H. Bradley (1846–1924), Bernard Bosanquet (1848–1923) and J. E. McTaggart (1866–1925). All these men were at the height of their influence at the turn of the century, and Bradley's *Appearance and Reality* (1893) was not without reason regarded as 'the most original work in British metaphysics in the 19th century'. But already a reaction was in preparation, against the 'Ideas' in the Hegelian sense, and in favour of a very different apprehension of reality.

Two men, neither of whom was a Christian, have profoundly influenced British philosophy in the first half of the twentieth century—G. E. Moore and Bertrand Russell. At the time at which these two men began to be interested in philosophy Kant and Hegel filled

[44] Paul Tillich, *Theology of Culture* (1959), p. 108. Tillich, for all his learning, does not know England as he knows Germany and America, and I would not subscribe to every word of his analysis. Nor am I convinced that it is quite true that the Existentialists 'are the expression of the great revolution within and against Western industrial society which was prepared in the nineteenth century and is being carried out in the twentieth'. op. cit. p. 111.

the heavens; but, according to the testimony of Russell, 'Moore, first, and I closely following him, climbed out of the mental prison and found ourselves again at liberty to breathe the free air of a universe restored to reality'. A philosopher who could write an Essay called 'A Defence of Common Sense',[45] is clearly on the Existentialist side in the controversy between 'the System' and the fullness of human experience. To quote again from Russell's testimony:

It is difficult for the present generation to realize what academic philosophy was like when he and I were young. . . . With Moore, British philosophy returned to the kind of work in which it had been pre-eminent in former centuries. Those who are too young to remember the academic reign of German idealism in English philosophy after T. H. Green can hardly appreciate what Moore achieved in the way of liberation from intellectual fetters.

Much has happened in British philosophy since 1940. And the sense of the brokenness of life, which has been so strong on the continent, is perhaps beginning to be felt in Britain as it was not felt in earlier years. It may be that 'the angry young men' are the beginnings of a peculiarly British form of Existentialism; it is clear that their leaders have learned much from Camus and from Sartre. If this understanding of 'the angry young men' is correct, it is to be hoped that they will encounter something other than uncomprehending hostility in the Christian Churches.

For, deeply as we may at points disagree with them, there are many things in the Existentialists that all Christians must recognize as admirable. Best of all, perhaps, is their determination to be done with nonsense, to look at all things with a calm, appraising, disillusioned eye, and to accept the reality of things, however disagreeable and discouraging it may be. Admirable also is the courage which will follow a line of thought to its ultimate and bitter conclusion; admirable the courage which refuses to accept the comforts of God and religion, if acceptance involves in any degree a surrender of intellectual integrity.

Many of the contentions of the Existentialists are true.

It is true that ethical standards and norms and the traditions of society cannot be relied on to give man the guidance that he needs. Every moment is different from every other moment, and each one

---

[45] G. E. Moore, in *Contemporary British Philosophy* (2nd. ser., 1925).

makes its own special and individual demand which cannot be reduced to any rule.

It is true that thought which does not lead to action is barren. It is the business of the thinker not merely to understand the world but also to change it.

It is true that truth is not something that can be done up in a package and learned in a formula. Communication of any truth that matters can only be indirect, and it can be apprehended only by a process which is more than merely intellectual.

It is true that life can be lived only in the atmosphere of decision; what is meant is a readiness for constantly renewed decision, and not a decision that can be taken once for all. Every decision involves a risk—a risk of losing oneself; but this risk has to be accepted as a part of human living.

It is true that man can live only in freedom. But this freedom implies freedom to be in revolt, to rebel against convention that time has made unreal, against everything that is insincere and hypocritical, against the partial idea that would set itself up as absolute truth.

None of this need be strange for Christians, since it is all contained, though not in such terms as these, in the doctrine of the Holy Spirit. If Existentialists could understand what is meant by the doctrine of the Holy Spirit, they might find that many of their objections to the Christian faith and even to the Christian Church would fall to the ground. If the Church were to take this doctrine seriously, it would recognize itself as being in a state of continuous creation. Yesterday's truth is no longer sufficient for to-day; indeed it is no longer truth, unless it has been rediscovered to-day in its pristine reality. Christian life must be a continuous process of self-criticism, in a very real sense of self-creation. It is the task of the Holy Spirit to lead the Church into all truth. But there is no reason to suppose that this task has yet been accomplished. Once the Spirit is allowed free play, movement is recovered, and the Church becomes a living, breathing thing.

In the light of this doctrine, there are certain questions the Existentialist answer to which the Christian may rightly ask the Existentialist to reconsider.

1. The Existentialists, especially those of the type of Heidegger and Sartre, tend to assume that the reality of man is most clearly seen and experienced in his loneliness. But is this true? Is man in

his loneliness, the wolf-child, genuinely human? Is not the richest life that which is most fully related to other selves, in marriage, parenthood, friendship and the rest, and which has learned to find in the other not the enemy but the fulfilment of the self? 'The fellowship of the Holy Spirit' is no meaningless Christian phrase. Where the Holy Spirit is at work, the self ceases to be either aggressive or possessive. It has no desire either to subject other selves to itself or to rob them of their freedom. The self is willing to make itself the servant of the other. In such relatedness fellowship is the fulfilment and not the death of human freedom.

2. We fully accept the Existentialist dictum that a large part of a man's business is to make himself. The self is not given ready-made; it has to be acquired by disciplined and devoted effort. Much of this can be accomplished only by trial and error, and there is no certain and infallible guidance. Yet we may venture to suggest to the Existentialist that man is not left without any clue as he attempts to find his way in the maze of existence. The pattern of human existence is already there, not in a code or a manual of ethics but in the life and person of Jesus Christ. One life cannot give immediate guidance or direction to another life. But it can be inexhaustible in significance. This is the meaning of the Christian claim that the free man is being recreated by the Holy Spirit after the likeness of him who made him, namely Jesus Christ.

3. The Existentialist tends to rule out the possibility of grace. As we have seen, Sartre roughly and violently rejects it. But this is hardly a matter that can be settled on *a priori* grounds. The Existentialist first encloses himself in the loneliness of his own personal existence, in which he is shut off from any help that any human hand could give. Then, by a process of extrapolation, he concludes that there is no help anywhere in the universe. But this is circular reasoning. The reality of grace cannot be demonstrated in the same way as a proposition in geometry. In the last resort it can only be experienced. But those who have experienced life as full of kindness, who are themselves prepared to be the servants of other selves and are willing to ask the ultimate question as to the nature of a universe in which such things are present realities, may find it not unreasonable to think that human kindness exists because there is an ultimate kindness hidden at the heart of the universe. If this hidden kindness is not passive but active, the most appropriate term for the expression of its nature is 'grace'.

4. It is quite true that at the end of every man's life stands death. It is foolish to forget this. It is only right that man should have the courage to face his end, to recognize the limits that death will impose on all that he can do here, and so learn like the Greeks to think only mortal thoughts. He must be prepared also to face the *possibility* that death may mean total extinction—the end of everything. But the Existentialist must not be surprised if some of his interlocutors are not prepared to accept in this connexion mere dogmatic assertion offered without proof. In a matter where demonstration is impossible, we do well to keep a mind open in either direction. The Christian has no right to ask for more than this. If he feels within himself a joyful certainty that death is a beginning rather than an end, this must come from his assurance that a living Spirit is at work within him. For himself he can confidently believe that 'if the Spirit of him who raised Jesus from the dead dwells in you, he who raised Christ Jesus from the dead will give life to your mortal bodies also through his Spirit which dwells in you' (Rom. 8.11). He cannot convey this faith to the Existentialist by any form of direct communication; he has the right to affirm that that alone is a true Existentialism which takes account of all the possibilities of human existence, without excluding any.

CHAPTER IX

CHRISTENDOM

IF we speak in terms of the comparative study of religions, it is not easy always to arrive at an understanding of what it is that is to be compared. There is always a tendency on the part of the student to become an apologist—to compare the best in what he knows and professes with the worst and weakest of the systems other than his own, and so to win cheap and insignificant victories that settle nothing. It is to be hoped that in this book we have avoided this danger; we have honestly tried to set out the other religions of the world as their adherents see them, recognizing that there can be no real dialogue until the best in one is confronted by the best in the other.

It is true, however, that in our exposition we have tended to by-pass one solid and inescapable fact—the existence of Christendom. The Christian faith is not an ideal or a memory; it is not a theory or a set of convictions. It is a faith that for good and evil has become incorporate in a body, a Church, which has had a long and complex history, which is mainly situated in the West and is inextricably linked with the history of the nations of the West, and which manifests many of the strengths and weaknesses of other human societies and corporations.

Many Christians resent these painfully material associations of their faith, and in one way or another refuse to recognize them.

Some have maintained that Christianity is not a religion, and that therefore, while purely outward comparison of the Christian Church with other religious bodies may be possible, the Gospel is incommensurable with anything else, and therefore cannot be compared with anything else. The question whether Christianity is or is not a religion is very largely a matter of definition. If by religion we mean man's attempt to make himself at home in his own world, to justify himself, to lift himself up to the level of God, naturally the Gospel belongs to an entirely different world.[1] But if we think in

---

[1] Dr. Hendrick Kraemer seems in many contexts to take this view of 'religion', e.g. in *Religion and the Christian Faith* (1956), p. 334, he writes: 'Man wants God, but somehow he wants Him in his own way. Therefore the deepest *Ahnungen*, the highest flights, the sincerest contrition, remain in the sphere of a lofty moralism or spirituality. Nowhere do we find a radical repudiation of every possible man-made spiritual world.'

terms of such concepts as revelation, worship, obedience to the divine, we must recognize that there are such similarities between the Christian way and other ways as enable those who are walking in the various ways to talk to one another with at least some possibility of mutual understanding.

Some would fall back, in self-defence, on the old distinction between the visible and the invisible Church. The visible Church may be poor and wretched and naked and blind; the invisible Church is without spot or wrinkle or any such thing. For Christians this is a useful, indeed almost a necessary, distinction. It is of no interest whatever to non-Christians. For them the Gospel cannot be separated from its integument; it presents itself to them in terms of that which they can see and hear and experience in relation to the visible Church.

Other Christians feel that the empirical Church is involved in so grave a betrayal of true Christian faith that the only way to live Christianly is to go out from the Church and start again. Certain individuals may have experienced a real vocation to make such a radical break with the past. But when we are face to face with the non-Christian world, the attempt to make such a break will avail us nothing. We cannot deny our own past; we are what the history of centuries has made us. Whatever we try to make of ourselves, the Gospel will always take the shape of that vessel in which it is carried. This has always been the experience of those who have gone out to preach the blessed Gospel of salvation without particular forms or attachments; they have ended by reproducing with singular exactness the form of Christian life to which they have been themselves accustomed, even when they believe themselves to have given their converts the fullest scope to develop in liberty.

Theologically, we have been discovering anew that the Church is not an appendage to the Gospel; it is itself a part of the Gospel. The Gospel cannot be separated from that new people of God, in which its nature is to be made manifest. Practically, this has always been known to everyone who has ever attempted to talk with the adherents of faiths other than his own. Even where it is only two individuals who meet to talk, each brings with him the whole of what he is and of what his faith has made of him. The community is implicit in the individual, the Church in the believer. We may feel that the Gospel towers over us, judging us; yet, as far as the world is concerned, we are ourselves the Gospel; there is no other.

Christian faith, then, always presents itself as a strange amalgam of the divine and the human; it nowhere exists in its purity, but always in conjunction with very human and imperfect Christians. If we are prepared to recognize this, it behoves us to take a sternly realistic view of the perils to which the Christian society, just like every other religious society, is exposed by the mere fact of living in the world.

1. In the first place, there is an inevitable tendency for the living experience of faith to harden down into doctrinal formulae. The Gospel starts from the tremendous Person and the glowing poetry of Jesus of Nazareth. It passes through the imaginative and still mainly poetical interpretation of Paul and John. But even before the end of the New Testament period the original inspiration is beginning to die away; the faith once delivered to the saints is already thought of in doctrinal rather than in existential terms. It is not long before we come to the complexities of the Athanasian Creed, and the barren logomachies of the sixth and seventh centuries about matters which are in any case beyond human ken.

2. Secondly, experience becomes frozen in an institution. We start with the glad freedom of voluntary service, in which greatness and authority are measured only by devotion to the cause and by willingness to take the place of a servant. Already in the second generation permanent officials are beginning to appear. The charismatic is being replaced by the institutional. A hierarchy develops. The whole-time servants of the Church expect to be paid for their service and the ecclesiastical career begins to attract. The Church acquires property and even wealth. As early as the fourth century a pagan historian, Ammianus Marcellinus, remarks that no doubt the larger bishoprics, especially that of Rome, are natural objects of ambition to those who hope to acquire them. By this time the Church is not very much different from any other property-owning society. It claims protection from the law and must enter into litigation if its rights are threatened. There is one further stage of possible degradation—if the Church, not content with equality, begins to claim privilege as against other societies. The whole of Christian history shows that this is a temptation to which the Church has always been peculiarly vulnerable; it acquires privileges in time of prosperity, and will then move heaven and earth to see that these privileges are in no way diminished.

3. The life of the Church soon comes to be determined by

tradition. It is taken for granted that those born within the Christian society will be Christians. Provided that they show a minimum of conformity to the rules and practices of the community, they may expect to enjoy its privileges. The ordinances of the faith—baptism, confirmation and the rest—take on a social rather than a religious character, and are observed with little regard to their Christian significance.

4. Finally, the faith comes to be identified with a certain culture. Christianity, dominant so long in the West, is one of the ingredients in Western culture. The Church tends to identify itself with that culture and with the nations in the life of which it finds expression. Then to be a Christian means primarily to be a Western man, and has very little to do with any personal relationship to the Gospel of Jesus Christ.

It is at this point that demonic powers can take hold of a religion, and use it for purposes very different from those to which it ought to be consecrated. For four centuries Western culture has been explosive, dynamic and expansive. It has spread itself abroad through the world. This has been also the period of the great expansion of the Christian Church. However honest Western man may be with himself, there is always the danger that he may desire the propagation of this culture and this faith, because they are his and therefore in his judgement superior to all others. This danger is particularly great when a supposed cultural superiority is associated with economic, or still worse military, power. One who interests himself in the spread of the faith on such terms as these has made himself the master of the Gospel instead of its servant; he is using it to further his own ends. The extent to which Christian missionaries have been imbued with imperialistic aims has doubtless been greatly exaggerated by their critics.[2] Yet there is enough substance in the criticism to make the thoughtful Christian acutely uncomfortable.

Having said all this, we must go on to recognize that each of these four developments—dogma, institution, tradition, culture—

[2] I think that Dr. H. Kraemer is right in his criticism of K. M. Panikkar's *Asia and Western Dominance* (1954): 'This able Indian historian says many cruel, indubitably true things, which should be fully digested, and passes judgments that deserve close attention. It must, however, also be said that the lack of understanding of Christianity and the ultimate motives of its missions is appalling, and leads this erudite Indian . . . into an injustice and superciliousness which can only issue from an unconscious burning resentment.' *Religion and the Christian Faith*, p. 29, n.1.

is inevitable, and that similar phenomena are to be traced in every religion.

1. Religion, we may say, is an experience and should not attempt to be more. But man is by nature a reflective animal, and nothing can prevent him from reflecting on that which he has experienced and attempting to understand it. Every man has in some degree or other the analytic gift; it is through question and analysis that understanding is reached. The moment that this process is applied to religion, the formulation of doctrine has begun. Once the questioning spirit has been aroused, it is no use saying that this or that question must not be asked; sooner or later it will be asked, and some attempt at least to provide an answer must be made.

Islam starts with the tumultuous experience of the Prophet on the mountain. Its technical creed is the shortest and simplest in the world. Yet Islam too has had its period of scholasticism, when subtle question and interpretation grew into a mountain of erudition. The Jews produced the Talmud. In India the Bhagavad Gita is 'revelation'. But questions of interpretation arise; the commentators get to work. Samkara and Ramanuja have both left their classic commentaries, and have shown the diversity of meaning that one text can be made to yield.

The believer is inclined to sigh over the immense outpouring of human labour that has gone into these books, and to wonder whether the scholars have done anything but crush living faith under their mountainous productions. But this is a narrow and unjust view. The importance of doctrine must not be exaggerated; but rightly understood it can serve two useful purposes. It can save later generations from having to do the whole work of question and answer for themselves and from the start. And against certain possible roads it can place a warning that these have been explored and found to lead nowhere. And even doctrine, if it takes such a form as the *Te Deum*, can be turned into an instrument of praise.

2. Almost every new Christian group starts with the idea that it will not become an institution; it will return to the simplicity of the primitive days and will refuse to be weighed down by the worldly considerations that come with wealth and property. Some such groups have been more successful than others in avoiding the steps by which a society is turned into an institution; but the beginnings of the process are observable in almost all of them. At the start there

is no ordained ministry. But ere long one or two begin to stand out as specially gifted, and responsibility comes more and more to fall into their hands. As numbers grow, the work of the ministry becomes more exacting, and can hardly be carried out in the spare time of those who are already earning their daily bread in the world. A demand for a better-educated ministry begins to make itself felt and men must be trained. Most groups find it necessary to own some kind of place of meeting—and at once are launched on all the problems involved in the possession of property. It is possible to watch with interest the development of all these phenomena in the Pentecostal groups, some of which seem to be moving rapidly from 'the sect-type' to 'the Church-type' of organization.

Religions, such as Christianity and Islam, which have regular services of worship and expect the faithful to attend them, are specially faced by the problems of institution and property. The mosque and the church are among the most familiar buildings in the world. Hinduism and Buddhism have a much more flexible organization. Yet every Hindu village has its shrines, probably communally owned by the villagers and maintained by their joint efforts. Every shrine must have its ministrant, though his duties may be few and occasional, and for the fulfilment of those duties he will expect some renumeration.

3. It is impossible to resist the growth of tradition. There is bound to be a difference between one who has been born into the Christian fellowship and the one who has joined it from without of his own free volition. Those who have long worked in a rapidly growing Christian community, like the late Bishop Azariah in the villages of Dornakal, are wont to lament the decline in the second and third generation. Where is the enthusiasm of the first converts? Why have acquiescence, and even apathy, taken so quickly the place of personal conviction and the willingness to suffer? The answer really is obvious. There are two distinct problems and they must be handled quite differently. Nor must it be supposed that all is loss, when the day of first beginnings is over and a new Christian group has moved forward into the life of a settled community. In the first generation everything is discovery and conflict—a situation which lends itself both to high achievement, and also to certain traumatic divisions within the human personality. There is something to be said for the calmer period in which a number of things can be taken for granted, moral standards are accepted in principle though not

always observed in practice, and a deeper process of spiritual development can begin.

As soon as a Christian community is formed it is faced by the problem of the coming generation. In Russia this is settled for the Church by the Government—no religious instruction of any kind may be given to a young person under eighteen. In certain families in the West, in which the parents are of different religion or confession, for the sake of peace and quiet in the home agreement has been reached to keep religion out of it, and 'to let the children make up their own minds, when they are old enough to think for themselves'. But most people would not regard this as a satisfactory solution. Even those Christian bodies which practise only adult baptism do not regard the children of Christian parents as entirely outside the covenant; in fact in many cases infants are solemnly dedicated to God though not baptized. In almost all religious bodies some provision is made for the instruction of the young in the tenets of their religion; it is notable that at the present time even Hinduism, which has relied so much on practice and the externals of devotion, is beginning to feel the need of more formal religious teaching.

Now, it has to be recognized that there is an immense difference between teaching, which can be directly apprehended and even memorized, and that real religious communication which, as Kierkegaard so clearly saw, can be made only indirectly. But to say that one is not the same as the other is not to say that either is unimportant. And, even if no such regular teaching is given, it is impossible to keep religion away from the children. They will ask questions about it, even in Russia. Impressions are forming in them, far below the level of conscious response. Memory may recall only such marginal things as hot-cross buns on Good Friday. Yet probably there are few Jews who are not stirred by some recollection of Passover meals in the old home; and, even in secularized America, there are not a few who recall that Thanksgiving is intended to be a thanksgiving to Almighty God, and is declared to be so every year by the President. Tradition and traditional observance may become the chief obstacles to true religion. They can also form the channels in which the streams of true religion will flow, if the windows of heaven should again be opened.

4. It is vain to imagine that religion can be kept uncontaminated by the process of cultural development. It cannot be kept separate from culture, and it ought not to be kept separate from culture.

Religion is so many-sided a thing that it is bound to affect the life of man at every point. All Western law is in its origin most deeply indebted to the Romans; yet no one concerned with the common law in England can fail to observe the effect on it of the Judaeo-Christian tradition, with its insistence on moral, as distinct from merely legal, responsibility. We take it for granted that Sunday will be a day of rest, but this is a Judaeo-Christian cultural assumtion, and not a universally accepted principle.[3] It is only if he comes to live in a non-Christian country that the Christian will realize to the full the difference between Christendom and the rest of the world. The cultural significance of the weekly rest, quite apart from the question of worship, cannot possibly be exaggerated.[4] This was constantly observed by the non-Christian villager in India, who would call out after the Christian inquirers, 'Go and become Christians, and get a rest on Sunday'. And it was interesting to note, in a partially Christian city like Madras, how many Hindu shopkeepers had come quietly to accept the Christian example.

Religion and culture *ought* not to be separated. This is the point on which Christopher Dawson has so admirably insisted.[5] If religion tries to live in a world of its own, unrelated to the other aspects of the life of man in society, it becomes anaemic, precious and uninteresting, the plaything of those who have a special penchant for that kind of thing. If culture tries to exist without religious sanctions, it becomes demonic; it is then the expression of the titanic in man, of his unbridled lust for self-expression and self-development, unchecked by any higher norms in the light of which man is held to be answerable. In the past religion and culture have always dwelt together as sometimes somewhat uneasy bedfellows. The tragedy of our own day is that for the first time in history they seem irremediably to have fallen apart. Christopher Dawson ends his book with two acute and pregnant observations:

We are faced with a spiritual conflict of the most acute kind, a sort of social schizophrenia which divides the soul of society between a non-moral will to power served by inhuman techniques and a religious faith and moral idealism which have no power to influence human life. There

---

[3] Islam, of course, has its one day of rest in seven, in this following the Judaeo-Christian tradition.

[4] G. von Rad rightly points out that the Jewish sabbath is primarily the day of *rest* for man and beast, and that it is only much later that we hear of religious services being held in connexion with it. *Moses* (Eng. trans. 1960), p. 52.

[5] Notably in *Religion and Culture* (1948), Chapters I and III.

must be a return to unity—a spiritual integration of culture—if mankind is to survive. . . . This does not mean a new religion or a new culture but a movement of spiritual reintegration which would restore that vital relation between religion and culture which has existed at every age and on every level of human development.[6]

If we set out to look for true religion and undefiled, we are not likely to find it. Wherever we encounter it, the gold of pure religion is likely to be mixed with a certain measure of alloy. But this means that every religious faith must live in a state of perpetual self-criticism. The alloy may serve to make religion workable. Carried beyond a certain measure it will assuredly make it unworkable.

Critics of Christendom have an easy task ready to hand. The principles of the Gospel are so lofty that it is not difficult to represent the Churches as in a state of permanent treason against their Lord. It would be unfair, however, not to look at the other side and not to recognize the immense travail of self-criticism which has been going on within the Christian Churches, and precisely along the line of the four developments or dangers which we have been analysing.

1. The Church has inherited a vast system of doctrine, mainly deriving from the contact between Greek and biblical thought in two stages; first directly in the days of the great Greek Fathers and the Christological controversies of the fourth and fifth centuries; secondly in the Middle Ages, when Aristotle came back to the West via Arabia, and the re-fertilization of the Western mind found its most perfectly proportioned expression in the *Summa* of Thomas Aquinas. Almost till our own day Christian doctrinal thinking has moved within the limits of the traditional questions and the categories derived from the enquiring mind of the Greeks. We live in a period of reaction. Those questions and answers were right and necessary at a certain stage of Christian development. Must we not now get behind them, and learn again to think *biblically*, in categories more directly derived from the Christian revelation itself?

In this connexion it is natural to think of the work of Karl Barth. Barth deliberately set himself to eliminate Greek ideas and metaphysical concepts, and to express the whole Christian faith in the framework of the dominating idea of the Word of God as revelation. Even those who least agree with Karl Barth have been compelled to take him seriously; even Roman Catholics have admitted that

[6] Op. cit. pp. 217–18.

he, by his writings, has awoken in them a new enthusiasm for dogmatic theology.

But it would be a grave error to limit the movement of contemporary theology to the Barthian school. Everywhere there is a sense of freedom and discovery. Part of this is due to the new schools of interpretation of the Old Testament, and to a recognition of the special Hebrew genius in its relatedness to the Christian revelation. The Greek mind does not work in the same way as the Hebrew.[7] The answers to our questions to some extent depend on the way in which the questions are framed, and this in turn depends on certain linguistic and psychological structures. Is it not likely that, if we go back to the less abstract, more pictorial, way of thinking of the Hebrew, we shall ask of revelation different questions from those propounded by the Greeks? This point will come before us again in connexion with the right of peoples with an entirely different background, such as the Chinese, to ask of the biblical revelation such questions as would never occur to a Western thinker.

2. In the Churches radical questions are being asked as to the relevance and adequacy of old forms of organization and ministry to contemporary situations.

One of the very oldest structures of the Christian society is the parish, a geographical area within which every soul is the pastoral responsibility of a single shepherd, or of a group of shepherds. This worked admirably in a rural society, when the vast mass of the people lived in small villages and could be personally cared for by the resident parson. Is such a structure relevant in the days of industrial civilization and of the concentration of men in the enormous cities of the modern world? I do not think myself that the parish will ever be superseded. Yet it is reasonable to ask whether the Church should not relate itself to some of the other structures of human life—to the place in which men work as well as to the place in which they sleep. The system of industrial chaplains in Britain and elsewhere is still tentative; but it may claim at least to have drawn attention to possibilities that need to be further worked out.

---

[7] An interesting study of the contrast is T. Boman's *Das Hebräische Denken im Vergleich mit dem Griechischen* (1954) (Eng. trans. *Hebrew Thought Compared with Greek*, London, 1960). This book, valuable as it is, needs to be read in the light of the criticisms directed against it by Professor James Barr in his work *The Semantics of Biblical Language* (1961). There is a difference, but it is less absolute than Boman supposes.

Traditional ministries are not adequately meeting the needs of Christian witness in the world to-day. In this field to-day radical thinking is going on in many places.

Even those who through prejudice or conviction are opposed to the ordination of women to the ministry of the Church are fain to recognize that the Church has failed to make adequate use of the gifts of one half of its membership. What ought to be the special contribution of women to the life of the Church? It may be that we do not know the answer to this question; it is something that the question is being seriously asked.

No Church is satisfied with the use that it is making of its laymen. In such days as these, do we not need a revival of the prophetic as against the more institutional forms of the ministry? And is it not likely that, as in the Old Testament, the majority of those called to exercise this ministry will be laymen? Many of the existing lay movements tend towards an increasing clericalization of the faithful layman, and this is exactly the opposite of what is needed. It is the merit of the Department on the Laity of the World Council of Churches that it has passed beyond this narrow view-point, and tried to view the problem of lay ministry as a function of the total life of the *Laos*, the people of God.

3. The Church of Christ can never completely separate itself from its traditions. But in many areas the simple fact of opposition is making plain to the Churches the truth that they cannot live on their past.

This is most plain in the communist countries, and, in this field as in others, our best evidence seems to come from East Germany. There the traditional structure has been that of the *Volkskirche*, in which everyone is baptized and confirmed and pays Church taxes. Now the communists, with their secular alternative to Confirmation, have rudely broken through all that, and have made it plain that the characteristic dimension of Christian faith is not consent but decision.

This is one of the sharpest instances. But in many other tradition-ally Christian countries the Church has been reminded that it is now in a minority situation. It cannot rely on the general stream of public opinion to carry it forward; it can rely, humanly speaking, only on the wills and the determination of those who have made a definite and personal commitment of themselves to Christ. The traditional is yielding to the existential. This is all to the good, provided that in recognizing the difference between their genuinely committed and their uncommitted adherents the Churches do not develop the faults of a minority which feels itself to be on the defensive. At all times the deeply committed Christians have been a minority; in times when that minority has felt itself to be a dynamic minority, with the future in its hands, its achievements have been sensational, and quite out of proportion to the numbers of those engaged in the Christian enterprise.

4. The Western world is almost morbidly obsessed by a guilt complex over its identification of Christian faith with its own culture. This is so strongly felt by the younger generation as to make difficult any presentation of the call to missionary service overseas. 'When we have made such a mess of things in the West, have we any right to export our culture overseas, and offer it to these others?' If the question is put in this form, clearly the answer can only be 'No'. Yet the whole course of this chapter excludes the other obvious and simple explanation, that we do not go abroad to spread our culture but only to preach the pure Gospel of Jesus Christ our Lord. As we have seen, this is precisely the thing that we can never do—we can go only as ourselves, and that means as specimens of Western man.

It is hardly too much to say that the Western Churches are at the present time making almost frenzied efforts to disentangle the Gospel from the Western habiliments in which it has been clothed.[8] It is not clear that these Churches are as yet fully aware of the complexity of the problem that they have taken in hand. We may note four points which must be kept separate and distinct:

On the whole the Western Churches are now penitent Churches. They have come to recognize that 'empirical Christianity', the Churches as they now are, with their all too human elements and their involvement in the things of this world, stand under the judgement of God, no less than other human structures and organizations, religious or secular. In this sense at least Christianity is 'one of the religions', and must accept the fact that judgement is to begin at the house of God.

The immediate task is to discover how the Gospel can again become the vivifying force in Western culture, how the gap of

---

[8] But note the paradox: 'It is amazing that while the Christian evanglist talks about the need for proclaiming the faith dissociated with the cultural forms which are part of the Western heritage, Hindu religious leaders advocate the dissemination of just these cultural forms as separated from their Christian foundations.' P. D. Devanandan, *The Gospel and Renascent Hinduism* (1959), p. 36.

which Mr. Dawson has so poignantly spoken can be bridged. This is a different task from that of winning back the individual to the faith. It demands the penetration of whole populations by the Christian idea on the emotional and subconscious level, so that the ordinary man comes again to think and to feel in a Christian way even when he is not making any conscious profession of Christian faith. In a word, we have to reverse the process which Nietzsche alleged to have taken place without men's knowing it. Instead of 'God is dead' we must be able to affirm that 'God is alive again in the Western consciousness' or at least that 'God is again striving to be born'.

But the Western Churches cannot hold over their offer of the Gospel to all the world until the process of the recovery of the West has been completed. The dialogue between the religions has begun; it is essential that the Christian voice should be heard in it with ever-increasing clarity; and in many parts of the world the Christian voice can only be a Western voice. But, in their new humility, the Western Churches are prepared to learn from the mistakes of the past. They are better able than they were to distinguish between the essentials of the Gospel and the fortuitous accretions which are dear to the West, but have nothing to do with the central issues of faith in Christ. They go now to offer and not to impose.

In the past it was too readily assumed that out of the seed of of the Gospel only one kind of tree can grow—sow the Word, and what you will see emerge is something like the culture of the Western world. So it was natural for the early Portuguese missionaries to give their converts Portuguese names, some of which their descendants still proudly bear, and to expect them to conform as nearly as possible to the habits of their teachers and their rulers.

Now to a certain extent the analogy of the seed and the tree is correct. The possible forms of Christian living are not infinitely variable. For instance, the Christian society will always be a strictly monogamous society.[9] Such a society is different at its heart from one in which polygamy is permitted and encouraged. Monogamy is more than a Western sociological ideal.

Nor is it necessary to suppose that the West should withhold from others all the good things that have come to it from other than strictly Christian sources. A careful study of Plato and Aristotle

[9] I know that some of my African friends will take me up on this. But a society like our own, which permits a rather wide range of promiscuity and a good deal of secret concubinage, is not thereby constituted a polygamous society.

might be for the Indian theological student an invaluable introduction, by way of contrast, to the stern discipline of learning to think in genuinely biblical categories.

Yet, when these reservations have been made, we are now willing to recognize as never before that the creative powers of the Gospel are greater than we had supposed, and that its working in the kingdoms of men may be more flexible than we have allowed for. Vines are vines all over the world; but the vine has exceptional powers of drawing difference and variety from varying conditions of soil and sun and rain. What a Chinese Christian culture, with a genuinely Chinese and not a Graeco-Roman background might become, we are as yet hardly able to imagine. Yet we have become convinced that such a development would be according to the will of God, and that, if very widely differing patterns of Christian living were to develop in different parts of the world, that would tend to the enrichment and not to the impoverishment of the Church, and to the glorification of Christ and not to His dishonour.

Now it has to be noticed that this Christian tendency towards self-criticism and consequent liberation from the past runs directly counter to what is happening in many other areas of the world. All great cultures in the past have been dependent on a religion. All great religions of the past have expressed themselves in a particular and recognizable pattern of culture. With the rise of nationalism in Asia and Africa, there has been an inevitable tendency to identify national pride, religious tradition, the cultural heritage, and sometimes even the language which has been the vehicle of religion and culture in the past. We noted earlier the way in which Ceylon was brought to the very brink of complete disaster by the attempt of the Buddhist priesthood to insist on Sinhalese as the sole official language of the country. It is true that the emissaries of these faiths in the West sometimes deny the cultural affiliations of their faith. But in the homelands of these faiths there seems to be the beginning of what can only be called a totalitarian outlook, in which nation, state and Church are merged into one single complex unity.

If this is true, it may be that the Christian process of self-criticism which we have been describing will come to be seen in retrospect as one of the great spiritual happenings of our time, and one that can render immense service not only to the Christian faith but to all the other living faiths of the world.

If we are moving into a totalitarian era, as there is good reason to fear that we are, it is essential that there should be one body which recognizes as the principle of its life that, beyond all claims that may be made by the state or any other human structure or society, there are supramundane values to which it is committed, and to which it must be loyal whether in life or in death. In the past, the Church has often been content to be the handmaid or the servant or the ally of the state. If anything has been clearly learned in this century, it is that no such alliance can ever be more than conditional. The state, as one of the orders instituted or permitted by God, is entitled to the loyalty of men. But there is another loyalty which may not in any circumstances be circumscribed or compromised. Faith is coming to be recognized in a new way as the guardian of the freedom of the soul of man.

This may be felt on the national, or the local, or the individual level.

Throughout the whole of the Christian Western tradition, from Constantine onwards, the state has taken the Church under its protection and in various ways made use of it for its own purposes. Gradually and painfully the battle for toleration has been won in most Western countries; but still in most of them there is one dominant form of the Christian religion, which is in some form of association with the state.

It is its radical departure from this tradition that lends its importance to the American experiment of the total separation of Church and state—an importance not yet adequately realized by historians outside the United States.[10] Even in the United States this situation was reached only by a somewhat painful process of trial and error. Most of the Colonies started with established Churches, and were most averse from the principle of toleration. But gradually the other view prevailed. What was granted to all forms of faith and of no-faith was not toleration but equality within the broad limits of the operation of the common law.

No solution of the relation of Church and state is perfect. Even when there is no legal bond, Churches can become subservient to public opinion, to social pressures and to the will of a majority. If

---

[10] One of the merits of Professor Hermelink's great history of the nineteenth century: *Das Christentum in der Menschheitsgeschichte* (3 vols. 1951, 1953, 1955) is his clear recognition of the independent contribution that American Christianity has in this respect made to the progress of the Christian world as a whole.

the state is completely safeguarded against the influence of religion, it may become secularized, and government may come to be regarded as the field of the operation of unbridled power politics without reference to any supposedly higher laws and powers. Churches, even though they have no legal status, can organize themselves to bring considerable pressure to bear on any democratically-elected government. Yet on the whole it must be recognized that the American experiment has worked well. The Churches flourish. Deeply secularized as it is, the nation seems yet to regard itself as in some sense 'a nation under God', a phrase which taken seriously helps to mitigate the light-hearted blasphemy of 'God's own country'.

It is significant that on the other side of the world another great nation has organized itself somewhat on the American pattern. India has declared itself to be a *secular* democratic republic. But the word 'secular' needs careful interpretation. Those who framed the Indian Constitution declared that they did not intend to disregard religion or to deny its significance in the life of man. But this state would not ally itself with any religion, would not claim for itself any authority in the name of religion or over any man's religion. As we have already seen, not everyone in India is satisfied with this solution; certain Hindu elements are pressing strongly for the recognition of India as Hindustan, the land in which Hindu religion and Hindus have a pre-eminent right to exist and to dominate. But in spite of these elements of resistance, it may be taken as reasonably certain that the present constitution will be upheld.

This is the most favourable situation for the maintenance of the spiritual independence of the faith and of the Church. It must not, however, be forgotten that the Church is called to maintain that independence in all circumstances, however unfavourable, and that some of its greatest services to the freedom of the human spirit have been rendered precisely when its faithfulness has led it into conflict with the state, and on to the bitter road of persecution.

At the level of man in community the local Church should have the answer to the gnawing problem of the insignificance of the individual man. We cannot set the clock back. More and more our destinies are controlled by forces over which we have no control; we feel ourselves carried away like straws on a stream. But, in order to be a man, a man needs a place in which his voice is listened to with respect, in which his vote counts, in which he has a share in making the decisions by which he consents to live. If every other outlet is denied him, the local Church should survive the flood as that community in which precisely these necessities of the human spirit are offered to the ordinary man.[11]

Here, perhaps, the Churches of the Baptist and Congregationalist orders have the most to offer to our need. From the beginning they have professed and maintained the absolute equality of believers in the sight of God. They have taken it for granted that at any moment the right word might be given through the Holy Spirit to any member of the community, however insignificant. In the solemnity of the Church meeting every member feels that momentous things are being decided, that his voice counts, and that the decisions he shares in making will have significance for time and for eternity. Such things add space and dignity to human existence. And perhaps all this may prove of special value where men are passing out of the collective anonymity of the tribe into the collective anonymity of the great city.

At a third point the Church can safeguard the integrity of human beings. Kierkegaard held that a man realizes the true nature of his being only in immediate confrontation by the living God. There no one can help him. This is the moment of supreme loneliness in human life. He comes to a point at which a decisive 'Yes' or 'No' has to be said. Certainly at the moment the individual cannot understand all that is implicit in the decision; he is of necessity entering into an uncharted future. His new life will be marked by that openness to the future, of which Bultmann speaks. But the decision, if made, is his and no one else's. This is not individualism. On the contrary, it marks the advance from the mere individual, conditioned by his past, his tradition, and the ceaseless levelling processes of modern society, into full personal existence, in which a man takes full responsibility for his own decisions and is prepared to stand to them, come life come death. Anyone who has been led to make such a decision knows well that it will be costly, and is likely to bring down upon him the criticism and hostility of the society in which he lives, even though that be a Christian society. Such is the price that almost always has to be paid for a genuinely personal existence.

No claim is here being made that the Christian Churches are the only body in the world to concern themselves with the contemporary

[11] For this principle to be effective, it is essential that the local Church should not be too large. Ministers and lay leaders alike, especially in America, tend to be hypnotized by the bourgeois siren of *size*, and so quite possibly to defeat their own excellent intentions.

threat to personal existence. There are other groups, mainly human-istic in character, which share the same concern, and give roughly the same answer, though naturally translated into secular terms. The Churches, however, may claim that in the last quarter of a century they have made considerable discoveries in all these fields, and, that though much is yet experimental and tentative, results have been sufficiently impressive to encourage further experiment in all these directions. They may maintain that in this period, in which all over the world there are evident such strong tendencies towards the totalitarian deformation of human existence in the political, the social, the economic and the intellectual fields, these are the kind of problems with which all the religions ought to be occupying themselves. They have, perhaps, the right to ask the representatives of the other religions how far they have occupied themselves with such problems, and what their experiences have been. This will not lead to a comparison of ideas and doctrines; it may fruitfully lead the dialogue on to the much deeper level of what may be called existential attitudes. What is our judgement on human life as a whole and on the value of the human person? It is on this level that discussion between the faiths may come to be truly creative.

At this point we have suggested that Christians may come with questions to their friends in the other faiths. Dialogue becomes dialogue only when question is met with question. We must expect and welcome the questioning of others. It is for them to formulate their questions. But, in the light of our study, we may perhaps identify five regions in which questions are almost certain to be presented, and in which Christians must be prepared to think out an answer.

1. The Christian faith has, as we have seen, laid claim from the beginning to a universal destiny. How far is it to-day a genuinely international body?

On the purely superficial level, our answer lies ready to hand. There is no race and no religion in the world which has not yielded converts to the Christian faith.[12] But such an answer will not satisfy the questioner. He is concerned to know how far the Western

---

[12] This is a careful statement. As far as is known, there are no Christians in Tibet. But in Ladakh and elsewhere men of Tibetan *race* have become Christians, and have even been ordained to the Christian ministry.

dominance in Christianity has receded, how far in fact, to put it bluntly, the Christian faith is still the faith of the white man.

The question is a fair one. The Christian can only reply that almost all the Christian Churches in the world are now penitently aware of the pungency of the question, and are doing what they can to set right one of the gravest defects in the Christian pattern as it now presents itself. Racial pride and exclusiveness have played a terrible part in the Christian consciousness, and they will not be exorcized overnight. But we really are making progress.

One line of advance is seen in the ecumenical movement. The progress made in sixty years is somewhat precisely measurable. At the great Edinburgh Missionary Conference of 1910, only seventeen out of more than twelve hundred people who took part were of non-Caucasian origin. At the fourth Assembly of the World Council of Churches held at Uppsala in 1968, and even more at the Conference on Church and Society held at Geneva in 1966, the voice of the younger Churches was plainly heard, and the representatives of those churches felt, perhaps for the first time, that they were being taken seriously by the leaders of the older churches. The majority of the delegates still come from the West, and this is inevitable in view of the fact that by far the larger number of Christians in the world live in Western countries. But the principle of complete spiritual equality has been established, and will never again be questioned.[13]

There are, however, things in the Christian Churches which are hard to defend, and which are rightly criticized by non-Christian friends. The reality of racial and colour prejudice spreads far beyond the limits of those areas in which it is specially a problem, is present in a great many people who have never been challenged by it as a practical issue, and has very deep roots in human nature. It is good to be reminded of this; at the same time it is important not to forget the progress that has been made. If a complete list could be made of all the colleges in the United States which during the last twenty-five years have admitted Negro students for the first time, of all the areas in which segregation in the schools has been abolished, of all the positions of distinction to which Negroes have been called in these years, it would be possible to argue that a revolution in the

---

[13] The Roman Catholic parallel to this development has been the great development of the indigenous episcopate, and the appointment as Cardinals of bishops from almost every major country in the world.

Christian consciousness, comparable to that which marked the period of the Reformation, has come about in our time.

The situation is far more difficult when, as in South Africa, a method which the greater part of the Christian world holds to be wrong is defended as though it were itself a part of the Christian faith. Racial discrimination goes back as far as the beginning of history. Sparta had its helots, India its scheduled castes. The situation becomes really serious when religious conviction is called in to hallow the forces of fear, of prejudice and of dislike. Yet even here it is possible to see the beginnings of a change. The younger theologians of the Dutch Reformed Church are not so sure as their fathers were that the doctrine of *apartheid* can be directly derived from the biblical revelation. When the religious foundations of a conviction give way, it is likely that the conviction itself is on the way to substantial modification.

2. The Christian Churches are challenged to show that they can really produce such fellowship, such community, as should be the natural fruit of the principles that they profess. Have we, in point of fact, done as well as the trade union, the social club, the regiment, the Antarctic expedition, and other forms of association in which men have come together for the promotion of common aims?

Here we must honestly admit our gravest weakness. Yet we can modestly claim that we have been more aware of the problem than our critics, and have taken certain steps to meet the criticism.

In the first place we may note the way in which the doctrine of forgiveness has come back into the centre of Christian thinking—we noted earlier that in Hinduism it seems to be completely absent. No society can hold together in any intimacy, unless men and women are willing to forgive one another. This is as true of the family as of any other society; where a family has broken up, again and again the cause is found to have been the denial of forgiveness where it ought to have been granted. It is not easy to forgive. The one thing that more than any other helps men to forgive is the knowledge that they themselves have received forgiveness when they had done nothing to deserve it. This is the message that has come to them through Jesus Christ; the challenge of the apostle is that Christians should live 'forgiving one another, even as God also for Christ's sake hath forgiven you'.

Secondly, there is the new emphasis on the whole worshipping community as the instrument for evangelistic work. In the past 'evangelism' has been regarded as the special call or prerogative of a limited number of people. Now the weight of the challenge rests on the Christian people as a whole. And a people that is divided within itself cannot hope to go forward to effective and powerful witness.

Within the Christian world there has been over the last few years a remarkable development of new experiments in various forms of Christian life in community. These have sprung up spontaneously and independently in many parts of the Christian world. One of the best known is the Reformed brotherhood of Taizé in France. At the Reformation the Reformed Churches vigorously repudiated the monastic life and everything connected with it; one could hardly imagine a more unfavourable soil for the growth of what is in fact a monastic order. Yet Taizé has survived the first thirty years of its existence, has grown, has drawn in brothers from several countries, and has exercised a profound influence on many who have not actually joined it.

3. Our friends have the right to ask us whether we are absolutely honest in our self-criticism, and in our presentation of the faith that we claim to profess.

In this area it seems to me that we can stand up fairly well to criticism. The Christian Churches have lived through two centuries of crisis, and though weather-beaten they seem on the whole to have survived remarkably well.

Two centuries ago, men began to ask new questions, and to devise new critical methods for the advancement of knowledge.[14] When once these methods had been evolved, it was quite certain that in course of time they would be applied to questions of religion and to the Christian faith in exactly the same way as to everything else. Some Christians naturally regarded such an approach as blasphemous. There were cries of alarm and despair. But neither alarm nor despair would stay the flood. And gradually the majority of thoughtful Christians have accepted the legitimacy of the critical approach. It is not a question of this or that solution to a particular problem; it is the new conviction that the Christian faith has nothing

[14] The initial impulse had been given nearly a century earlier, in the decade 1680–90, which saw the publication of Newton's *Principia* and Locke's *Essay on the Human Understanding*. But it was from about 1760 onwards that the new scientific movement began to gather weight and impetus. Teilhard de Chardin, in his fascinating *The Phenomenon of Man* (Eng. trans. 1959) recognizes this as one of the great crises in the evolution of the human species.

to fear from the humble and reverent use of those same methods that have proved so useful for the advancement of knowledge in other spheres.

Professor Clement Webb, no mean authority, has given it as his judgement that this is the greatest revolution in Christian thought, since in the course of the first century the Church was compelled to recognize that the expectation of the immediate return of the Lord in glory would not be literally fulfilled. Certainly a great gulf separates us from our fathers in the eighteenth century. We may read the ancient classics of Christian theology for education and edification; it is not until we come to the works of Schleiermacher (1768–1834) that we feel ourselves to be listening to a man who might almost be our own contemporary.

The Church has had to experience a number of shocks. First came the assault on the infallibility of Scripture, in many cases associated with the doctrines of the mythological school of interpretation, as in D. F. Strauss's *Life of Christ* (1835–6). Then followed physical science in the hands not so much of Darwin (*The Origin of Species*, 1859) as of his followers. Next came the comparative study of religions, of which E. B. Tylor's *Primitive Religion* (1871) was the first gospel. At about the same time the Marxist assault on all religion as 'ideology' began to be acutely felt. Sigmund Freud began his great series of publications in 1894, though the possible consequences of his discoveries for religious faith did not become apparent to many until after the First World War. Now we are facing the challenge of the quasi-religious humanists, to whom we have devoted a number of pages earlier in this book.

At every fresh alarm there have been further cries of anxiety and despair. There have been false formulations of problems and defences which really defended nothing. There has been the inveterate tendency to confuse outworks with the very citadel of the faith. Some Christians have made far too many concessions in the name of progress to the supposedly progressive spirit; others ostrich-like have denied that there really was any problem. And yet the Church of Christ is still there. Under the guidance of prophetic spirits, who have believed that God might have new truths to reveal through science or psychology and who have refused to be afraid of any challenge or any evidence, after the period of strain the Churches seem to have settled down to a period of relative tranquillity. We have learned not to mistake a skirmish for a battle, and not to suppose that, because some ancient formulation will not stand examination, the whole structure of the faith is in peril.

Yet it remains true that in 1970 we cannot present the Christian faith as our predecessors presented it in 1870, or theirs in 1770. Some things have been lost and others gained, and there will not be an unanimous judgement as to loss and gain. But what is certain is that all things have been changed. Part of the embarrassment of the modern missionary is that, having himself been exposed at least vicariously to these processes of change, he finds himself speaking to Christians and non-Christians to whom the questions are unintelligible, and the answers therefore necessarily irrelevant.

For the moment this seems to turn to our disadvantage. But this may be only a temporary drawback. For this tremendous effort of Christian honesty over two centuries puts us in a position from which we can demand of our partners in the dialogue that they should exercise equal honesty. Are they prepared, as we are, to submit the sources of their faith to the most minute critical examination, and to abide by the results?

It is hard for the Christian to approach the Bible, the Word of God, in a critical spirit, and many preachers reveal every Sunday the schizophrenia under which they still labour. But far more difficult is it for the Muslim even to think of applying criticism to the Qur'an. For him this is the very word of God, eternal and uncreate; how then subject it to the probe and scalpel of the surgeon? A beginning has been made with the *ḥadith*, the traditions of the life and words of Muhammad; Muslim scholars are prepared to recognize the distinction between those which are probably authentic, those which may have a kernel of authenticity much overlaid by interpretation, and those which rest only on the pious imagination of later Muslim generations. But the Muslim scholar may rest assured that sooner or later he will be driven, by the same irresistible impulse as the Christians, to look on the Qur'an with the same critical eyes as have been trained in other fields. What the consequences for his faith may be it is not for a Christian even to imagine.

Critical work on Hindu sources has so far been carried out almost exclusively by Western writers. Hindus themselves are bound sooner or later to be drawn into the enquiry. The Bhagavad Gita is the most popular of all Hindu classics. Both Samkara and

Ramanuja have written commentaries on it, Saṃkara in terms of rigid *Advaita* monism, Ramanuja in terms of what Rudolf Otto has taught us to call India's religion of grace. They cannot both be right. Which is right? Or is it possible that both are wrong, and that neither of their philosophies in reality bears any relation to the Gita? Such questions cannot be indefinitely postponed. It is not for the Christian to attempt to do the work of the Hindu or the Muslim for him; but when the Hindu and the Muslim and others are prepared to do such work, they will find that their dialogue with the Christian has moved into a new and unexpected dimension.

4. The fourth question will relate to our willingness to accept new light, from whatever direction it may come, and to believe that other faiths may enshrine truths to which we ourselves have been blind.

Once again, the Churches can point to their own record in support of the view that, slow as they may be to learn, they are not wholly unwilling to learn from others. They believe that all truth is present in Christ; but they are bound also to admit their blindness, and to recognize that they have sometimes owed to critics and enemies the discovery of vital truth that was all the time implicit in the life and teaching of Christ.

There is much that is not admirable in the modern feminist movement. Men and women of my age, after sixty years, still look back with shamed disgust on the tactics of the suffragettes in the reign of King Edward VII. All too often it has seemed that the one aim of the feminists has been to show there is nothing which a man can do which a woman cannot do also, forgetting that perhaps God made them male and female precisely because a woman can do certain things that a man can never do. Yet, when all this has been said, who will maintain that the position of women in Britain a hundred years ago was worthy of a Christian civilization? It was a great deal better than it had been in the reign of the first Queen Elizabeth. But did it bear any relation to the revelation of God in Jesus Christ?

The *Magnificat* is a great paean in favour of social righteousness.[15] But how much attention had the Churches paid to it in the four centuries that followed the break-up of the medieval world? How much do we owe to Karl Marx and his friends for the quickened social consciousness in almost all the Churches? To follow the

---

[15] But not, as is sometimes inferred, a programme of social action!

declarations of Christian Conferences, from the Birmingham Conference on Christian Politics, Economics and Citizenship of 1924, and the Stockholm Conference on Life and Work in 1925, down to the Assembly of the World Council of Churches at Uppsala in 1968 is to see how this sense of social responsibility has deepened and broadened in the Churches. The violent accusation, constantly repeated by some conservatives, that the ecumenically-minded Churches are no better than lackeys of Moscow both indicates the source of some of the lessons that they have learned, and suggests that they have learned their lessons well.

Now, this being the attitude of the modern Churches, we may affirm that we are prepared to open ourselves in fullest measure to every challenge that the Hindu or the Muslim or the Buddhist can present. We may make in our minds the reservation that, if he convinces us of depths of mystical experience or ethical achievement of which we now know nothing, we shall find in the end that this was still an aspect of the message of Christ that we had somehow overlooked. But we can honestly say that at every point he will find us open to conviction.

5. If this is a true and honest statement of the attitude of the Christian Churches, his last question will be whether we are prepared for a recasting and restatement of Christian truth in the light of the new knowledge that may come to us. The answer to this question has already been given, when we were speaking of the possibility of new forms of Christian culture and of new Christian discoveries in the lands that are now non-Christian. We must be, and are, prepared for such restatement.

But here, too, it may be well to throw in a word of caution. It is possible to restate Christian faith in such general terms that it is reduced to a vague theosophy from which the particular challenge presented by Christian faith is eliminated. There are certain basic convictions which must be maintained, if Christianity is to be recognizably Christian. Of these I have listed seven:

1. There is only one God and Creator, from whom all things take their origin.

2. This God is a self-revealing God, and he himself is active in the knowledge that we have of him.

3. In Jesus the full meaning of the life of man, and of the purpose of God for the universe, has been made known. In him the alienated world has been reconciled to God.

4. In Jesus Christians see the way in which they ought to live; his life is the norm to which they are unconditionally bound.

5. The Cross of Jesus shows that to follow his way will certainly result in suffering; this is neither to be resented nor to be evaded.

6. The Christian faith may learn much from other faiths; but it is universal in its claims; in the end Christ must be acknowledged as Lord of all.

7. The death of the body is not the end. Christ has revealed the eternal dimension as the true home of man's spirit.

To make these affirmations is not to deny the right of any of our interlocutors in the debate to challenge or to criticize any one of them. It is simply to state the limits of concession. If any one of these cardinal points came to be seriously modified, Christianity would become something unrecognizably different from what it is.

We now move back to the other leg of the dialectic. Throughout this chapter we have seen the Christian Churches doing a great deal of house-cleaning, and preparing themselves, though still very inadequately, for their tasks in the modern world. Now it is time for the Christians to put a few questions to the other side. How does the Christian, after all this preparation, enter to-day into the dialogue with his friends of the other faiths?

The answer is admirably given us by Dr. Hendrik Kraemer:

Therefore Christ's ambassadors in the world, in order to preach the Gospel, can and must stand in the world of non-Christian religions with downright intrepidity and radical humility. And the same applies to the Christian standing in the world of culture, wherever it may be.[16]

Kraemer speaks here, as he has spoken earlier, of a 'congenial understanding' of the other faiths. This is the first and great requisite. But our problem, our razor's edge, is the combination of this openness with the conviction that the message of Jesus Christ is proclamation, challenge, and judgement. We shall come to the other faiths to-day not as dogmatists or critics, but in the spirit of humble questioning, entitled to ask our questions, because we have first submitted ourselves to theirs.

Our first question, perhaps, will be whether these other faiths have ever really heard of a God who acts. If the answer is 'No', is

---

[16] *Religion and the Christian Faith* (1956), p. 335. The whole section pp. 335–9 needs to be read.

their thought about God in any way commensurable with ours? Where are we to find any common denominator of thought?

It is clear that one of the battle-grounds is going to be the nature of history. It may well be that we do not ourselves yet fully understand what we mean when we speak of God as Lord of history. But we do know that, in contrast to the Greek idea of history as cyclic, in which all things come back to that which they were before, and to the Hindu-Buddhist concept in which history is necessarily meaningless, we hold that history has a meaning. It is the sphere in which God is at work. This does not mean simply that he interferes cataclysmically at certain given moments; the whole of history is the loom of his weaving. All nations and events are related to his purpose, though they may vary in their distance from the centre of that purpose. Now only one kind of God could be active in history in this kind of way; and no other kind of God could be the object of Christian faith.

This leads directly to our second question. Have our interlocutors ever really looked at Jesus Christ and tried to see him as he is? For, if we take the Gospels seriously (and at the same time as critically as you will), Jesus is not the least like anyone else who has ever lived. The things that he says about God are not the same as the sayings of any other religious teacher. The claims that he makes for himself are not the same as those that have been made by any other religious teacher. His criticisms of human life and society are far more devastating than any other man has ever made. The demands he makes on men are more searching than those put forward by any other religious teacher.

To say all this does not necessarily mean that Jesus was right. It is simply a plea for plain honesty. The danger of the approach of 'congenial understanding' is that we may all get lost in a fog of geniality. The first period is that of approximation, in which we find out the similarities between the faiths. This must be followed by a period of reflection, in which we face with ruthless honesty the reality of the differences. Dr. Kraemer is right in warning us of this:

It is . . . illegitimate to speak of a rectilinear transition from the world of religion (or philosophy or whatever you will) to the world of revelation. Becoming a disciple of Christ means always a radical break with the past. Christ is, as we have repeatedly said, the *crisis* of all Religion (and philosophy, good and bad); this is to say, as well the Judge as the great Transformer of all religion. It never means a gradual transition.[17]

So, when we invite our friends of the other faiths to look at Jesus Christ, we may do so with a full sense of responsibility for what it may mean for them, if they should look on him and really see him. That would be for them the ending of an old world and the creation of a new; for if any man be in Christ, there is a new creation.

Nor are we allowed, by the truth of Christ, to say 'Look at him, and do not look at us'. Dr. Vicedom has recently written trenchantly of the way in which the messenger of the Gospel is identified not merely with his message but with his God:

God comes to the people through His messengers. It is by their behaviour that God is judged. If the missionaries succeed in entering into the life of the people, in adapting themselves to their way of living, if they learn the language and become in many ways the advisers, friends and helpers of the Papuans, gradually confidence in the missionaries is established. This confidence is at once transferred to God. God is always judged in the light of what the missionaries are. Unless this comes to pass, even in New Guinea we shall hear people say, 'Your God is a foreign God. He demands new ways of doing things. He speaks our language so badly that it makes us sick even to listen to you'.[18]

It is not only in New Guinea that such things are true. For the Christian, every study of his relationship to the other faiths and their adherents must end with the ancient words of the New Testament, 'What manner of men ought ye to be?'[19]

---

[17] Op. cit. p. 338.
[18] G. F. Vicedom, *Church and People in New Guinea* (World Christian Books, 1961), pp. 16-17.
[19] 2 Peter 3, 11.

BIBLIOGRAPHY

THERE is an immense and ever-growing literature on every aspect of the subject. This bibliography includes only a small number of books, most of which have been published fairly recently, and almost all of which contain more extensive bibliographies, by means of which the reader who wishes to carry his studies further can find his way to other sources of information.

General

BOUQUET, A. C. *Sacred Books of the World*. London: Penguin Books, 1954.

BOUQUET, A. C. *Comparative Religion*. London: Penguin Books, 5th ed. revised, 1956.

BOUQUET, A. C. *The Christian Faith and Non-Christian Religions*. London: Nisbet, 1958.

JURJI, E. J. (ed.). *The Great Religions of the Modern World*. Princeton University Press (London: Oxford University Press), 1946.

KITAGAWA, J. M. (ed.). *Modern Trends in World Religions*. La Salle, Illinois, 1959.

KRAEMER, H. *Religion and the Christian Faith*. London: Lutterworth Press, 1956.

KRAEMER, H. *World Culture and World Religions*. London: Lutterworth Press, 1960.

LEEUW, G. VAN DER. *Religion in Essence and Manifestation*. London: Allen and Unwin, 1964.

LEWIS, H. D., and SLATER, R. H. L. *World Religions: Meeting Points and Major Issues*. London: C. A. Watts, 1966.

PERRY, E. *The Gospel in Dispute: the Relation of Christian Faith to other Missionary Religions*. New York: Doubleday, 1958.

RINGGREN, H., and STRÖM, A. V. *Religions of Mankind, Today, Yesterday*. London: Oliver and Boyd, 1966.

SMART, N. *A Dialogue of Religions*. London: S.C.M. Press, 1960.

WACH, J. (ed. J. M. Kitagawa). *The Comparative Study of Religions*. New York: Columbia University Press (London: Oxford University Press), 1958.

ZAEHNER, R. C. (ed.). *The Concise Encyclopaedia of Living Faiths*. London: Hutchinson, revised ed., 1964.

Judaism

ELLISON, H. L. *The Jew* (Christian Approach Series). London: Edinburgh House Press, 1958.

EPSTEIN, I. *Judaism: A Historical Presentation.* London: Penguin Books, 1959.

HEDENQUIST, G. (ed.). *The Church and the Jewish People.* London: Edinburgh House Press, 1954.

HERBERG, W. *Judaism and Modern Man.* New York: Farrar, Straus and Young, 1952.

JOCZ, J. C. *The Jewish People and Jesus Christ.* London: S.P.C.K., revised ed., 1951.

OESTERREICHER, J. M. (ed.). *The Bridge: A Yearbook of Judaeo-Christian Studies,* 4 vols. New York: Pantheon Books, 1955, 1956, 1958, 1961.

PARKES, J. *The Foundations of Judaism and Christianity.* London: Mitchell, 1960.

SCHULTZ, H. J. (ed.). *Juden, Christen, Deutsche.* Stuttgart: Kreuz Verlag, 1961.

Islam

ANDERSON, J. N. D. *Islamic Law in the Modern World.* New York University Press, 1959.

CRAGG, K. *The Dome and the Rock.* London: S.P.C.K., 1964.

CRAGG, K. *The Call of the Minaret.* New York (and London): Oxford University Press, 1956.

CRAGG, K. *Sandals at the Mosque.* London: S.C.M. Press (New York: Oxford University Press), 1959.

GIBB, H. A. R. *Modern Trends in Islam.* Chicago University Press, 1947.

GIBB, H. A. R. *Mohammedanism.* Home University Library, London (and New York): Oxford University Press, 1953.

GRUNEBAUM, G. E. VON. *Islam.* London: Routledge, 2nd ed., 1961.

GUILLAUME, A. *Islam.* London: Penguin Books, 1959.

HOURANI, A. *Arabic Thought in the Liberal Age.* London: Oxford University Press, 1962.

MARRISON, G. E. *The Muslim* (Christian Approach Series). London: Edinburgh House Press, 1959.

RONDOT, P. *L'Islam et les Mussulmans d'Aujourd'hui.* Paris: Editions de l'Orante, 1958.

SMITH, W. C. *Islam in Modern History.* Princeton University Press (London: Oxford University Press), 1957.

Hinduism

DEVANANDAN, P. D. *The Gospel and Renascent Hinduism.* London: S.C.M. Press, 1959.

DIEHL, C. G. *Church and Shrine: Intermingling Patterns of Culture.* Uppsala, 1965.

GONDA, J. *Die Religionen Indiens.* 2 vols. Stuttgart: W. Kohlhammer Verlag, 1961.

MANIKAM, R. B. *Christianity in the Asian Revolution.* Methuen, 1954.

MORGAN, K. W. (ed.). *The Religion of the Hindus.* New York: Ronald Press, 1953.

RADHAKRISHNAN, S. *The Hindu View of Life.* London: Allen and Unwin, 1927.

RADHAKRISHNAN, S. *Eastern Religions and Western Thought.* Oxford: Clarendon Press (New York: Oxford University Press), 2nd ed. 1940.

RADHAKRISHNAN, S. *East and West in Religion.* London: Allen and Unwin, 1933.

SAMARTHA, S. J. *Introduction to Radhakrishnan: the Man and his Thought.* Y.M.C.A., New Delhi, 1964.

SARMA, D. S. *Hinduism Through the Ages.* Bombay, 1956.

SPEAR, P. *India, Pakistan and the West.* London (and New York): Oxford University Press, 4th ed., 1967.

THOMPSON, E. W. *The Word of the Cross to Hindus.* Madras: Christian Literature Society, 1956.

WINSLOW, J. C. *The Hindu* (Christian Approach Series). London: Edinburgh House Press, 1958.

WOLFF, O. *Christus unter den Hindus.* Gütersloh: Mohn, 1965.

ZAEHNER, R. C. *At Sundry Times.* London: Faber and Faber, 1958.

ZAEHNER, R. C. *Hinduism.* London: Oxford University Press, 1962.

Buddhism

APPLETON, G. *The Buddhist* (Christian Approach Series). London: Edinburgh House Press, 1958.

CONZE, E. (tr.). *Buddhist Scriptures.* London: Penguin Books, 1959.

FROMM, E., SUZUKI, D. T., DE MARTINO, R. *Zen Buddhism and Psychoanalysis.* New York: Harper, 1960.

HUMPHREYS, C. *Buddhism.* London: Penguin Books, 2nd ed. revised, 1958.

KRETSER, B. DE. *Man in Buddhism and Christianity.* Calcutta: Y.M.C.A. Press, 1954.

MORGAN, K. W. (ed.). *The Path of the Buddha.* New York: Ronald Press, 1956.

SCHECTER, J. *The New Face of Buddha.* London: Gollancz, 1967.

SLATER, R. H. L. *Paradox and Nirvana.* Chicago University Press, 1951.

SUZUKI, D. T. *An Introduction to Zen Buddhism.* New York: Philosophical Library, 1949.

The Revolt in the Temple. Colombo: Sinha Publications, 1953.

Primitive Religion

BARRETT, D. B. *Schism and Renewal in Africa*. Nairobi: Oxford University Press, 1968.

EVANS-PRITCHARD, E. E. *Nuer Religion*. London (and New York): Oxford University Press, 1956.

EVANS-PRITCHARD, E. E. *Theories of Primitive Religion*. Oxford: Clarendon Press, 1965.

FRANKFORT, H. and others. *Before Philosophy*. London: Penguin Books, 1949.

HARRIS, W. T. and PARRINDER, E. G. *The Animist* (Christian Approach Series). London: Edinburgh House Press, 1960.

KENYATTA, J. *Facing Mount Kenya: The Tribal Life of the Kikuyu*. London: Secker and Warburg, 2nd ed., 1953.

LAWRENCE, P. *Road Belong Cargo*. Manchester University Press, 1964.

LESSA, W. A. and VOGT, E. Z. (eds.). *Reader in Comparative Religion: An Anthropological Approach*. New York (and London): Harper, 1965.

MEAD, M. *New Lives for Old: Cultural Transformation in Manus, 1928–53*. New York: Morrow; London: Gollancz, 1956.

RUTHERFORD, J. *Darkness and Light: an Anthology of African Writing*. London: Faith Press, 1958.

TAYLOR, J. V. *The Growth of the Church in Buganda*. London: S.C.M. Press, 1958.

TEMPELS, P. *La Philosophie Bantoue*. Elizabethville, 1945.

VICEDOM, G. F. *Church and People in New Guinea* (World Christian Books no. 38). London: Lutterworth Press, 1961.

Marxism

CAREW-HUNT, R. N. *The Theory and Practice of Communism*. London: Geoffrey Bles, 1950.

CROSSMAN, R. H. S. (ed.). *The God that Failed: Six Studies in Communism*. London: Hamish Hamilton, 1956.

MILLER, A. *The Christian Significance of Karl Marx*. London: S.C.M. Press, 1946.

ROGERS, E. *A Commentary on Communism*. London: Epworth Press paperback ed., 1958.

WEST, C. C. *Communism and the Theologians: the Story of an Encounter*. London: S.C.M. Press, 1958.

Scientific Humanism

HUXLEY, J. *Religion without Revelation*. London: Parrish, 1957.

HUXLEY, J. (ed.). *The Humanist Frame*. London: Allen and Unwin, 1961.

Secularization

GOGARTEN, F. *Verhängnis und Hoffnung der Neuzeit: Die Säkularisierung als theologisches Problem*. Stuttgart, 1953.
LEEUWEN, A. T. VAN. *Christianity in World History: the Meeting of the Faiths of East and West*. London: Edinburgh House Press, 1964.

Secularism

BARRY, F. R. *Secular and Supernatural*. London: S.C.M. Press, 1969.
GREGOR SMITH, R. *Secular Christianity*. London: Collins, 1966.
MACQUARRIE, J. *God and Secularity*. London: Lutterworth Press, 1968.
MARTIN, D. *The Religious and the Secular*. London: Routledge, 1969.
OGDEN, S. M. *The Reality of God and Other Essays*. London: S.C.M. Press, 1967.
VAN BUREN, P. M. *The Secular Meaning of the Gospel*. London: S.C.M. Press, 1963.

Existentialism

BLACKHAM, H. T. *Six Existentialist Thinkers*. London: Routledge, 1952.
HEIDEGGER, M. *Sein und Zeit*. Tübingen: Niemeyer, 8th ed., 1957. Eng. trans. *Being and Time* (trs. John Macquarrie). London: S.C.M. Press, 1962.
HERBERG, W. *Four Existentialist Theologians*. New York: Doubleday, 1958.
MACQUARRIE, J. *An Existentialist Theology*. London: S.C.M. Press, 1955.
MARCEL, G. *Être et Avoir*. Eng. trans. *Being and Having*. London and New York, 1965.
MARCEL, G. *Le Mystère de l'Être* (Gifford Lectures) I: Réflexion et Mystère. II: Foi et Mystère. Paris: Aubier, 1951.
MIEGGE, G. (trs. S. C. Neill). *Gospel and Myth in the Thought of Rudolf Bultmann*. London: Lutterworth Press, 1960.
ROBERTS, David E. *Existentialism and Religious Belief*. New York (and London): Oxford University Press, 1957.
SARTRE, J.P. *L'Être et le Néant*. Eng. trans. *Being and Nothingness* (trs. H. E. Barnes). London: Methuen, 1957.
TILLICH, P. *Theology of Culture*. New York (and London): Oxford University Press, 1959.

INDEX

Acre, 42
Adriatic, 43
Advaita monism, 230
Africa, 43, 125 ff., 138, 140 ff., 220;
  Central, 131; East, 46; North, 42;
  South, 78, 226; tropical, 42, 46
Ahiṃsā, 119
Ahmadiyya movement, 63
Al-Azhar University, 46
Algeria, 44
Alice movement, 148
America, 103, 107, 138, 221, 223
Anatta, 107, 109
Animism, 71
Ankara, 47
Anicca, 107
Apartheid, 226
Appleton, George, 103 n.
Aquinas, Thomas, 215
Arabia, 45; Arabic language, 46; Arab
  League, 46; Arabs, 26, 41, 45, 144
Aristotle, 168, 170, 215, 219
Arjuna, 79, 92
Armenians, 21 n.
Arya Samaj, 74
Ashanti, 140
Asia, 29, 43, 70, 220
Asoka, 102
Atlantic, 42
Augsburg, Diet of, 42 n.
Augustine, 41
Azariah, Bishop, 212
Aztec, 136

Bach, Johann Sebastian, 179
Balfour, A. J., 25; Declaration, 25
Balkans, 43
Baly, Denis, 26 n.
Bandaranaike, Solomon, 104
Bantu, 133 f.
Barker, Ernest, 58
Barth, Karl, 215
Basham, A. L., 80 n., 97
Beauvoir, Simone de, 189, 193 n.
Bhagavad Gita, 71, 79, 92 f., 211,
  229 f.
Bhakti, 70, 92, 102 n.
Bhave, Vinoba, 81
Boddhisattva, 100, 123
Boman, T., 216 n.
Bonhoeffer, Dietrich, 165
Bosanquet, Bernard, 202
Bouquet, A. C., 85, 104 n., 111 n., 120 n.,
  122 n., 132, 143
Bradley, F. H., 202
Brahma Sūtra, 88 n., 97

Brahmans, 73, 96, 100, 110 n., 135
Brahmo Samaj, 75, 76 n.
Brazil, 127
Buber, Martin, 33 f., 37 f., 130, 191 n.
Buddha, 100 f., 104 ff., 110, 113 n., 118,
  122, 125
Buddhism, 44, 97, 99–124, 212; gospel of
  peace, 119 ff., Zen form of, 113 ff.,
  philosophy, 116 ff.
Buddhist, 28, 101, 117 n., 231; Society,
  106; World Council, 105
Bultmann, Rudolf, 9 n., 37 n., 188 n.,
  199 ff., 223
Burma, 103 f.
Byzantium, 57

Camus, Albert, 192 ff., 196 f., 203
Cargo cult, 147
Caribbean, 126
Ceylon, 102, 104, 220
Chardin, P. Teilhard de, 90, 159, 227
Chandran, J. R., 75 n.
China, 42, 46, 103, 114
Christian faith: dialogue with Judaism,
  29–39; with Islam, 62–69; with Hindu-
  ism, 89–98; with Buddhism, 120–4;
  with Primitive Religion, 143–52; with
  Marxism, 155–178; with Existentialism,
  201, 203–6
Christianity, basic convictions, 231–2
Christendom, 207–34
Church, 23 f., 27, 31, 40 f., 57, 94, 96,
  151, 155, 156, 166, 207 ff., 213 ff.;
  Baptist, 223; Congregational, 223;
  Roman Catholic, 160; Reformed, 227
Communist régimes, 151
C.O.P.E.C., 231
Congo, 142
Congress, 80 n.
Constantinople, 42
Conze, E., 103 n., 105, 111 n., 123 n.,
  125 n.
Coptic language, 45
Cortes, 136
Cournos, John, 30 n.
Cragg, Kenneth, 60, 62 n., 69 n.
Crusades, 42, 58
Czechoslovakia, 158

Dante, 173
Darwin, Charles, 228
Datta, Narendranath, 76
Davids, Rhys, 109
Davis, J. Merle, 165–6
Dawson, Christopher, 164, 214, 219
Dehqani, Hassan, 28

Dernier des Justes, Le, 20
Descartes, 198
Devanandan, P. D., 71 n., 75 n., 78 n., 81 n., 87 n., 96 n.
Dhamma, 101 f., 103 n., 116, 119, 125
Dharma, 97
Diehl, C. G., 71 n., 129 n.
Diwakar, R. R., 96 n.
Donne, John, 14
Dutch, The, 43

East *v.* West, 51–2, 58, 63, 68
Edersheim, 27
Edinburgh 1910, 225
Edward I, 20
Egypt, 42 f., 45, 51
Emunah, 37 f.
England, 21; Buddhism in, 106
Entscheidung, 200
Europe, 138
Evans-Pritchard, E. E., 128
Evanston, 157 n.
Existentialism, 180–206
Existenz, 186

Faraday, Michael, 167
Farmer, H. H., 127 ff.
Fatiha, 59 f., 61 n.
Fear, 137, 146–8
Ferdinand and Isabella, 21
Feuerbach, 164, 184
Fioretti, 101
France, 44, 158, 189; the French, 43
Francis, St., 101
Frankfort, Henri, 131
Frazer, Sir James, 129
Freud, Sigmund, 228

Galileo, 168
Gandhi, M. K., 76 ff., 86 f., 92
Gautama, 99 f.
Germany, 21, 43, 80, 105 f., 158; missionaries, 149; occupation of France, 158, 189
Ghana, 140
Gibb, H. A. R., 46 n., 53 f., 56
Gogarten, Friedrich, 161
Gollancz, Victor, 31
Golwalker, Shri, 74
Gospel, background of, 24
Greece, 43; Greeks, 9, 87, 204; Greek thought, 215
Green, T. H., 202 f.
Guillaume, Dr., 65
Gujerati, 80 n.

ḥadith, 53, 229
Haiti, 126
Hallaj, 55

Hamann, J. G., 181
Handel, 179
Harijan, 79
Head-hunting, 136, 146
Hebrews, 87; Epistle to the, 26
Hegel, 156, 179, 195, 202
Heidegger, Martin, 185–8, 190, 197, 200 f., 204
Henry VIII, 57
Herberg, Will, 32
Hindu, 28, 48, 104, 160, 222, 230 f.
Hinduism, 28, 44, 70–98, 102, 110, 125, 212, 226
Hindu Mahasabha, 74
History, nature of, 231
Hitler, 21, 171
Hobsbawm, E. J., 156
Holmes, Edmund, 117 n.
Holsten, Walter, 106 n.
Horner, I. B., 112 n.
Hoyle, F., 174 n.
Humanism, 158–160, 166
Humphreys, Christmas, 106, 107 n., 108 n., 117 n.
Hungary, 42 n.
Hussain, Kamel, 62
Huxley, Aldous, 92
Huxley, Sir Julian, 158–9

Ijmā, 53 f.
Ijtihād, 53 f.
Immediacy, 114 ff.
India, 42 f., 46, 49 f., 100, 125, 149, 156, 162, 163, 166, 167; Muslims in, 49 f.
Indonesia, 42 f., 46
International Missionary Council, 28
International Committee on the Christian Approach to Israel, 28
Iqbal, Muhammad, 40 n., 54
Iraq, 43, 51
Ireland, Republic of, 50
Iroquois, 127
Ishtadevātā, 83, 92
Islam, 3, 40–69, 74, 83, 95 n., 97, 142, 144, 154, 211 f.
Islam in Modern History, 55
Israel, 22 f., 25 f., 32, 35, 146, 161
Italians, 43, 125

Japan, 103, 114
Jaspers, Karl, 185 n., 197
Jerusalem, 42 n., 160
Jewry, 23, 26, 29
Jews, The, 20–39, 50, 58, 211, 213
Jordania, 43
Jowett, Benjamin, 202
Judaism, 28 f., 83, 102, 154
Judaism and Christianity, 24 n.
Junod, H. A., 145

Kabir, 97
Kalighat, 70
Kant, 202
Kapilavastu, 99
Karma, 86, 97, 119
Kellerhals, Emmanuel, 68 n.
Kennedy, President J. F., 173
Kenya, 147
Keshub Chander Sen, 75, 97
Keysser, Christian, 137, 149 n.
Khandhas, 107 f., 120 f.
Kierkegaard, Søren, 180–85, 190, 213, 223
Kivebulaya, Apolo, 145
Korea, 103
Koran, *see* Qur'an
Kosmala, Hans, 30 n.
Kraemer, H., 2 n., 3, 82 n., 207 n., 210 n., 232 f.
Kretser, Bryan de, 108, 109 n.
Krishna, 79, 92
Kshatriya, 99 f.
Kumasi, 140

Laos, 217
Laplace, 168, 172
Leeuwen, A. van, 161–6
Levi, Rabbi Yom Tov, 20
Libya, 43
Life and Times of Jesus the Messiah, 27
Littlewood, J. E., 172–3
Liverpool, conference, 1, 6
Liyaqat Ali Khan, 48
Locke, John, 166

Macdonald, D. B., 59 f.
Mackinnon, D. M., 179
Macquarrie, J., 162 n., 176 n., 188, 201 n.
McTaggart, J. E., 202
Madras Christian College, 82
Maha Thera U Tittila, 121
Mahayana, 119
Malik, Charles, 61
Manickavasagar, 102 n.
Manimekhalai, 102
Marcel, Gabriel, 189, 191 n., 192 n., 197 ff.
Marcellinus, Ammianus, 209
Martin, C. A., Bishop, 27
Martineau, James, 75
Marx, Karl, 8, 104, 155–7, 184, 228, 230
Mau Mau, 147
Maurice, F. D., 157
Maury, Pierre, 170 n., 178
Maya, 87
Mecca, 44 f.
Medina, 50
Mehta, 98 n.
Mesopotamia, 42
Mettiya, Ananda, 103 n.

Middle East, 43, 47
Mill, John Stuart, 78
Mishnah, 30
Mohacs, 42 n.
Moltmann, Jürgen, 157, 158 n.
Montefiore, C. J., 30
Montezuma, 136
Moore, G. E., 202 f.
Morocco, 43
Morris, William, 78
Moscow, 231
Muꜥahadah, 50
Muhammad, 1, 40 f., 44, 53, 64, 67 f., 105
Muhammad Farid Wajdi, 52
Muir, Sir William, 1
Mukallaf, 48
Mulago, Vincent, 133
Müller, Max, 1
Murti, Professor, 85
Muslim, 28, 40, 42 ff., 47, 49 ff., 54, 87, 97, 104, 160, 229 ff.
Mussolini, 171

Nāma, 108
Napoleon, 168
Nasser, President, 47
Navajos, 127
Negro, 225
Neher, André, 36 n.
New Guinea, 137 f., 140, 149, 234
Newton, Isaac, 166, 168
Nicholson, R. A., 56 n.
Nichtung, 187
Niebuhr, Reinhold, 27
Nietzsche, 191 ff., 219
Nile, 43
Niles, D. T., 122 n.
Nirvana, 103 n., 111 f., 118, 123, 125
Nkrumah, Kwame, 140
Nuer, 128
Nyerere, Julius, 139
Nygren, Anders, Bishop, 22, 37

Obote, Milton, 139
Olsen, Regin, 183
Operation Reach, 63
Otto, Rudolf, 230

Pacific Ocean, 42
Pakistan, 48 ff., 52, 54, 57
Palestine, 25 f., 43
Panikkar, K. M., 210 n.
Papuans, 234
Parliament of Religions, 77
Parkes, James, 23 f.
Pascal, 9, 180 n.
Paul, 23 f., 37 f., 153, 174
Perry, Edmund, 66 n:, 69, 119 n., 122 n.
Persia, 42 f., 46
Plato, 29, 219

Plotinus 15, 112
Porteus, S. D., 137
Portuguese, 217
Primitive religions, 124–52
Pygmies, 131, 145

Questions of King Milinda, 109
Qur'an, 4, 45, 46, 48 f., 52 f., 55, 61 n.,
    64, 66 f., 227; translation of, 46

Radhakrishnan, S., 76, 81 ff., 84 n., 85 f.,
    88, 96 f.
Ramakrishna Paramahamsa, 76
Ramanuja, 211, 230
Ram Mohan Roy, 75
Rashtriya Sevak Sangh, 74
Reformation, the, 42, 56 f., 226 f.
Religion and magic, 129 f.
Reinach, Salomon, 2
Rig-Veda, 70
Roberts, D. E., 180 n., 187 n.
Romans, Epistle to, 22, 37
Rome, 22, 57, 135
Roosevelt, President Franklin, 78
Rosenzweig, Franz, 31 f.
Runciman, Sir Steven, 58 f.
Rūpa, 108
Ruskin, 78, 81
Russell, Bertrand, 202 f.
Russia, 80, 103, 142, 154, 213

Samkara, 92, 211, 229 f.
Sankhara, 108
Sanna, 108
Sannyāsi, 86
Saraswati, Dayananda, 74
Sartor Resartus, 86
Sartre, J. P., 189 ff., 203 ff.
Sarvāgamaprāmānya, 85
Sarma, D. S., 97
Sarvodaya, 81
Schleiermacher, 228
Schmidt, W., 131 f.
Schopenhauer, 105
Schwarz-Bart, André, 20
Secularism, 162, 166–76, 178
Secularization, 162–3, 166
Sen, P. K., 75 n.
Senghor, Léopold, 139
Shari'ah, 47, 56
Siam, 103
Sinhalese, 104
Slater, R. H. L., 110 n.
Smith, Robert, 30 n.
Smith, W. Cantwell, 40, 44 n., 47, 50, 52,
    55 ff., 61
Söderblom, Nathan, 2, 129 n.
Spain, 21, 42, 57
Spear, Percival, 73, 75 n.
Stevens, G. H., 27 n.

Stockholm, 231
Strauss, D. F., 228
Sufism, 55; Sufis, 62 n.
Sunnah, 48 f.
Süssman, Cornelia and Irving, 30 n.
Swahili, 46
Syria, 42

Tagore, Rabindranath, 76 n.
Taizé, 227
Talmud, 211
Tambaran, 3
Tamil, 104
Tanzania, 142
Tao, 111
Taylor, J. V., 143 f.
Tayumanavar, 70
Tel Aviv, 25
Telugu, 149
Tempels, P., 133 ff., 139 n., 140
Temple, the (Solomon's), 25
Temple, William, Archbishop, 14, 155
Theravada, 111
Thomas, M. M., 75 n.
Tibet, 102
Tillich, Paul, 180, 184 n., 185 n., 202
Tithonus, 15
Tolstoy, 78
Tours, Battle of, 42
Troeltsch, 2 n.
Tunis, 43
Turkey, 43, 47 ff; Turks, 42, 173
Tylor, E. B., 128, 153, 228

U Chan Htoon, 120
Udāna-Sutta, 110
Uganda, 142
Ulema, 52, 54
UNESCO, 158
U Nu, 104
Upanishads (Taittiriya and Chandogya,
    70), 83, 86, 95, 99
Urdu, 46

Van Buren, P., 169–70
Vedana, 108
Vedanta, 77, 82 ff.
Vedas, 74
Vernichtung, 187
Vicedom, G. F., 105, 106 n., 149 n., 234
Vienna, 42
Vihāra, 106, 107 n.
Vinnāna, 108
Vivekananda, Swami, 76, 83
Volkskirche, 217
Voodoo, 126
Vorhandenheit, 186

Wajdi, Muhammad Farid, 52
Warren, M. A. C., 62 n.

Webb, C. C. J., 89, 228
Weizmann, Chaim, 25
Whitehead, A. N., 15
Willey, Basil, 91 n.
Wilson, Edmund, 127
Wisdom, 37
Wolff, Otto, 78
Wordsworth, 91

World Council of Churches Assembly, 1,
  157n., 160, 225, 231
World Missionary Conference, 160

Yoga, 91

Zaehner, R. C., 63, 91
Zambia, 142
Zionism, 25